THE NEW NORTHERN DIMENSION OF THE EUROPEAN NEIGHBOURHOOD

EDITED BY

PAMI AALTO
HELGE BLAKKISRUD
HANNA SMITH

FOREWORD BY

MICHAEL EMERSON

CONTRIBUTORS

PAMI AALTO
AADNE AASLAND
MORTEN ANKER
HELGE BLAKKISRUD
BJØRN BRUNSTAD
IRINA BUSYGINA
MIKHAIL FILIPPOV
JAKUB M. GODZIMIRSKI
ALF HÅKON HOEL
SIGVE R. LELAND
KARI LIUHTO
KATRI PYNNÖNIEMI
HANNA SMITH
NINA TYNKKYNEN
INDRA ØVERLAND

D1350887

The Centre for European Policy Studies (CEPS) is an independent policy research institute based in Brussels. Its mission is to produce sound analytical research leading to constructive solutions to the challenges facing Europe today. The views expressed in this publication are those of the authors writing in a personal capacity and do not necessarily reflect those of CEPS or any other institution with which the authors are associated.

ISBN 978-92-9079-834-7

Centre for European Policy Studies
Place du Congrès 1, B-1000 Brussels
Tel: 32 (0) 2 229.39.11 Fax: 32 (0) 2 219.41.51
e-mail: info@ceps.eu
internet: http://www.ceps.eu

Cover photograph of Longyearbyen, the Svalbard Archipelago, printed with permission from Tommy Dahl Markussen ©

CONTENTS

Part III. Towards a New Northern Agenda

FOREWORD
MICHAEL EMERSON

The Centre for European Policy Studies greatly appreciates having been invited to publish this book on the new Northern Dimension, which serves as an important piece in the jigsaw puzzle of the European Union's multiple policies towards its neighbours.

The puzzle has many pieces indeed. To the north there is the EU's uneasy relationship with Russia, for which the new Northern Dimension is seen by the EU as its north-west regional adjunct (but I comment in a moment on the role of Norway and Iceland in this initiative); to the east a newly baptised Eastern Partnership is currently being shaped against the background of the eastern branch of the European Neighbourhood Policy (ENP), and which also has its regional dimension in the Black Sea Synergy initiative; to the south-east there is the stabilisation and association process for the Balkan states that are not yet members of the EU; and to the south the Barcelona process has morphed into the southern branch of the ENP, which is in turn now morphing into the Union for the Mediterranean. This multiplicity of constantly changing initiatives is already telling us that there is an intense but complex search process going on, seeking the optimal arrangements between the EU and its very different neighbours. To put this in a somewhat dramatised historical perspective, this is the story of the newly post-modern contemporary Europe trying to shape its relationship with the former Russian empire and Soviet Union, and the former Ottoman and Arab empires.

To this vast landscape of neighbourhood relations the new Northern Dimension brings a number of interesting particularities, which this book shows to be a combination of qualities and limitations.

First, it is an exercise in neighbourhood policy, in which Norway, Iceland and the EU ally to try to do something useful with north-west Russia. Within the EU, Finland took the first initiative in 1998 to launch the (old) Northern Dimension policy, and it sustains a highly active role in the (new) Northern Dimension. This book is sponsored jointly by the Finnish and Norwegian ministries of foreign affairs, in itself a discreet message. The new Northern Dimension sees the EU and the two non-EU partners of the European Economic Area join in a foreign policy initiative with the EU.

Second, it is an exercise in what the introductory chapter to this book brands as 'small-but-smart' policies, and third, an operation that seeks to 'fly below the radar' of the high politics of EU–Russian relations and of Russian geo-politics. Can this work? This is the question the book addresses.

The small-but-smart test seems to have been passed quite successfully. Should this remark seem to be vague and lacking in vivid interest, remember what 'small-but-not-smart' policies in Russia's neighbourhood means. This summer's war in Georgia gives the perspective, in which this tragic episode resulted from the underlying lack of trust between Russia and Georgia, and then miscalculation in response to provocation. By contrast, for Finland and Norway the new Northern Dimension is an extension of consistent bilateral policies of engagement with Russia.

The new Northern Dimension also ranks as small but smart in relation to the EU, in that Finland and Norway have exercised leading roles while smoothly securing joint ownership of it with the EU, which brings larger political and financial resources into play. The tensions that arose within the EU in the last year over French President Nicolas Sarkozy's initiative on the Union for the Mediterranean shows that regional leadership and EU ownership are not always the easiest of qualities to combine.

The test on flying below the radar, however, reveals limitations. As the book shows, sectoral programmes for public health and the environment have made substantial progress, and these can rank as largely de-politicised activities. They could indeed fly below the radar. In two other respects, however, the limitations are seen to be significant. The energy sector is of outstanding importance and potential for the Northern Dimension area, with huge new investments due in oil and gas fields (the offshore Shtokman field and the Yamal Peninsula). But here the new Northern Dimension has not been able to achieve real traction. The big action has been taking place elsewhere in dealings between Moscow and major European oil companies with national governments (including Norway) behind them. Also, at the level of foreign investment in Russia more generally, the experience of Finnish and Norwegian companies shows that Russia's current policies of economic nationalism in favour of 'strategic' sectors are a serious hindrance, which the Northern Dimension cannot overcome.

On the other hand, the new Northern Dimension would seem to score positively as a confidence-building or confidence-deepening measure with Russia. Here flying below the radar has seen adoption of a work programme jointly with Russia, even if in practice this has meant the exclusion of some topics of the highest interest to the European parties, such as democracy and its many component parts. So this is a plus and a minus at the same time.

Michael Emerson
Senior Fellow, CEPS
Brussels, December 2008

ACKNOWLEDGEMENTS

For good collaboration and funding we wish to thank the Finnish and Norwegian ministries of foreign affairs, and in particular Matti Anttonen, Maimo Henriksson, Eija Limnell, Markus Lyra, Petri Salo, Merja Silvennoinen, Marja-Leena Vuorenpää; and Gyrid Celius, Robert Kvile, Sven Svedman, Olav-Nils Thue and Geir Westgaard.

Warm thanks are also due to Otto Mamelund of the Consulate General of Norway in St. Petersburg, Rune Aasheim of the Consulate General of Norway in Murmansk, Olli Perheentupa of the Consulate General of Finland in St. Petersburg, Polina Tsikoreva of the Norwegian University Centre in St. Petersburg, and Marja Koskela and Sari Rautio of the Embassy of Finland in Moscow, as well as the Finnish Ambassador to Norway, Peter Stenlund and the Norwegian Ambassador to Finland, Leidulv Namtvedt.

We are likewise greatly indebted to several high-ranking Russian officials who participated in the events organised by the project team: Andrei Avetisyan, Deputy Head of the European Cooperation Department, Ministry of Foreign Affairs of the Russian Federation; Evgenii Lukyanov, Deputy Plenipotentiary Envoy of the President of the Russian Federation to the North-West Federal District, Valentina Gortshakova of the North-West Development and Investment Promotion Agency and Slava Hodko of the Coordination Council on Cross-border Cooperation under the Presidential Plenipotentiary Envoy to the North-West Federal District. Our thanks also go to Jaakko Henttonen of the European Bank for Reconstruction and Development.

Marja Riikonen and Anna Salonsalmi provided considerable help with administrative matters at the Aleksanteri Institute, and Susan Høivik of the Norwegian Institute of International Affairs did the language editing. Jeremy Smith from the University of Birmingham also read and commented on several of the chapters. At the Centre for European Policy Studies (CEPS), Kathleen King and Els Van den Broeck worked very efficiently with manuscript preparation. Tommy Dahl Markussen kindly made a photo available for the cover of the book from the spectacular archives of SvalbardPictures. For their support, we thank the directors of the Aleksanteri Institute, Markku Kivinen, and the Norwegian Institute of International Affairs, Jan Egeland.

We also warmly thank the numerous researchers and policy-makers who commented on our continuing work at a series of seminars in Oslo, Helsinki and St. Petersburg during 2007–08, fully acknowledging that the list is not complete: Michael Emerson, who in addition to expertly overseeing this book's publication process at CEPS commented extensively on the chapter drafts, Johan Petter Barlindhaug, Pertti Joenniemi, Jahn-Otto Johansen, Kadri Liik, Andreas Ljunggren, Nikita Lomagin, Viljar Lubi, Arild Moe, Viatcheslav Morozov, Iver Neumann, Ingmar Oldberg, Tatiana Romanova, Pekka Sutela, Teija Tiilikainen and Stanislav Tkachenko.

1. INTRODUCTION
PAMI AALTO, HELGE BLAKKISRUD &
HANNA SMITH

1. A new northern dimension of Europe's neighbourhood?

In this book, we examine regional cooperation in Europe's northern neighbourhood. Regional cooperation remains an important part of European integration and the external relations of the European Union. In northern Europe in particular, the numerous formats of bilateral collaboration and multilateral policy initiatives during the past decade and a half have served to keep the agenda for northern regional cooperation a busy one.

By speaking of a 'new northern dimension' of Europe's neighbourhood in the title of this book, we wish to indicate how some old features have persisted in the northern regional agenda while others have changed in character and new issues have emerged. The old features include continuing collaboration among the Nordic states and their role as motors of regional cooperation. Today, however, EU funding has long since replaced Nordic funds as the most significant provider of practical means and incentives. At the same time, the Nordics have taken very different paths in their efforts at bolstering regional cooperation.

Finland and Norway look to intensify economic and political relations with Russia, now re-emerging as a great power. Additionally, for Finland, business and other forms of integration with Estonia is a natural and continuing process. Denmark's relations with Russia largely pertain to economic and agricultural cooperation, whereas the political aspects remain somewhat troubled. Iceland's geographical remoteness could be overcome with the new focus on Arctic energy and transport cooperation.

The severe economic problems Iceland is experiencing at the time of writing (autumn 2008) may dampen such hopes or alternatively the proposed Russian investment/loans to Iceland may bolster mutual ties. Sweden has been a notable investor in regional cooperation with Russia, but its interest has begun to shift more exclusively to the Baltic area. And together with the Baltic EU member states and Poland, Sweden is seeking to facilitate the Ukrainian aim of European integration and simultaneously to approach the western part of former Soviet territory in general, largely omitting Russia from these activities. The Balts and Poles, for their part, have longstanding conflicts with Russia on the interpretation of history – an issue that has again become pivotal as a side effect of the souring of their energy trade relations with Russia.[1]

This new situation presents a clear challenge for engaging Russia positively in northern European regional cooperation. We also feel that it is extremely important for the new northern dimension of Europe's neighbourhood to cultivate its good record and continue to include Russia as a natural and essential partner. Any work towards that goal can in turn pave the way for finding better working relations between the EU, its member states and Russia. Regardless of growing disillusionment, or a reality check on all sides compared with the promises of the early 1990s, a European–Russian partnership remains a widely shared goal in the wider European area. The webs of economic and energy policy interdependence between the two sides make such a partnership imperative.

The means by which this policy goal of ensuring Russia's place in the northern dimension of Europe's neighbourhood can be facilitated and the limitations along the way are our main concerns in this book.[2] We propose

---

[1] For more on these divisions, see P. Aalto and N. Tynkkynen, "The Nordic Countries: Engaging Russia, Trading in Energy or Taming Environmental Threats?", in P. Aalto (ed.), *The EU–Russia Energy Dialogue: Europe's Future Energy Security?*, Aldershot: Ashgate, 2007, pp. 119–29; and E. Berg, "The Baltic Gateway: A Corridor Leading towards Three Different Directions?", in P. Aalto (ed.), *The EU–Russia Energy Dialogue: Europe's Future Energy Security?*, Aldershot: Ashgate, 2007, pp. 145–62.

[2] The book is based on the Finnish–Norwegian research project, "The New Northern Dimension and the Possibility of an Energy Partnership – Cooperation between Finland and Norway", funded by the Ministry of Foreign Affairs of Finland and Ministry of Foreign Affairs of Norway, 2007–08.

a practical agenda that is in line with the evolving policy environment in Europe's wider neighbourhood and one that relies on the legacy of – as well as several recent tendencies in – northern European regional collaboration. We also offer our own policy recommendations for setting further priorities on this agenda. Yet, to identify where the northern experiences of regional cooperation can generate broader insights, we first need to situate the northern agenda in the wider framework of the European neighbourhood.

2.   A pragmatic approach to Europe's neighbourhood

In the contemporary policy debate on Europe's neighbourhood, grand designs are transforming into more pragmatic considerations. This process also means that the northern, eastern and southern directions are re-emerging as distinct policy platforms. One reason for the re-emergence of such 'dimensionalism' is the current internal dissonance within the EU.[3] Among other things, this obstructs the Union's ability to take a concerted look at its borders and make decisions on its institutional arrangements pertaining to relations with neighbours, such as the division of competencies, use of funds and setting of priorities.

Especially the 2004 'big bang' enlargement into an EU-25 highlighted and aggravated the Union's internal heterogeneity. By 2008, the number of member states had grown to 27, with several Balkan countries waiting in the wings for entry. The rejection of the EU's Constitutional Treaty by French and Dutch voters in 2005, and Ireland's rejection of the Treaty's watered-down version in 2008 for their part, meant dropping or at least postponing institutional reforms geared towards enhancing the conduct of relations with neighbours. For some disillusioned observers, the Union's internal integration is on the verge of collapse, while the associated enlargement fatigue is forcing EU policy-makers towards a practical, incremental or even minimalist policy agenda.[4]

---

[3] For 'dimensionalism' within the EU, see H. Haukkala, *A Hole in the Wall? Dimensionalism and the EU's New 'Neighbourhood Policy'*, UPI Working Paper No. 41/2003, Finnish Institute of Foreign Affairs, Helsinki, 2003.

[4] See A. Clesse, "The Enlargement Mess", *Europe's World*, No. 8, Spring 2008 (retrieved from www.europesworld.org/EWSettings/Article/tabid/191/Article Type/articleview/ArticleID/20805/Default.aspx).

These gloomy views may best be understood as wake-up calls rather than accurate reflections, as the EU is nevertheless continuing to attract many of its neighbours in the Balkans and beyond. On balance, it is fair to say that the practicable but very necessary work with the neighbourhood that we are witnessing in the current difficult conditions is leading to sector-specific, regional initiatives and to more clearly delimited policy agendas. To some extent, this merely reflects the enlarged form and territory of the EU, where it is only natural that regional interests should surface. Each corner of the EU has something special to it. This means encountering different neighbours and consequently having some region-specific needs for policy-making across the EU's borders.

One policy that is under pressure from these developments is the European Neighbourhood Policy (ENP), launched in 2004 for developing a zone of prosperity and a friendly neighbourhood. The grand goal of developing a coherent strategic view of the Union's environs continues to exist in the EU's parlance and policy-making machinery, but for example the policy's funding instrument still consists of regional components reminiscent of the previous fragmented instruments. The policy has also met increasing scepticism on the part of partner countries. Many of them have difficulties in finding their own priorities reflected in the policy's action plans, regardless of the declared principles of differentiation according to each partner's own individual merits and predicaments, and joint ownership of the policy.[5] Russia, for one, has opted not to become a party to the ENP even though it benefits from the funds available through the policy's funding instrument. At the same time, there is a debate on whether a new and more realistic strategic package should be introduced into EU–Russian relations,[6] or whether it is still possible to continue on the basis of the old 'common' (albeit strongly EU-defined) values including

---

[5] See P. Aalto, *European Union and the Making of a Wider Northern Europe*, London: Routledge, 2006(a), pp. 55–56; E. Barbé and E. Johansson-Nogués, "The EU as a Modest 'Force for Good': The European Neighbourhood Policy", *International Affairs*, Vol. 84, No. 1, 2008, pp. 86–89 and 95–96.

[6] See e.g. M. Emerson, *Time to Think of a Strategic Bargain with Russia*, CEPS Policy Brief No. 160, Centre for European Policy Studies, Brussels, May 2008; M. Leonard and N. Popescu, *A Power Audit of EU–Russia Relations*, European Council on Foreign Relations, London, 2007; R. Lyne, "Blueprint for a New Relationship with Russia", *Europe's World*, No. 9, Summer 2008, pp. 52–58.

democracy and human rights, alongside the somewhat less controversial principles of rule of law and market economy.[7]

In this book, we take a note of these sobering events, which instruct us to examine the merits of a *pragmatic approach* to issues of neighbourhood and regional cooperation across borders. A pragmatic approach should ideally be based on *common interests* shared by all parties and should include *realistic short-term targets within clearly defined areas of policy*. In the new northern dimension of Europe's neighbourhood, it is possible to test such an approach and develop it further. We suggest that although Europe's north is on the whole a well-researched topic, in current policy research it is not adequately covered as an example of practical, country- and sector-specific collaboration.

When it comes to engaging Russia, the northern experiences offer a mixture of bilateral and multilateral ties. Especially the latter have remained insufficiently covered in the recent policy literature. For example, a widely read blueprint for re-focusing the EU's Russian relations mentions how the bilateral track can be used to enforce common EU objectives instead of each member state striking its own selfish deals with Russia.[8] Although this may help in advancing objectives defined on the EU side, the authors fail to take note of the potential offered by multilateral platforms in regional cooperation with Russia.[9] And in northern Europe, there are many platforms of that kind.

We thus suggest that drawing lessons from practical bilateral *and* multilateral regional cooperation with Russia in the north can prove highly relevant not only for developing the northern policy agenda, and but also for engaging Russia on a more general level. Bilateral collaboration on northern environmental and natural resource issues was initiated in the 1970s, across the political divides of the cold war. Environmental and other scientific cooperation between Finland and the Soviet Union was paralleled by Norwegian–Soviet fisheries research and joint management of the fish stock within the Barents Sea. Since the early 1990s, collaboration has extended to various forms of soft security issues in both the Baltic and

---

[7] For a slightly different interpretation, see H. Haukkala, *False Premises, Sound Principles: The Way Forward in EU–Russia Relations*, UPI-FIIA Briefing Paper No. 20, Finnish Institute for International Affairs, Helsinki, April 2008(a).

[8] See Leonard and Popescu (2007), op. cit.

[9] Ibid.

Barents Sea areas, which has helped to expand bilateral work to the multilateral level.

Our primary research task in this book is to assess these well-established examples of practical regional cooperation in northern Europe, in both bilateral and multilateral formats. Our second research task is to assess new challenges of a more strategic nature that northern cooperation faces, for example as a result of the increasing role of the Baltic Sea in the transit of energy and other raw materials from resource-rich north-western Russia to European markets. Moreover, there are clear prospects for Norwegian–Russian energy sector cooperation, making the Barents Sea a similar playground of economic opportunities and environmental risks. The possible freeing of the Arctic Sea from multiyear ice in perhaps at most some 15–20 years as a result of global warming adds new opportunities for shipping from the North Atlantic to the Pacific. Such circumstances would make it easier for Russia to expand the currently minor northern energy transit route from Murmansk and its other northern territories, while also reducing its dependence on the Baltic and Black Sea ports. Even more notably, it will make the potentially huge energy resources in the Arctic's seabed available for exploitation, if the necessary technologies can be developed.

Many of these issues pertain, or may do so in the future, either implicitly or explicitly to the new Northern Dimension policy of the EU, Iceland, Norway and Russia, which was launched in a revamped format in 2006 to sharpen both sectorally and geographically the policy's old format initiated in the late 1990s (see Figure 1.1).

Figure 1.1 The Northern Dimension – Geographical scope

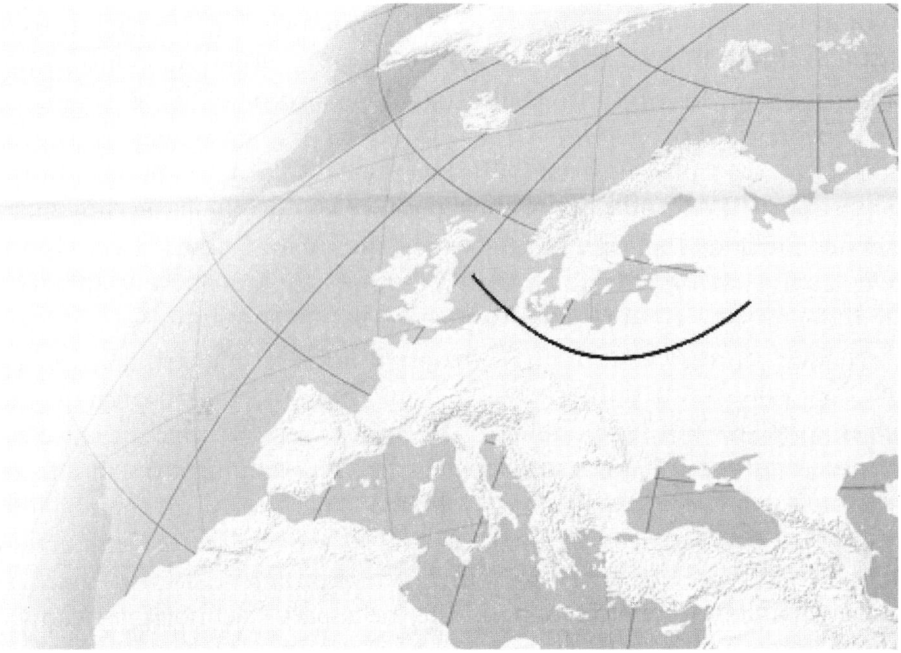

Source: The Northern Dimension Partnership in Public Health and Well-being
(retrieved from www.ndphs.org/?about_nd).

3.   New policy framework for Europe's north

The old Northern Dimension was an EU-defined policy aimed at creating a
policy framework and at introducing coherence, efficiency and added value
to the mosaic of existing northern policies. It has been claimed that the first
versions of the ENP picked up on these intentions, while the ENP's joint
ownership principle is also reminiscent of the Northern Dimension's
'partner-oriented' approach.[10]

On the initiative of Finland, the old Northern Dimension was
adopted by the EU as its policy in 1998. The birth of the policy has been
attributed to various factors – for example, that it represented Finland's

---

[10] See E. Lannon and P. van Elsuwege, "The EU's Northern Dimension and the
EMP-ENP: Institutional Frameworks and Decision-Making Processes Compared",
2004, p. 69 (retrieved from www.fscpo.unict.it/EuroMed/EDRC5/euneighbours
01.pdf).

response to the collapse of the cold war era 'Nordic balance' and that Finland's accession to the Union in 1995 created a new 1,300 km long EU–Russian border, and thus there was an urgent need to engage Russia actively in foreign and regional policy issues.[11] Simultaneously, the initiative reflected a need to institutionally coordinate the network of regional organisations in which the EU enjoyed a growing role as an agenda-setter: the Council of the Baltic Sea States (CBSS), the Barents Euro-Arctic Council (BEAC) and the Arctic Council (AC) (in the latter, however, the involvement of the United States has diminished the EU's weight). Some 600 sub-state organisations with a capacity for transborder activity[12] add to the sense of a vivid regional landscape in northern Europe.

The old Northern Dimension prompted a lively scholarly and policy debate, including both positive and critical assessments.[13] Especially the EU's action plans for the Northern Dimension for the years 1999–2006 encountered criticism from various angles, but perhaps most notably from the Russian government for not taking its views properly into consideration. The political declarations and lists of projects in the action plans failed to translate into tangible, practically implemented and financed projects. The Northern Dimension Environmental Partnership (NDEP), launched in 2001, improved the situation in the sector of environmental protection and nuclear safety. Today, the NDEP remains a workable model for concrete project collaboration in these spheres, having a special fund for which €243 million has already been pledged and which is eventually set to reach over €2 billion. The Northern Dimension Partnership in Public Health and Social Well-being (NDPHS) is also in operation. Unlike the NDEP, it does not have a special fund and its projects are mostly financed by a single

---

[11] See e.g. P. Aalto, S. Dalby and V. Harle, "The Critical Geopolitics of Northern Europe: Identity Politics Unlimited", *Geopolitics*, Vol. 8, No. 1, 2003, pp. 7–13; D. Arter, "Small State Influence within the EU: The Case of Finland's 'Northern Dimension Initiative'", *Journal of Common Market Studies*, Vol. 38, No. 5, 2000, pp. 679–81.

[12] See J.W. Scott, "Baltic Sea Regionalism, EU Geopolitics and Symbolic Geographies of Co-operation", *Journal of Baltic Studies*, Vol. 33, No. 2, 2002, p. 142.

[13] See Aalto, Dalby and Harle (2003), op. cit.; P. Aalto, "The Northern Dimension's Role in EU–Russia Relations", in H. Smith (ed.), *The Two-Level Game: Russia's Relations with Great Britain, Finland and the European Union*, Aleksanteri Institute, Helsinki, 2006(b), pp. 104–17.

source. Yet it represents an important experiment in creating a regional forum for the joint management of cross-border health challenges.

The new Northern Dimension that got underway in 2007 has a less EU-centric and more flexible framework. For the first time, Russia, Norway, Iceland and the EU are *equal partners*. As the partners declared in 2006:

> The present policy framework document is a joint achievement of the partners. The Northern Dimension partners recognize that their cooperation framework can only be driven by the spirit of partnership and based on shared confidence. The Northern Dimension policy is henceforward a common project and a common responsibility. It will help to ensure that no dividing lines are established in the North of Europe.[14]

Russia's longstanding concerns are addressed in the introduction of the notion of equality along with the reference to not creating dividing lines. This is what the Russian side has repeatedly asked for in the post-cold war era, but without becoming adequately understood in the enlargement frenzy of Western alliances.

Although the new Northern Dimension is declared to be founded on 'internationally recognised principles', it does not operate on the basis of conditionality, otherwise so typical of EU neighbourhood and external policies. Alongside the partners, other actors include the CBSS, BEAC, AC and the Nordic Council of Ministers as well as international financial institutions such as the European Bank for Reconstruction and Development (EBRD), the European Investment Bank and Nordic Investment Bank. In addition, various sub-state regional organisations participate. Moreover, in the new, more inclusive format of the policy, the US and Canada have become observers.[15] Still, the real centre of gravity in the new policy is the EU–Russian interface in the north:

---

[14] See the Northern Dimension Policy Framework Document (Helsinki, 24 November 2006), p. 1 (retrieved from http://ec.europa.eu/external_relations/north_dim/doc/frame_pol_1106.pdf).

[15] See C. Browning, "A Multi-Dimensional Approach to Regional Co-operation: The United States and the Northern European Initiative", *European Security*, Vol. 10, No. 4, 2001, pp. 84–108; C. Browning, "Competing or Complementary Policies? Understanding the Relationship between the NEI and ND", paper presented at the ISA conference, New Orleans, 24–27 March 2002.

> The Northern Dimension will be a regional expression of the Common Spaces EU/Russia. Russia and the European Union will make the Northern Dimension policy a cross-cutting topic and a tool where appropriate for the implementation of the road maps for the Common Spaces with full participation of Iceland and Norway in matters relevant to [the] Northern Dimension.[16]

Much like the old Northern Dimension, the new policy "will seek complementarity among its partners and participants" and "will focus on areas of cooperation where a regional and sub-regional emphasis brings added value". Nevertheless, priority is now to be given to "result-oriented proposals".[17] All this reflects the down-to-earth, practical nature of the policy that is very clearly based on concrete projects with a strong Russian focus. It is hence logical that the tried and tested NDEP and NDPHS partnerships remain at the policy's core. In the course of autumn 2008, the *logistics and transport sector* will become the next new area for setting up a formal partnership. The possibility of an *energy* partnership is being explored. The political declaration on the new Northern Dimension states that the partners "will ask [the Northern Dimension senior officials] to examine enhanced cooperation in the field of energy efficiency and renewable energy, inviting for this purpose also experts and international financing institutions".[18] Although not mentioned in the founding documents, debate at the policy-maker level indicates that a *cultural* partnership may also enter the picture.

4.   The policy challenges of the new Northern Dimension

The policy challenges facing the new Northern Dimension include matters relating to principles, policy environment, institutional structures and implementation, as discussed below.

1) Principles: How to put the equality principle into practice? The predecessor to the new Northern Dimension already had a partner-oriented aim. Even so, real equality remained unlikely as long as Russia struggled economically and the regional aid paradigm from the Nordics to Russia persisted. Only the strong growth of the Russian economy since

---

[16] See the "Political Declaration on the Northern Dimension Policy" (Helsinki, 24 November 2006), pp. 3–4.

[17] Ibid., p. 3.

[18] Ibid.

1998, which by the new millennium had made it a capable investor in regional cooperation, helped to institute the equality principle properly not only at the level of rhetoric but also in the more solid form of co-financing projects.

The EU–Russia 'common spaces' became a concrete manifestation of the EU–Russian strategic partnership in 2003, which were bolstered by the road maps in 2005. The notions of 'common spaces' and 'strategic partnership' in themselves imply the concept of an equality of sorts. At this grand level of EU–Russian relations we encounter Russia's goal of re-establishing itself as a great power of equal standing with the European power(s). The cornerstones of the EU–Russian relationship prior to the common spaces project – the Partnership and Cooperation Agreement (PCA), the TACIS funding instrument and the EU's ill-fated common strategy on Russia – were mostly built on EU-defined principles, despite ostensibly being jointly agreed.[19] Today, many of these principles are contested in Russia. The implementation of the common spaces has encountered problems as well (see chapter 2 in this book).[20] Given this situation, the Northern Dimension has a big task ahead if it is to act as a 'face-saver' and a reminder of successful cooperation.

2) Policy environment: How to compete/coordinate with other initiatives? The new Northern Dimension is to function as a coordinating policy within northern European regional cooperation, in the midst of other fora and initiatives. It has mediated the work of the regional councils CBSS and BEAC with increasing success.[21] Nonetheless, there is a notable challenge in the form of the planned Baltic Sea strategy for the EU. This strategy was initiated by the European Parliament during 2006–07. The European Commission is to give a report in the course of autumn 2008, with the strategy supposed to be adopted during Sweden's EU presidency in 2009. The beginning of the drafting process for the Baltic Sea strategy was geared largely towards solving problems in which Russia is an important party, but unfortunately, the process was initiated without consulting Russia. The considerable geographical overlap between the Baltic Sea strategy and the

---

[19] For a detailed analysis, see H. Haukkala, *Multi-Causal Social Mechanisms and the Study of International Institutionalisation: The Case of EU–Russia Strategic Partnership*, University of Turku, 2008(b).

[20] Ibid., ch. 8; see also Leonard and Popescu (2007), op. cit.

[21] See Aalto (2006a), op. cit., pp. 24–27.

Northern Dimension poses the dilemma of how to link the two fruitfully without damaging the Northern Dimension's promising start in engaging Russia constructively.

3) *Institutional structures: How to coordinate institutionally?* Institutionally, the successful implementation of the Northern Dimension relies on using flexible coordination mechanisms.[22] Within the EU, the Northern Dimension is part of the Union's external relations but cuts across all its three pillars: the funding instruments stem from the first pillar of the single market, the objectives come at least partly from the second pillar of external relations and some of the problems relate to the third pillar of justice and home affairs, including management of border regimes. Furthermore, the Northern Dimension includes cooperation among the EU, EU member state governments, regional organisations, international financial institutions and businesses.[23] The core activities of the new Northern Dimension – the partnerships – are flexible and open in terms of their composition. To handle all this, the institutional framework of the Northern Dimension involves ministerial meetings every two years and senior official meetings at least on every alternate year between them. Partners, observers and participants are invited to both sets of meetings. A steering group spearheaded by the partners meets three times a year and can invite participants and observers into its work. This all means that motivated and well-resourced parties can exert considerable influence on policy, and that there is relatively little institutionalisation in the formal sense for a policy with EU involvement.

4) *Implementation: How to develop existing partnerships and put into effect new and planned partnerships?* The new Northern Dimension promises to extend the experiences gained from the NDEP and NDPHS into the transport and logistics sectors, and possibly into the sphere of energy. Energy is set to remain one of the key themes in European policy. The geographical area covered by the Northern Dimension represents a significant reservoir of mostly untapped energy sources. Energy transport routes that are increasingly important cross the area. The region is home to some innovative experiments in environmentally friendly energy technology and boasts the example of the avant-garde Nordic electricity

---

[22] See Council of the European Union, *Full Report on Northern Dimension Policies*, 9804/01, Brussels, 12 June 2001.

[23] See Lannon and van Elsuwege (2004), op. cit., pp. 25–26.

market Nordpool and its related NORD-EL grid and regulatory mechanisms. The harsh northern conditions also create a suitable environment for testing energy efficiency policies and technical solutions. In short, it would be foolish not to consider the role energy can and should play in the Northern Dimension, as energy is already part and parcel of the northern policy agenda. Yet, extending Northern Dimension cooperation into the energy and transport sectors (which in Russia are increasingly viewed in a strategic light) may strip the policy of some of its uncontroversial and pragmatic qualities.

5.   A policy research challenge

The goal we set concerning the Northern Dimension in policy research is to move beyond the commonplace debate on the policy's overall merits. To this end, we analyse specific policy questions and sectors of northern European collaboration.

To situate the Northern Dimension in its wider context, in chapter 2 Hanna Smith discusses the policy as part of the broader picture of regionalism in international politics, in particular towards the former Soviet territory and Russia. Russia's efforts of building regional cooperation frameworks in its former Soviet sphere of interest have largely backfired. The new Northern Dimension's focus on advancing practical objectives enables Russia to maintain its great-power status as it does not push integration on unacceptable terms. At the local level in Russia, there is a demand for even more intensive practical collaboration. The deeper involvement of Canada and the US, two countries with some interests in the region, has been limited by Canada's fairly explicit Arctic focus and the shifting of US programmes from the Baltic Sea area towards the western parts of post-Soviet space. Nuclear safety cooperation represents a field in which they can meaningfully be involved regardless of the sensitive nature of this sector. Finally, Smith contends that gearing the Northern Dimension towards workable and sectoral partnerships may provide a model for how to resolve some of the problems in the PCA negotiations between the EU and Russia.

Part I of this book moves on to assess existing practical forms of northern cooperation. In chapter 3, Sigve R. Leland and Alf Håkon Hoel discuss the experiences of cooperation in the Barents region since the early 1990s. Problems of coordination between the two Barents councils – the intergovernmental and the regional ones – and their various working groups finally led to the establishment of an international secretariat in 2007 to complement national secretariats. In the health sector, there is a pattern of cooperation and potential competition prevailing between the Barents Health and Social Programme and the Northern Dimension's NDPHS. The chapter concludes by noting how regional cooperation also remains important for its own sake: actors 'learn by doing', and more time invested is likely to generate more of the trust and mutually shared objectives that Leland and Hoel deem important conditions for success.

In chapter 4, Alf Håkon Hoel deepens the examination of collaboration in the 'High North', to use the Norwegian term, into the cooperation in fisheries management between Norway and the Soviet Union/Russia from the 1970s onwards. The best practices accounting for the relative success in this case have included a robust but flexible legal regime at the wider international and the bilateral levels; learning over time; scientific cooperation to develop a joint framework acceptable to both parties; deliberately limiting cooperation to technical matters; and the ability and willingness to update the focus and working formats as necessary, not forgetting to synchronise actions with other relevant fora.

In chapter 5, Nina Tynkkynen analyses six cases of environmental cooperation in the Barents and Baltic Sea areas with a special focus on Finnish–Russian experiences. Concerning drivers of success, she stresses the role of common interests, shared objectives, expert-level collaboration, a learning-by-doing approach and trust, very much as Leland and Hoel concluded in the analysis of the Barents cooperation and the Norwegian–Russian fisheries management cases. In addition, she accentuates the benefits of finding partners and working formats that can be relatively independent from the central authorities. Joint funding is crucial as well. Additionally, Tynkkynen takes note of the very real effects of differences in cultural backgrounds that can hamper efforts at collaboration.

Aadne Aasland finds in chapter 6 that the relatively decentralised organisation of Russia's health sector has helped to stimulate cooperation in this sphere. He also mentions Russia's increasing financial capability, which will probably prove far more significant for addressing communicable diseases in the region than for example the NDPHS can ever do, regardless of the useful extra attention it assigns to the issue. That HIV/AIDS has been accepted as an issue at the political level in Russia has been a precondition of progress. Still, Aasland considers the overlapping Barents and Northern Dimension health-sector programmes to be hardly an ideal arrangement. He concludes by recommending greater involvement by research communities to foster the emerging expert and practitioner consensus in the field.

In chapter 7, Katri Pynnöniemi notes that two of the EU's five major trans-European transport axes pass through northern territories: the Motorways of the Seas and the Northern Axis. On the Russian side, however, policy planning has shifted from EU-defined corridors/axes to developing Russia's own 'international transport corridors' to facilitate energy exports, including pipelines and oil terminals. Unilateralism by the EU and Russia has similarly hampered efforts to solve the problems of the infamously long lorry queues on the Finnish–Russian border, and the Siberian overflight fees continue to be enforced for European aviation companies. Overall, Russian actors are in need of Western investments in this sector, but the new Northern Dimension transport and logistics partnership faces a daunting task if it is to succeed in helping to find acceptable formats and priorities.

In part II of this book, we turn to the second research task of assessing the new challenges facing northern cooperation. In chapter 8, Indra Øverland presents two major gas projects that increase the strategic significance of the European north and which can cover Russia's gas exports to Europe for decades: the Yamal Peninsula and the Shtokman fields in the Barents Sea. Whereas Yamal may eventually prove to be a predominately Russian project, in Shtokman the Russian actors will have a greater need for foreign partners owing to their own lack of expertise. French Total and Norwegian StatoilHydro have preliminarily acceded as minority shareholders in the company developing the fields. Although the Shtokman project will generate considerable cross-border activity in the north, Øverland laments how it has been conspicuously absent from the Northern Dimension, the main initiative for coordinating such issues among the EU, Russia and Norway.

Jakub M. Godzimirski's discussion of Russia's energy strategy in chapter 9 sheds further light on the difficulties of bolstering the Northern Dimension's take on energy. The Russian state has been consolidating its hold over the energy sector, limiting the role of foreign companies, co-opting the economic and political elite, using energy as a political tool and attempting to establish tighter control over energy transit routes. Foreign access to the Russian energy sector is being limited or closed, while Russian companies are aggressively trying to invest in the European downstream sector. In the midst of all this, especially the Russian military continues to view the Murmansk area, which is pivotal for Shtokman's development, as strategically significant. This means that at best the Northern Dimension can play a role in improving the energy efficiency of the Russian economy, and to a somewhat lesser degree, in promoting renewable energy technology in Russia. Local Russian actors have a particularly keen interest in these matters. Renewable energy technology companies in the Nordic states and Germany complement the potential partnership, which should have a strong public–private component.

In chapter 10, Morten Anker and Bjørn Brunstad survey the experiences of Norwegian companies working in Russia. They draw important conclusions regarding what policies like the Northern Dimension can offer for the inclusion of companies into public–private partnerships. In general, Western companies can enter into large-scale energy projects in the Russian energy sector only with considerable political support. In the energy services sector, however, the outlook is less restricted. Overall, considerable risks remain in the Russian economy. If the Northern Dimension can help with business risk mitigation by assisting in partner selection, project support, infrastructure development and moving administrative barriers, it will be of use. That being stated, in terms of project support, large companies have their own sources and direct contacts with top-level decision-makers in Russia. As for project funding, Norwegian companies have several already existing channels – and often even these are not used to their full potential.

Kari Liuhto concludes our review of possibilities for new public–private partnerships in chapter 11 by dividing the Russian economy into the strategically non-sensitive, economically sensitive, militarily sensitive and top-sensitive sectors. He also notes that in addition to Russia's new law on the strategic sectors of the economy, economic nationalism has many other features that Western investors must take into account, such as state corporations and Kremlin-supported oligarchs. Any Northern Dimension activities in the fields of transport, logistics and even electricity generation will be subject to the rising strategic significance of these sectors. Nevertheless, that consumer goods remain outside the strategic realm opens up good prospects for cross-border economic activity in the region. Interestingly, according to Liuhto, the Russian leadership will sooner or later have to consider re-opening Russia's economy.

In the end comment we invited for this book, Irina Busygina and Mikhail Filippov revisit the connections between the strategic and regional levels in EU–Russian relations. They contend that for reasons related to the respective internal politics of Russia and the EU, tensions at the strategic level are likely to continue. To ensure that the Northern Dimension is insulated from this unfortunate cycle, it should be limited to localised and non-politicised matters where it can make a real difference. Issues such as democracy, human rights and the strategic aspects of energy security are best left out. Keeping the Northern Dimension tightly focused would best recognise the effectiveness of 'small and smart' strategies that various northern actors have utilised in their relations with Russia, and this approach is likely to benefit Russian regional actors most directly. In this way, those living in the Northern Dimension area could also best ensure a degree of 'subsidiarity' and ownership of the policy.

Finally, in the conclusions to the book, we briefly evaluate the degree to which the Northern Dimension can respond to the four policy challenges identified above. We also summarise our policy recommendations for developing each of the existing and planned Northern Dimension partnerships.

6. References

Aalto, P. (2006a), *European Union and the Making of a Wider Northern Europe*, London: Routledge, pp. 24–27 and 55–56.

—————— (2006b), "The Northern Dimension's Role in EU–Russia Relations", in H. Smith (ed.), *The Two-Level Game: Russia's Relations with Great Britain, Finland and the European Union*, Aleksanteri Institute, Helsinki, pp. 104–17.

Aalto, P. and N. Tynkkynen (2007), "The Nordic Countries: Engaging Russia, Trading in Energy or Taming Environmental Threats?", in P. Aalto (ed.), *The EU–Russia Energy Dialogue: Europe's Future Energy Security?*, Aldershot: Ashgate, pp. 119–29.

Aalto, P., S. Dalby and V. Harle (2003), "The Critical Geopolitics of Northern Europe: Identity Politics Unlimited", *Geopolitics*, Vol. 8, No. 1, pp. 7–13.

Arter, D. (2000), "Small State Influence within the EU: The Case of Finland's 'Northern Dimension Initiative'", *Journal of Common Market Studies*, Vol. 38, No. 5, pp. 679–81.

Barbé, E. and E. Johansson-Nogués (2008), "The EU as a Modest 'Force for Good': The European Neighbourhood Policy", *International Affairs*, Vol. 84, No. 1, pp. 86–89 and 95–96.

Berg, E. (2007), "The Baltic Gateway: A Corridor Leading towards Three Different Directions?", in P. Aalto (ed.), *The EU–Russia Energy Dialogue: Europe's Future Energy Security?*, Aldershot: Ashgate.

Browning, C. (2001), "A Multi-Dimensional Approach to Regional Co-operation: The United States and the Northern European Initiative", *European Security*, Vol. 10, No. 4, pp. 84–108.

————— (2002), "Competing or Complementary Policies? Understanding the Relationship between the NEI and ND", paper presented at the ISA conference, New Orleans, 24–27 March.

Clesse, A. (2008), "The Enlargement Mess", *Europe's World*, No. 8, Spring, pp. 10–12.

Council of the European Union (2001), *Full Report on Northern Dimension Policies*, 9804/01, Brussels, 12 June.

Emerson, M. (2008), *Time to Think of a Strategic Bargain with Russia*, CEPS Policy Brief No. 160, Centre for European Policy Studies, Brussels, May.

Haukkala, H. (2003), *A Hole in the Wall? Dimensionalism and the EU's New 'Neighbourhood Policy'*, UPI Working Paper No. 41/2003, Finnish Institute for Foreign Affairs, Helsinki.

————— (2008a), *False Premises, Sound Principles: The Way Forward in EU–Russia Relations*, UPI-FIIA Briefing Paper No. 20, Finnish Institute for International Affairs, Helsinki, April.

————— (2008b), *Multi-Causal Social Mechanisms and the Study of International Institutionalisation: The Case of EU–Russia Strategic Partnership*, University of Turku.

Lannon, E. and P. van Elsuwege (2004), "The EU's Northern Dimension and the EMP-ENP: Institutional Frameworks and Decision-Making Processes Compared", p. 69 (retrieved from www.fscpo.unict.it/EuroMed/EDRC5/euneighbours01.pdf).

Leonard, M. and N. Popescu (2007), *A Power Audit of EU–Russia Relations*, European Council on Foreign Relations, London.

Lyne, R. (2008), "Blueprint for a New Relationship with Russia", *Europe's World*, No. 9, Summer, pp. 52–58.

Scott, J.W. (2002), "Baltic Sea Regionalism, EU Geopolitics and Symbolic Geographies of Co-operation", *Journal of Baltic Studies*, Vol. 33, No. 2, p. 142.

2. RUSSIAN FOREIGN POLICY, REGIONAL COOPERATION AND NORTHERN RELATIONS
HANNA SMITH

1. Introduction

Since the late 1980s, various forms of regionalism have emerged throughout the world. The concept of 'new regionalism' is often connected with developments in the Asia–Pacific region. But looking at developments especially during the past 10 years in Europe and the European Union, we can start talking about a new regionalism in Europe as well.

The widening and deepening of European integration is perhaps the most pronounced example of this trend. Regional cooperation now also forms part of the external relations of the EU. Examples here include the Northern Dimension policy, the Black Sea cooperation initiative, the Mediterranean Union, the Barcelona process and the proposal for a specific eastern dimension in the European Neighbourhood Policy (ENP). Each of these initiatives involves different partners and operates within varying remits, but they all fall into the category of regional cooperation. It is against this background and the broader context of Russia's relations with the West that this chapter examines the place of the Northern Dimension.

2. Regional organisations in the former Soviet space

Some EU-led initiatives involve partners from the post-Soviet space, although we also find patterns of regional cooperation and attempts at multilateral action without EU involvement. Such Eurasian regionalism has generally been dominated by Russian initiatives. References to a "social construction of Europe" that emphasise "polity formation through rules and norms, the transformation of identities, the role of ideas and the uses of language" are not so different from the way in which Russia has attempted to build regional cohesion on the ruins of the Soviet Union.[1] In these arrangements, Russia would naturally be the patron.

The most notable attempt at economic and political integration has been the Commonwealth of Independent States (CIS), set up to manage the collapse of the Soviet Union peacefully. Today, however, it has the weakest prospects of all the integration projects in this area. Another attempt – this time at total integration – has been the proposed union between Russia and Belarus. Today, that process also seems further from its initial goal than ever before, and the idea of Belarusian statehood has grown stronger.

In the field of economic cooperation, the idea of a Single Economic Space (SES) among Russia, Belarus, Kazakhstan and Ukraine has been on and off the agenda. At first, the SES gathered momentum as each of the four members ratified the deal quickly. But then, just as rapidly as it had been initiated and pushed forward, it came to a halt and is now fading away. The Eurasian Economic Community (EurAsEC) is a more successful project. Growing out of the CIS customs union, it was established by Belarus, Kazakhstan, Kyrgyzstan, Russia and Tajikistan in 2001. The Organisation of Central Asian Cooperation merged with EurAsEC after having been an international organisation from 1991 to 2006, consisting of Kazakhstan, Kyrgyzstan, Tajikistan, Uzbekistan and Russia. Georgia, Turkey and Ukraine had observer status in the latter.

Yet, economic cooperation and integration in the Eurasian region has proven difficult, owing to highly differing approaches and notions of identity. The current leadership of Ukraine, being the only potential rival power to Russia (besides Kazakhstan), has a clear Western orientation and robustly challenges Russian initiatives and motives for integration. For reformers in Ukraine, the idea of European integration is closer to their hearts than is the Russian version.

In the area of security, it has been easier to find a common approach, since in security matters smaller states will often join the bandwagon of a stronger one. The Eurasian organisations on security cooperation are the Collective Security Treaty Organisation, which is a Russian-led defence alliance of Russia, Belarus, Armenia, Kazakhstan, Uzbekistan, Kyrgyzstan and Tajikistan; and the Shanghai Cooperation Organisation, which is

---

[1] See T. Christiansen, K. Jørgensen and A. Wiener, "The Social Construction of Europe", *Journal of European Public Policy*, Vol. 6, No. 4, 1999, p. 528.

composed of China and five post-Soviet states – Russia, Kazakhstan, Kyrgyzstan, Tajikistan and Uzbekistan. Regional integration processes in the former Soviet space that are clearly moving away from Russian domination include GUAM (Georgia, Ukraine, Azerbaijan and Moldova) and the Community of Democratic Choice that was established in 2005 (Georgia, Ukraine, Estonia, Latvia, Lithuania, and Moldova). The latter also includes full members from outside the post-Soviet area, i.e. Romania, Slovenia and the Republic of Macedonia, as well as members with observer status: Azerbaijan, Czech Republic, Bulgaria, Hungary, Poland, the United States, the EU and the Organisation for Security and Cooperation in Europe. Eurasian regional cooperation has been rich in ideas since the collapse of the Soviet Union, but has also largely been a rollercoaster ride, with the best forms of cooperation not yet agreed.

3.   Russian foreign policy and the new regionalism

Developments in the post-Soviet space have influenced Russian foreign policy and brought regionalism to prominence on the Russian foreign policy agenda. Arguably, there are two main principles driving Russian foreign policy – great-power politics and regionalism. Under these two main headings are four sub-themes: multilateralism, *ressentiment*, imperialism (in various forms and meaning more of a mindset than actual action) and the principle of sovereignty.[2]

The Northern Dimension framework is a case in which Russia engages in regional cooperation as an equal partner – and crucially, outside the post-Soviet space. At the same time, the Northern Dimension includes both of the main principles of Russian foreign policy: great-power politics and regionalism. In this manner, the Northern Dimension can facilitate the identification of overlapping interests and best practices in achieving common goals and mutual interests on two different levels. Furthermore, what makes the Northern Dimension framework different from most of the Eurasian initiatives is that practical cooperation, once begun, has been quite successful (see chapters 5 and 6). It also provides possibilities for new forms of collaboration, even during times when cooperation between Russia and the West is otherwise deadlocked (see chapter 7). Whether the Northern Dimension is looked at as a 'policy framework with projects' or

---

[2] See H. Smith, "Det förflutnas inflytande på rysk utrikespolitik", *Nordisk Østforum*, Vol. 19, No. 3, 2005, pp. 287–306.

as 'projects with a policy framework', the result is the same: projects expressing common interests are advanced much more effectively than in the former Soviet space. One reason is that the equality principle of the Northern Dimension does not readily give the upper hand to any of the partners. It also constitutes a new kind of regional cooperative framework – cooperation without expectations of integration – thereby minimising the effect of politics and questions of identity. On the other hand, this can also be seen as a drawback, since a member may choose not to participate in some initiatives, hence making it less effective.

'New regionalism' is situated at the interface of globalisation, regionalism and multilateralism. Of these, regionalism may be either a stumbling block or a building block to multilateralism.[3] As an expression of new regionalism, the Northern Dimension is variously used in Russian foreign policy: to achieve practical goals (on the environment, health, education, cross-border cooperation, etc.); as one type of identity marker (northern countries, northern identity); and as an important political tool (being an equal partner, obtaining inside access to EU politics and establishing a counterweight to other regional developments in the former Soviet region). Chief characteristics of new regionalism are its multidimensionality, complexity, fluidity and non-conformity, and that it involves a range of state and non-state actors, who often come together in fairly informal ways. This is the strength of the Northern Dimension, but it also poses a potential threat to its success. For the future, the test of the new regionalism is to go beyond 'safe' subjects that are not politically volatile. Issues commonly taken up in the framework of regional cooperation are environmental and health matters as well as cross-border cooperation on a small scale. Education and culture also fall into this category. It will be a challenge, however, to extend this cooperation to sectors like energy.

The Northern Dimension is not as such an organisation or an institution, which may be an advantage or disadvantage for the success of the framework. Either way, it serves as a case study of how new regionalism can offer solutions to longstanding problems in relations between Russia and Europe.

---

[3] See Y. Usui, "An Evolving Path of Regionalism: The Construction of an Environmental Acquis in the EEC and ASEAN", ISS Research Series, *Bulletin of Universities and Institutes*, No. 24, 2007, pp. 31–66.

4.   Neighbours for better and for worse[4]

Towards the end of 2007, there was more and more talk about stagnating, declining and troubled Russian–EU relations. Even the nomination of a new president for Russia, Dmitry Medvedev, with a reputation of being more 'liberal' than his predecessor Vladimir Putin, did not ameliorate the diplomatic climate. At the same time, economic ties were flourishing. As a result, there has been a widespread call to redefine the strategic partnership between the EU and Russia. In the West, Russia is seen as pursuing a more aggressive foreign policy. The Russian position, by contrast, is that the West cannot handle a revived Russia and shows no respect for Russian views. Several high profile analyses have appeared on the Russian side about the reasons behind the troubled times for Russia's relations with the West in general and for Russian–EU relations in particular since Putin's Munich speech in February 2007.[5] Foreign minister Sergei Lavrov has even used the term 'post-Munich era'. In an article for *Expert*, he put the principle of sovereignty at the core of Russian international politics together with international law and market principles.[6] Nevertheless, Lavrov defines the economy as the first priority guiding Russian foreign policy. The interesting aspect of Russian analyses in the post-Munich era is the emphasis on Russian traumas not being so much about the Soviet period as about the 1990s.

---

[4] At the time of writing, the Russian–EU relationship has been thrown into turmoil by the conflict between Georgia and Russia in August 2008. While this threatens to slow down the development of cooperation in the immediate future, the longer-term impact is unclear.

[5] Notable Western analyses on Russia were published in 2007 by bodies such as the Finnish Parliament's Committee for the Future (O. Kuusi, H. Smith and P. Tihonen (eds), *Russia 2017: Three Scenarios*, Committee for the Future, Parliament of Finland, Helsinki, 2007); the UK House of Commons Committee for Foreign Affairs (*Global Security: Russia Report*, UK Parliament, London, November 2007 (retrieved from www.publications.parliament.uk/pa/cm200708/cmselect/cmfaff/51/5102.htm); the European Council on Foreign Relations (M. Leonard and N. Popescu, *A Power Audit of EU–Russia Relations*, European Council on Foreign Relations, London, 2007); and in the US, by the Centre for Strategic and International Studies (A. Kuchins, *Alternative Futures for Russia to 2017*, Centre for Strategic and International Studies, Washington, D.C., 2007).

[6] See S. Lavrov, "The Foreign Policy of Russia: A New Phase", *Expert*, 17 December 2007.

Any frameworks launched or agreements made in the 1990s are mostly viewed in a negative light in Russia: it is argued that the West took advantage of a weak Russia. Such an analysis objects to any claims of the West as being the winner of the cold war. To the contrary, proponents of this argument claim that the West has lost its unity since the Soviet threat has disappeared. One reason many Western analyses are so keen to keep Russian domestic affairs on the international agenda is said to be that they need to continue portraying Russia as a threat. In Russian interpretations of world politics there is also a strongly stated desire to cooperate and avoid direct confrontation. Lavrov, in fact, has called for a new great power concert of the 21st century.[7]

Since the Munich speech, the rhetoric of Russian foreign policy has toughened considerably but three major areas appear especially problematic in Russian–Western relations. According to Konstantin Kosachev, chairperson of the State Duma's committee for international affairs,

> if we put aside the root cause of our present problems – that is, an adherence to winner/loser logic – and thoroughly examine the key points of our differences, we will find that none of them are truly systemic (that is, of course, if the West does not have a systemic desire to counter Russia under any circumstances). At this time, we will delineate the three major groups of differences – security, values, and the situation in the post-Soviet space – that are not insurmountable if their causes are correctly established.[8]

Kosachev's comments on differences in Russian–Western relations as culminating on questions of security, values and post-Soviet space also apply to the Russian–EU level. Let us first look at the question of values. Values are represented in common norms and rules. The 'values gap' originates in the weak normative framework of EU–Russian relations. The Partnership and Cooperation Agreement (PCA) is still the cornerstone of relations but it has lost much of its stature because both Russia and the EU have changed considerably since 1994. Indeed, the faith in and future of the Russian-EU PCA is also a central question for the future of the EU's

---

[7] Ibid.

[8] See K. Kosachev, "Russia and the West: Where the Differences Lie", *Russia in Global Affairs*, Vol. 4, No. 4, 2007, pp. 37–48 (retrieved from http://eng.global affairs.ru/numbers/21/1149.html).

external relations with the East. Here, first of all, the EU needs to form a clear vision of how it wants to develop its external policy on its eastern borders. This is not only a matter of Russian–EU relations but also how the EU sees its relations with Ukraine, Belarus, Moldova and the states of the South Caucasus. Coordination between these two spheres is essential. After that can we think about what the EU wants from Russia and vice versa.

For the Russian side, despite some contradictory statements, Europe and the EU are still the focal points with regard to Russia's modernisation. A part of Russian identity is also distinctively European. Yet, it can be argued that Russia's approach to Europe is still at a formative stage. When it comes to concrete issues, Russia would appear to have three main objectives towards the EU: a common economic area, a visa-free border and some possibility to participate in EU decision-making – along the lines of Russia's ties with NATO, for example. The EU has shown a positive attitude towards the idea of a visa-free border and the formation of a common economic area. But giving even a limited possibility of participating in EU decision-making to Russia seems impossible. The EU is unique as an international organisation and it does not even have observer members. Therefore, when drafting the future normative framework for Russian–EU relations, whether a new PCA or something different, sectoral and regional normative frameworks might well be the right paths to follow. Some of the lessons and successful practices from reviving the Northern Dimension process could well be used in the negotiation process between Russia and the EU for a new PCA.

Questions related to security and the post-Soviet space put a strain on Russian–EU relations. External actors and affairs have increased the stresses, most notably the US, which plays the leading role in several issues that also concern Russia and the EU: Kosovo, the former Soviet area, the Treaty on Conventional Armed Forces in Europe, missile defence and Iran. The US is a sensitive topic for the Russians. It is a reminder and the defining factor of Russia's own great-power aspirations. The gap between Russia and the US is no longer ideological, which for a while led to the illusion that trouble-free cooperation could emerge. Russia is an odd mixture, however, of Western-style culture and norms as well as uniquely Russian qualities, and thus a country where things that are impossible anywhere else seem possible there.

In many issues, Russia and the US are on opposite sides. Sometimes Russia is an enemy, sometimes an adversary, sometimes a competitor and sometimes a partner. This situation creates a challenge for the EU's Russian policies, since both countries are important partners to the EU. A clear example of where the role of the US has put even more strain on Russian–EU relations is the Georgian/Russian conflict in 2008. In fact, most of the hostile commentary towards the West coming out of Russia, whether from the president, prime minister, foreign minister or other officials, blamed the US for the situation, thereby putting the EU in the middle of a new battlefield of spheres of influence. For the US, Georgia has become what Cuba was for the Soviet Union during the cold war. The Russian Federation is not the same military force as the former Soviet Union was, but it still has the capacity to make the world a very dangerous place. During the cold war, small-scale cooperation was what kept hopes for a better future alive. There is also a place for a framework like the Northern Dimension to play a small but significant role in Russian–EU relations during difficult times.

Sergei Ryabkov, a representative of the Russian Ministry of Foreign Affairs, stated in December 2007 that Russia is ready for cooperation and integration with the EU as intensively and at as fast a pace as the EU wishes.[9] Yet, while Russia expresses a desire to integrate with the EU and Europe, it does not want to have rules dictated to it, and this also applies to Russia's domestic arrangements. A common viewpoint of what human rights are, for example, has not yet been achieved. Moreover, Russia and the EU member states have very different ideas regarding state intervention in civil society and on issues relating to freedom of the press.

Still, the principles that foreign minister Lavrov defined in his above-mentioned article constitute the framework within which Russia is ready to work. Practical cooperation comes before integration. Russia and the EU should both accept their mutual differences but also ensure that commonly agreed decisions are kept and honoured. A positive starting point is that both sides genuinely seem to want to do business together.

5. North America and the Northern Dimension

The US and Canada have observer status in the renewed Northern Dimension. The US is involved in the northern region through several

---

[9] Refer to S. Ryabkov's presentation at the Conference on "Russia and the European Union – Future of Cooperation", organised by Bertelsmann Stiftung, Konrad Adenauer Stiftung, the German Chamber of Commerce and Industry and the German–Russian Forum, Moscow, 17–18 December 2007.

multilateral frameworks. In the Barents Euro-Arctic Council, the US and Canada are observers, and they are full members of the Arctic Council. Within these frameworks, Russia and the US can meet without the same kind of pressure that accompanies more high-profile encounters. In addition to the European Northern Dimension, there is a second, different, Northern Dimension that is a key element of Canadian foreign policy. The Canadian Northern Dimension has four priority areas:

> support for the work of the Arctic Council; participation in the expanding international support for northern Russia; realizing the full potential of the University of the Arctic, and enhancing a Canadian and circumpolar policy research network; and promoting sustainable development through the pursuit of economic and trade opportunities across the circumpolar region.[10]

For Canada, the north equates to the circumpolar region and the Arctic, while the EU's framework focuses more on Russia and the Baltic Sea states. This has given rise to conceptual tension with some practical implications. Nevertheless, within the renewed Northern Dimension framework the Arctic element is much stronger than in the old format. This outcome stems not only from the equal partnership of Norway, Iceland and Russia, but also from the geopolitical importance that the Arctic has been gaining. While the 'north' of North America, Europe and Russia all have their distinct features, the underlying issues are generally the same. Strengthening the trans-Atlantic link especially with regard to the Northern Dimension would support both regional and global cooperation.

From the perspective of the US, the European north generally has not played a very important role. Yet, several reasons have prompted the US to pay more attention to the region. In September 1997, the US launched its Northern European Initiative (NEI). The official goal was to demonstrate that integration and cooperation in northern Europe would benefit Russia and its Baltic neighbours. The NEI articulated six specific priorities: trade and business promotion, law enforcement, energy, the environment, public health and efforts at building civil society. It included largely the same

---

[10] See Foreign Affairs and International Trade Canada, "The Northern Dimension of Canada's Foreign Policy", Communications Bureau Department of Foreign Affairs and International Trade, Ottawa, 2008 (retrieved from www.international.gc.ca/polar-polaire/ndfp-vnpe2.aspx?lang=en#16).

geographical area as the Northern Dimension.[11] While the Northern Dimension targets north-western Russia on issues like cross-border health challenges and the environment, the NEI funded similar projects in the Baltic countries. The initiative was not particularly successful, however, because of reservations on the part of Russia and the EU. Today, the emergence of a stronger Russia with a more assertive energy policy has refocused the US interest in the northern European region, especially its Arctic parts.

The latest vehicle for US policy targeting the Baltic Sea area is called the Enhanced Partnership in Northern Europe (e-PINE) Programme, introduced in late 2003. The US State Department claims that this represents an updated US policy for the area in the light of the NEI's successful implementation: "The [NEI] policy's foremost goal, the integration of Estonia, Lithuania, and Latvia into the western European community of democracies, has been achieved, as symbolised by offers of North Atlantic Treaty Organisation (NATO) and European Union (EU) membership for the three states."[12] The e-PINE organises US activity within and in cooperation with the eight Nordic and Baltic States (thus not including Russia) in three broad focal areas: cooperative security, healthy societies and vibrant economies. It also seeks to promote US business links in the region. Where the e-PINE differs significantly from the new Northern Dimension is in the area of political security.

E-PINE includes cooperation in the fight against terrorism, something almost completely alien to the Northern Dimension. Still, at least from the US perspective, e-PINE should only support the EU's Northern Dimension, not compete with it.[13] The e-PINE programme has taken on new forms and directions since its initial launch in 2003. The Baltic countries no longer

---

[11] See A. Sergounin, "The United States' Northern Dimension? Prospects for a US–Russian Cooperative Agenda in Northern Europe", PONARS Policy Memo No. 232, prepared for the PONARS Policy Conference in Washington, D.C., 25 January 2002 (retrieved from www.csis.org/media/csis/pubs/pm_0232.pdf).

[12] For more information on the e-PINE Programme, see the e-PINE website at www.state.gov/p/eur/rt/epine/c10621.htm.

[13] See the testimony of Heather Conley, Deputy Assistant Secretary for European and Eurasian Affairs, "U.S., Northern Europe Working to Advance Democracy", before the House Committee on International Relations, the Enhanced Partnership in Northern Europe, 21 April 2004.

wanted to be the focus of the programme, and consequently Belarus, Ukraine, Moldova and Georgia were taken on board.[14] E-PINE consultations have also taken place with an expanded agenda. In April 2008, for example, discussions in Riga within the e-PINE format focused on the assessment of the situation in the neighbouring regions of the EU and developments in the Balkans, Afghanistan, the Middle East and Cuba.[15] E-PINE appears more political in nature than the Northern Dimension is or seeks to be, but both have regional cooperation as their basic starting point.

The trans-Atlantic connection is extremely important for the north, and it is vital to explore the ways in which the US and Canada could be better connected to the new Northern Dimension framework. As major global powers, both Russia and the US set their political agendas differently from their northern neighbours. Big-power politics tends to play a key role, and as a rule global considerations overrule the purely regional ones. Therefore, engaging great powers in the regional context will depend on how the region fits into their global agendas. The Baltic and Barents Seas have assumed greater global strategic importance, and thus have attracted the interest of the US and Russia. In the future, the question of the Arctic areas and their exploitation will grow in importance, and with it the role of Norway and Iceland.

6.   Nuclear safety cooperation

Questions of nuclear safety are of global interest. Within the Northern Dimension framework, cooperation on nuclear safety takes place under the environmental partnership. Nonetheless, nuclear safety differs significantly from conventional environmental cooperation and is politically a more sensitive issue. It is also a subject that attracts interest beyond regional cooperation. Nuclear safety in the north is of interest to the US and Canada as well as to the European great powers – the United Kingdom, Germany, and France. For example, the support fund of the Northern Dimension

---

[14] See M. Evans, "The US-North European Partnership: Advancing Democracy beyond the Baltics", Keynote Address, University of Washington, 26 May 2005 (retrieved from http://depts.washington.edu/baltic/lectures/evans_2005_05_26.htm).

[15] See the Ministry of Foreign Affairs of the Republic of Latvia, "Foreign Ministry Political Director in e-PINE Washington Consultations Discusses Current International Issues", Ministry of Foreign Affairs, Riga, 2008 (retrieved from www.am.gov.lv/en/news/press-releases/2008/april/30-1).

Environmental Partnership (NDEP) includes a funding window earmarked for nuclear safety issues. Since it became operational in 2003, France, Canada, the UK, the Netherlands and Belgium have contributed funding through this window (although not through the non-earmarked window covering conventional environmental cooperation). Also, the EU contributes more to the nuclear safety window than to conventional environmental cooperation – €40 million compared with €30 million (see chapter 5).

The nuclear window of the NDEP was built on the Multilateral Nuclear Environmental Programme in Russia (MNEPR). This programme facilitated work in three main areas: radioactive waste management, spent nuclear fuel security and reactor safety. Signatories include Belgium, Denmark, Finland, France, Germany, the Netherlands, Norway, Russia, Sweden and the UK, plus the European Commission and the European Atomic Energy Community. The US signed one part of the accord, but not the protocol on questions of liability structures.[16] The MNEPR was also supported by the announcement of the G-8 initiative against the spread of weapons and materials of mass destruction (at the Kananaskis summit in Canada, 2002), which gave priority to the safe and secure decommissioning of Russian nuclear submarines.

The NDEP's nuclear safety window operates through two channels: the Strategic Master Plan (SMP) and the Strategic Environmental Assessment (SEA). The SMP is a top-level work programme that helps decision-makers to define and prioritise projects. The SMP has been developed as a document that can be continuously modified according to further experience gained. It enables critical actions to be launched in time without impairing the outcome of the whole plan. The same idea can also be found in the renewed Northern Dimension framework. The aim of the SEA, for its part, is to evaluate the potential environmental impact of the activities defined in the SMP for the decommissioning of nuclear-powered naval vessels and other radiologically dangerous facilities in north-western Russia.

Four of the most recent projects in the nuclear safety window of the NDEP were signed in June 2008 between the European Bank for Reconstruction and Development (EBRD) and the newly established

---

[16] The umbrella agreement for the Cooperative Threat Reduction programme remains the liability foundation for all US–Russian nuclear dismantlement projects.

Russian state corporation Rosatom. The largest of these is the decommissioning of the Lepse vessel currently moored at Atomflot in Murmansk. The project will involve moving the vessel into a shipyard at Nerpa before the spent fuel is removed from the ship, which will then be dismantled. Project costs are estimated at €43 million. Other projects are a €20 million grant to Andreeva Bay, where some 22,000 spent nuclear fuel assemblies need to be removed from deteriorating dry storage tanks, repacked and exported from the site for reprocessing; €5.6 million for de-fuelling of the Papa-class nuclear submarine; and €5.1 million to help improve the radiation monitoring and emergency response system in the Arkhangelsk region. Vince Novak, Director of Nuclear Safety of the EBRD, termed these projects a milestone in NDEP nuclear safety cooperation, and a clear sign that implementation of the SMP is underway. He also noted the great commitment of the Russian side.[17]

Nuclear safety cooperation has been slow to move forward in the Northern Dimension framework, but it is still a good example of how even more sensitive issues can be dealt with and moved forward, albeit slowly and through a lengthy process of negotiations. Although the international media increasingly refer to a 'new cold war' between the Russian Federation and the Western world, the gradual movement forward in regional cooperation and wide collaborative frameworks like the Northern Dimension ensure that the clock will not be turned back.

7.   Conclusion

The vulnerability of cooperative frameworks between Russia and the West has been demonstrated by the events of August 2008 in Georgia. Within the former Soviet space there is also tension in regional cooperation, given the usually undisguised aim of Russia to dominate and given its perceptions – rightly or wrongly – of the national interests of the US being far too often taken into account. While it remains to be seen whether the Northern Dimension will be affected by the sudden deterioration in overall relations, so far it has proven a more stable cooperation framework than many others. In part, this is because the Northern Dimension has mostly been concerned with 'soft' issues. The Northern Dimension is also unique in assigning equal status to each of its partners and operating according to

---

[17] See the *NDEP Newsletter*, No. 16, July 2008.

consensus around individual issues, but without any strict veto rights, in addition to being particularly flexible.

The Northern Dimension remains a relatively unknown concept in Russian foreign policy. The same is true within the larger context of the EU. For those who are in touch with the concrete actions and practical cooperation within the Northern Dimension, especially in Finland and Norway, the benefits are relatively clear. Working with Russia on an equal footing is a fairly new experience both in the West and in Russia, and the Northern Dimension is often wrongly interpreted as a multilateral framework in which Russia has veto rights. It is true that most of the practical projects launched within the framework of the Northern Dimension have to involve consensus among all the partners. Yet, once this consensus has been achieved, the results have generally benefited all partners.

The factor that makes the Russian side somewhat slow in responding to proposals is that the Northern Dimension should not contradict or duplicate actions at the strategic level. This means that the local and state levels should be on the same page, and that process – as is widely acknowledged – is still far from working smoothly in Russia. Both the local and federal levels see the Northern Dimension as an important tool, but there seem to be some significant differences, for example over whether cross-border cooperation is included in the Northern Dimension or not. Differences of opinion also prevail with regard to project prioritisation. The local level prefers practical local cooperation where knowledge and technology from the outside can be brought in, while the federal level prefers high-profile projects that attract attention.[18]

In Russian–EU and Russian–US relationships, security issues have taken over the platform of cooperation and turned it into a conflict zone. The situation has started to favour such negative elements of Russian foreign policy as imperialistic thinking and *ressentiment* as well as realist thinking in great-power relations. The multilateralist element and sovereignty principle still exist, however, and the importance of regionalism will grow. These weak but persistent elements can act to provide a workable framework in Russian–EU relations and in Russian–US

---

[18] Refer to the "The New Northern Dimension: Regional Co-operation, Business and Energy", Expert seminar, Norwegian University Centre, St. Petersburg, 17 January 2008.

relations as well. Once dampening Russian–EU tensions allow PCA negotiations to advance seriously, the lessons learned from the Northern Dimension can prove valuable. Nuclear safety issues provide an example of how security-related matters can be dealt with under this framework, and have drawn the attention of the EU's larger powers to the achievements of the Northern Dimension. Regional cooperation and sectoral agreements may well provide the working formula for the future of Russian–EU relations.

Russia is not an easy partner for the West, but even during the cold war cooperation was possible. As talk of a 'cold peace' is starting to emerge, regionally based forms of cooperation are more important than ever. The US and Canada also have interests in the European north. Common ground on which the Northern Dimension and e-PINE programme could work together does exist. There is plenty of evidence that working constructively with Russia is possible and indeed the Northern Dimension framework provides an ideal setting for putting forward matters that are important for the West as well as for the future development of Russia. North-west Russia may well become an example for other Russian regions of how to develop their regions in collaboration with the central power and international actors.

8.   References

Christiansen, T., K. Jørgensen and A. Wiener (1999), "The Social Construction of Europe", *Journal of European Public Policy*, Vol. 6, No. 4, p. 528.

Conley, H. (2004), "U.S., Northern Europe Working to Advance Democracy", Testimony before the House Committee on International Relations, the Enhanced Partnership in Northern Europe, Washington, D.C., 21 April.

Evans, M. (2005), "The US–North European Partnership: Advancing Democracy beyond the Baltics", Keynote Address, University of Washington, 26 May (retrieved from http://depts.washington.edu/baltic/lectures/evans_2005_05_26.htm).

Foreign Affairs and International Trade Canada (2008), "The Northern Dimension of Canada's Foreign Policy", Communications Bureau, Department of Foreign Affairs and International Trade, Ottawa (retrieved from www.international.gc.ca/polar-polaire/ndfp-vnpe2.aspx?lang=en#l6).

Kosachev, K. (2007), "Russia and the West: Where the Differences Lie", *Russia in Global Affairs*, Vol. 4, No. 4, pp. 37–48 (retrieved from http://eng.globalaffairs.ru/numbers/21/1149.html).

Kuchins, A. (2007), *Alternative Futures for Russia to 2017*, Centre for Strategic and International Studies, Washington, D.C.

Kuusi, O., H. Smith and P. Tihonen (eds) (2007), *Russia 2017: Three Scenarios*, Committee for the Future, Parliament of Finland, Helsinki.

Lavrov, S. (2007), "The Foreign Policy of Russia: A New Phase", *Expert*, 17 December.

Leonard, M. and N. Popescu (2007), *A Power Audit of EU–Russia Relations*, European Council on Foreign Relations, London.

Ministry of Foreign Affairs of the Republic of Latvia (2008), "Foreign Ministry Political Director in e-PINE Washington Consultations Discusses Current International Issues", Ministry of Foreign Affairs, Riga (retrieved from www.am.gov.lv/en/news/press-releases/2008/april/30-1).

Ryabkov, S. (2007), Presentation at the Conference on "Russia and the European Union – Future of Cooperation", organised by the Bertelsmann Stiftung, Konrad Adenauer Stiftung, the German Chamber of Commerce and Industry and the German–Russian Forum, Moscow, 17–18 December.

Sergounin, A. (2002), "The United States' Northern Dimension? Prospects for a US–Russian Cooperative Agenda in Northern Europe", PONARS Policy Memo No. 232, prepared for the PONARS Policy Conference in Washington, D.C., 25 January (retrieved from www.csis.org/media/csis/pubs/pm_0232.pdf).

Smith, H. (2005), "Det förflutnas inflytande på rysk utrikespolitik", *Nordisk Østforum*, Vol. 19, No. 3, pp. 287–306.

UK House of Commons, Committee for Foreign Affairs (2007), *Global Security: Russia Report*, UK Parliament, London, November (retrieved from www.publications.parliament.uk/pa/cm200708/cmselect/cmfaff/51/5102.htm).

Usui, Y. (2007), "An Evolving Path of Regionalism: The Construction of an Environmental Acquis in the EEC and ASEAN", ISS Research Series, *Bulletin of Universities and Institutes*, No. 24, pp. 31–66.

PART I.
REGIONAL AND SECTORAL PARTNERSHIPS

3. LEARNING BY DOING: THE BARENTS COOPERATION AND DEVELOPMENT OF REGIONAL COLLABORATION IN THE NORTH
*SIGVE R. LELAND & ALF HÅKON HOEL**

1. Introduction

The collapse of the Soviet Union in 1991 presented Nordic decision-makers with a new set of challenges and opportunities in the 'High North': How can greater interaction with Russia be promoted, while at the same time avoiding a bilateralisation of relations? In 1992, Norwegian foreign minister Thorvald Stoltenberg launched the idea of setting up a multilateral framework for cooperation in the High North, and on 11 January 1993, the Barents cooperation was formally established with the adoption of the Kirkenes Declaration "to provide impetus to existing cooperation and consider new initiatives and proposals".[1]

Initial expectations of the Barents cooperation appear to have been rather unrealistic. For instance, official Norwegian statements at the time indicate a widespread belief that north-western Russians were 'really just

---

* For crucial support while working on this research, Alf Håkon Hoel would like to thank his institution, the Department of Political Science at the University of Tromsø, Norway.

[1] See the "Declaration on Cooperation in the Barents Euro-Arctic Region" (Kirkenes, 11 January 1993) (retrieved from www.beac.st).

like us' and that any differences had to be the result of Soviet oppression.[2] All the same, and despite some setbacks that are discussed below, the Barents cooperation has now been going on for 15 years. The experience amassed from this collaboration is interesting not only for those focusing on cross-border interaction and regional cooperation in the High North, but also in the wider context of the Northern Dimension policy.

How well has the Barents cooperation succeeded in achieving its stated goals? Any examination of this question is complicated by the relatively vague and open-ended objectives in the Kirkenes Declaration. Although the idea of "contributing substantially to stability and progress in the area and in Europe as a whole"[3] is certainly a noble goal, measuring the relative success of such an endeavour is difficult, to say the least. Isolating the effects of the Barents cooperation from those of all the other rapid developments taking place in contemporary Russia is in itself a daunting task.

Here we primarily examine of the evolution of the task structure and the organisational set-up. Drawing on documentary analysis and the experiences of those directly involved, we present some lessons learned from 15 years of cooperation. As regards the task structure, we look at the programmes and underlying projects carried out under the aegis of the Barents cooperation, and how these activities have developed over time. Concerning organisational evolution, the question is how the organisational structure has evolved in response to changes in needs and conditions.

Let us begin with a brief overview of the background to the establishment of the Barents cooperation and the Kirkenes Declaration.

2.   Background

The official motivation for the establishment of the Barents cooperation emphasised the need to promote positive developments in post-Communist Russia. These efforts, it was assumed, would in turn benefit Russia's neighbours. Such developments were to be supported through

---

[2] See G. Hønneland, *Barentsbrytninger: norsk nordområdepolitikk etter den kalde krigen*, Kristiansand, Høyskoleforlaget, 2005.

[3] See the 1993 "Declaration on Cooperation in the Barents Euro-Arctic Region", op. cit.

improving bilateral relations and the establishment of 'normal' cross-border interaction and cooperation in a region where the old East/West border had remained practically sealed during the cold war.

In addition, it has been held that Norway launched the Barents cooperation to avoid becoming marginalised in northern Europe after the establishment of the Council of Baltic Sea States in 1992, in which Norway played only a peripheral role.[4] Whatever Norway's initial intentions were, the proposition was also supported by then Russian foreign minister Andrei Kozyrev, which made it easier to get the other Nordic countries on board quickly. Finland had already been toying with similar ideas.

The region-builders cited close historical ties as an argument for the designation of the region. Jens Petter Nielsen points out that there was considerable cross-border trade and interaction within the region in the past, a tradition that continued even during long periods of border disputes, parallel taxation and other disagreements that tainted state-to-state relations.[5] Other scholars consider these claims about common history to be somewhat exaggerated by the region-builders. At the time of the establishment of the Barents cooperation, however, little was left of this joint heritage: there were significant cultural, linguistic, religious[6] and economic differences, factors that have hampered the renewal of cross-border cooperation in the region.

Geography

A central aspect of the cooperation has been to define the geographical scope of the 'Barents Euro-Arctic region' (commonly referred to simply as

---

[4] See Hønneland (2005), op. cit.

[5] See J.-P. Nielsen, "Russian-Norwegian Relations in Arctic Europe: The History of the 'Barents Euro-Arctic Region'", *East European Quarterly*, Vol. 35, No. 2, 2001, pp. 163–81.

[6] While culture, language and religion are often considered separately for analytical purposes, they tend to form more of a 'cultural complex'. For example, the belief that knowledge of the Russian language alone would be sufficient to overcome cultural barriers has often been criticised as a major flaw in early Norwegian–Russian cooperation; see Hønneland (2005), op. cit.

the Barents region).[7] From the very start, it was agreed to keep ocean territories and marine issues outside the cooperation, and to limit the region to land territories. Initially, the cooperation covered the seven northernmost counties of Norway, Sweden, Finland and north-west Russia, but it has since gradually been expanded to its current membership of 13 counties (Figure 3.1).

Figure 3.1 The Barents Euro-Arctic region

Source: The Barents portal (retrieved from www.barentsinfo.fi/barentsmap.htm).

Currently, the region covers an area of 1,755,800 km², i.e. a territory approximately the size of France, Spain, Germany, Italy and the Netherlands taken together. The total population, however, stands at just slightly less than 6 million, yielding a population density of only 3.5 inhabitants per km².

The Barents region is considered to be among Europe's richest in terms of natural resources, although it should be noted that exploiting these resources often requires considerable investment owing to the harsh

---

[7] The addition of 'Euro-Arctic' to the name has often been interpreted as part of the domestic debate over Norwegian EU membership, and as essentially an attempt to make Eurosceptic northern Norwegians feel more 'European'.

climate and remoteness of the region. On the Russian side, in particular there is already an extensive and highly profitable mining industry, extracting a wide range of minerals such as nickel, titanium and aluminium. There is also a substantial forestry industry across the region.

Recently, the petroleum industry has received the greatest interest, after the discoveries of several significant deposits of oil and gas in the Barents Sea. The vast Shtokman field is estimated to hold reserves of approximately 3.8 trillion cubic metres of natural gas,[8] more than twice the entire gas reserves of Canada. After years of indecision, in 2007 the Russian authorities decided to invite French Total and Norwegian StatoilHydro to participate in the development consortium led by Gazprom (the license and all marketing rights, however, will remain with the Gazprom subsidiary Sevmorneftegaz).[9]

Hopes are high that Shtokman will finally bring about the cross-border commercial ties and economic development that the Barents cooperation has, in the eyes of most observers, failed to create.[10] Shtokman has certainly helped to draw greater attention to the region as a whole in recent years. On the other hand, it may also have contributed to a certain sidelining of the Barents cooperation, as offshore activities fall outside its geographical scope. The Barents cooperation has an Energy Working Group (see below), but little involvement in the development of the petroleum industry in the region.

---

[8] This figure is Gazprom's most recent estimate at the time of writing.

[9] See the article, "All Shtokman gas belongs to Gazprom", *BarentsObserver.com,* 21 November 2007 (retrieved from www.barentsobserver.com/index.php?id=563162 &cat=91228&xforceredir=1&noredir=1).

[10] In the early 1990s, there were clearly unrealistic expectations in Norway, particularly in the northernmost counties, concerning the smooth introduction of capitalism in Russia and the potential for Norwegian companies in this new market. Geir Hønneland (2005, op. cit.) describes this period as gripped by "Barents Euphoria" and contrasts this with several examples of failed Norwegian business ventures from the same period. Hopes were dashed, however, upon encountering Russian bureaucracy and an unpredictable regulatory framework, as well as a tendency towards short-term profit-seeking among Norwegian actors; see E. Fløtten, *Barentssamarbeidet – hva nå? En kortfattet evaluering som tar for seg utfordringer og videre veivalg,* 2005 (retrieved from www.aksjonsprogrammet.no/vedlegg/barentssamarbeid.pdf).

Organisational structure

Membership in the Barents cooperation is made up of six states: Denmark, Finland, Iceland, Norway, Russia and Sweden, as well as the European Commission. Several other countries, including Canada, Germany, Japan, the UK and the US, participate as observers. The chair rotates every second year among Finland, Norway, Russia and Sweden, i.e. the countries considered physically part of the Barents region.

Cooperation is organised on two levels: the Barents Euro-Arctic Council (BEAC) is the forum for intergovernmental cooperation on issues concerning the Barents region. Representation in the BEAC consists of each member state's foreign minister or ministers responsible for the policy area to be discussed at a particular meeting. The BEAC meets at least once every two years, at the end of the term of office of the outgoing chair.

In addition, the Barents cooperation takes place at the regional level, underlining the goal of creating a transnational Barents region. The regional level cooperation is organised under the Barents Regional Council (BRC). Initially, membership of the BRC was made up of the three northernmost Norwegian counties of Nordland, Troms and Finnmark, plus Norrbotten in Sweden, Lapland in Finland and the Murmansk and Arkhangelsk Oblasts in Russia. Almost immediately after the establishment of the BRC, the Republic of Karelia (Russia) was accepted as a member. Since then, the Nenets Autonomous Okrug (Russia),[11] the Republic of Komi (Russia), and the counties of Oulu and Kainuu (Finland) and Västerbotten (Sweden) have become members. Furthermore, the indigenous peoples of the region have a representative on the BRC.

Both levels have committees responsible for handling administrative tasks and continuing work on prioritised issues between council meetings. These are the Committee of Senior Officials on the international level and the Barents Regional Committee on the regional level. The committees are made up of officials from the participating states and regional entities, respectively.

Moreover, in 2007, it was agreed to strengthen cooperation through setting up an international secretariat in Kirkenes. The secretariat will "provide technical support to the official bodies and working groups, as

---

[11] Nenets is geographically located in the territory of Arkhangelsk Oblast, but is nonetheless treated as a separate federation subject of the Russian Federation.

well as participate in project implementation and information activities".[12] Especially at the regional level, this step was warmly welcomed, as the lack of a permanent coordinating body has long been seen as one of the major flaws of the Barents cooperation.[13]

Both councils have in addition established several working groups dedicated to specific issues. The actual, substantive work under the Barents cooperation is often carried out in these working groups. The most important are arguably the *joint* working groups. These are co-chaired by state level and regional representatives and they have tended to be established along the lines of priority issues. Currently, there are four such working groups: the Joint Working Group on Energy, the Joint Working Group on Culture,[14] the Joint Working Group on Health and Related Social Issues, and the Joint Working Group on Education and Research. Particularly the latter two also represent areas in which the Barents cooperation has been relatively successful. In otherwise significant (but less successful) areas, economic cooperation in particular, there are no such joint working groups.

3. Assessing performance

As stated at the outset, the aim of this chapter is to assess lessons learned from the Barents cooperation by reviewing the development of the cooperation along two dimensions: changes in programmes and projects and changes in organisational structure. In doing so, it is important to keep the changes that have taken place in the international and domestic political context in the region as a backdrop.

The most fundamental change in recent years is undoubtedly the apparent revitalisation of Russia. Since the turn of the millennium, Russia's economy has strengthened greatly, fuelled by petroleum exports and rising

---

[12] See "Agreement on an International Barents Secretariat in Kirkenes", Press Release No. 135/07, Norwegian Ministry of Foreign Affairs, Oslo, 2007 (retrieved from www.regjeringen.no/en/dep/ud/Press_Contacts/News/2007/international _barents-secretariat.html?id=490271).

[13] See Fløtten (2005), op. cit.

[14] The Barents Regional Working Group on Culture became the Joint Working Group on Culture in late 2007. As it has thus only operated under its new mandate for a few months, we have opted to leave this joint working group out of the evaluation.

oil prices. Today, Russia also appears more politically stable than during the years of Boris Yeltsin's presidency. At the same time, economic growth during Vladimir Putin's presidency has been translated into a far more assertive foreign policy.[15] While the consequences for the Barents cooperation have not been as dramatic as for Russia's relations with some other states and organisations, the new Russian assertiveness is likely to have some impact on the room for international cooperation, especially where such cooperation involves foreign activities on Russian soil.

Political interest in the High North has been on the rise in recent years, notably in Norway. The potential for petroleum development also draws attention to the region in other national capitals. In 2007, Russian foreign ministry spokesperson Mikhail Kamynin commented on the potential for cooperation in the Barents region: "Energy is in the centre, and can function as a platform for joint action."[16] It is nonetheless still too early to say whether the focus on petroleum resources will ease or complicate cooperation in the region. With an apparent trend towards nationalisation of 'strategic' natural resources in Russia, the current dependency of the Russian economy on petroleum extraction, oil and gas might prove a source of conflict as much as cooperation.

Since the establishment of the Barents cooperation, both Sweden and Finland have become EU member states. The expansion of the Northern Dimension introduces some ambiguity. On the one hand, EU instruments often contribute funding to Barents region projects. Indeed, a great many projects could never have been realised without this support. Within the health sector, there is even explicit coordination between the Barents Health and Social Programme and the Northern Dimension Partnership in Public Health and Social Well-being (NDPHS). At the same time, the Northern Dimension could potentially be a competitor for the Barents cooperation, in the sense that it can draw political and financial resources away from the region to the wider geographical context of the Northern Dimension.

---

[15] See D. Averre, "'Sovereign Democracy' and Russia's Relations with the European Union", *Demokratizatsiya*, Vol. 15, No. 3, 2007, pp. 173–90.

[16] See the article, "Russia in Charge of Barents Cooperation", *BarentsObserver.com*, 15 November 2007 (retrieved from www.barentsobserver.com/index.php?id =558389).

4.   Programmes and projects

The Kirkenes Declaration specifies the prioritised areas of cooperation as follows: economy, trade, science and technology, tourism, the environment, infrastructure, cultural and educational exchange, and improvement of living conditions for the indigenous peoples of the region.[17] As discussed later, priorities have changed over time, with some formerly prioritised areas being shoved to the background while others have moved to the forefront.

The Regional Council seeks to operationalise the goals of the cooperation through the Barents Programme. The Programme is renewed at regular intervals, normally every three to four years, and serves as a framework and action plan for the cooperation, defining goals and priorities.

Projects carried out under the Barents Programme are primarily initiated by non-governmental organisations, educational institutions, businesses and other private actors, who apply to the relevant national institutions for funding to realise their proposed projects. The projects range in scale from the relatively small (conferences, concerts and other one-time events) to more expansive projects (primarily long-term cooperation in education, culture, business or other areas that require considerable resources). In the majority of cases, Barents cooperation institutions will provide only a relatively limited share of the funding required. EU initiatives like Kolarctic and the Interreg Programme tend to be important sources of supplementary funding, illustrating the frequent interweaving and overlapping of these initiatives. Occasionally, actors involved in the Barents cooperation also initiate projects themselves, by presenting ideas to potential participants and encouraging them to apply for funding.

Although the Barents Programme is multilateral, most projects have been implemented on a bilateral basis.[18] For example, the Norwegian

---

[17] See the 1993 "Declaration on Cooperation in the Barents Euro-Arctic Region", op. cit.

[18] See O.S. Stokke, G. Hønneland and P.J. Schei, "Pollution and Conservation", in O.S. Stokke and G. Hønneland (eds), *International Cooperation and Arctic Governance: Regime Effectiveness and Northern Region Building*, London: Routledge, 2007, pp. 78–112.

Barents Secretariat in Kirkenes is responsible for processing Norwegian project applications. A look at the Barents *Project Catalogue 2006* reveals that a majority of the projects that have received funding from the Barents Secretariat have solely involved Norwegian applicants and their Russian partners.[19]

Besides the Barents Programme, there are also other programmes under the Barents cooperation: the Regional Youth Programme, the Health and Social Programme (which receives additional funding from the EU and WHO) and the HIV/AIDS Programme. The latter two programmes in particular have been developed in coordination with the Northern Dimension.

The Health and Social Programme is by far the most extensive of these programmes. While most of the funding as well as the projects under the programme has come from Norway, the programme is nevertheless seen as one of the great successes of the Barents cooperation. Efforts have concentrated on halting the spread of communicable diseases, in particular tuberculosis and HIV/AIDS, which were spreading rapidly in north-west Russia in the late 1990s, and on the general improvement of the health infrastructure in north-west Russia.[20] The programme itself serves a function similar to that of the Barents Programme, although limited to "health and related social issues". The Working Group on Health and Related Social Issues is responsible for developing and following up on the programme, currently in its second period (2004–07) (it was preceded by the Barents Health Cooperation Programme 1999–2003).[21]

The increased emphasis on health and social issues is perhaps the most prominent example of the dynamic character of the Barents cooperation, as health issues were not even mentioned in the Kirkenes Declaration. As has often been the case in the Barents cooperation, Norway

---

[19] See the Norwegian Barents Secretariat, *Project Catalogue 2006*, Norwegian Barents Secretariat, Kirkenes, 2006 (retrieved from www.barents.no/getfile.php/403095.900.eswstrbvqs/Prosjektkatalog+2006.doc).

[20] See Hønneland (2005), op. cit.

[21] For more information, see the Barents Euro-Artic Region website (retrieved from www.barentshealth.org).

has provided the major part of the funding.[22] The establishment of a Task Force on Communicable Disease Control in the Baltic Sea region in 2000 by the Council of Baltic Sea States (CBSS) may have served to divert some funds away from the Health Cooperation Programme. On the other hand, there is general agreement that the Barents cooperation programmes and the CBSS Task Force, as well as its successor, the NDPHS, have complemented each other in the successful effort to stem the tide of tuberculosis in north-eastern Europe.

As noted earlier, the Health Cooperation Programme and the Health and Social Programme have often been singled out as the most successful initiatives under the Barents cooperation: participants on both sides have seemed satisfied with the collaboration, health cooperation involves relatively few controversies and the effects are easier to measure than in many of the other projects. The successful introduction of DOTS[23] in north-western Russia, the World Health Organisation's recommended treatment programme for tuberculosis, has been hailed as one of the greatest, most visible successes of the efforts (an honour that has to be shared with the CBSS Task Force).

The Barents cooperation can be said to develop according to a 'learning-by-doing' approach. Because of limited experience in dealing with Russia (or perhaps more accurately, with Russians), there have been many failed projects. As a result, the member states have chosen to focus their efforts on areas where they see results: the health cooperation has been successful and thus receives greater attention, whereas the Regional Working Group on Investments and Economic Cooperation, which experienced limited success, has been disbanded.

Another important aspect is the need for success stories to sell the Barents cooperation to the public. The Barents cooperation has received a great deal of negative press, especially in Norway. Particularly the projects related to business and industry have often been described in the media as disastrous failures, tarnishing the public image of the Barents cooperation.[24]

---

[22] See L. Rowe and G. Hønneland, "Communicable Disease Control", in O.S. Stokke and G. Hønneland, *International Cooperation and Arctic Governance: Regime Effectiveness and Northern Region Building*, London: Routledge, 2007, p. 54.

[23] DOTS refers to Directly Observed Therapy, Short-Course.

[24] This impression is also confirmed by some of the participants themselves in past evaluations of the Barents cooperation. See Fløtten (2005), op. cit.

By contrast, the health cooperation has experienced its fair share of successes and is now largely unassailable – it is very difficult to criticise anyone for fighting disease – and makes for nice headlines. This might be the reason the Norwegian government, which has the most prestige invested in the Barents cooperation, has also been the prime contributor to the health programmes.

5. Organisational development

The permanent structures of the Barents cooperation are the committees (the Committee of Senior Officials and the Regional Committee), the working groups and the secretariats. As the committees have remained largely unaltered except for the addition of new member regions to the Regional Committee, we focus on the working groups and secretariats, which have seen considerable changes in recent years.

The working groups

As regards the working groups, some of them have been around more or less from the beginning. These are the groups dedicated to economic cooperation, education, the environment, culture, transport and indigenous peoples.

Significant additions have, however, been made over time.[25] In 1998, for instance, the Barents Council established a Working Group on Energy – a step that reflected the growing interest in the energy resources of the Barents region. In practical terms, the working group has nevertheless served more as an auxiliary to the Working Group on the Environment. Most of the group's own work and supported projects have centred on reducing energy consumption, increasing energy efficiency and introducing bioenergy in north-west Russia. Petroleum development has been not been included in the Barents cooperation, reflecting the significance of the oil and gas resources in the economies of some member countries.

In 1999, an Exchange Programme for Higher Education and Research was established, and in 2003, the programme board was merged with the regional working group on education to form the Joint Working Group on Education and Research. The primary responsibilities of this group have

---

[25] Some very short-lived working groups are not included in this discussion.

been related to promoting and facilitating cooperation in education and research, as well as the exchange of students and researchers within the Barents region.

The same year, a Joint Working Group on Health and Related Social Issues was established in conjunction with the launch of the new Health and Social Programme. That the working group was only established after the original Health Cooperation Programme had proven successful perhaps reflects an initial unwillingness to invest too much in this new field of collaboration (indeed, there was no working group on health at either level until 2003). Since the launch of the new programme, the Joint Working Group on Health and Related Social Issues has nonetheless developed into perhaps the most active and well organised of the working groups, having come a long way in streamlining application procedures, providing information and facilitating communication among participants. Indeed, as mentioned above, health cooperation has become the new flagship of the Barents cooperation.

The concept of joint working groups is in itself an innovation, dating back no further than to 2003. As previously noted, the joint working groups have shared chairmanship with one chair representing one of the capitals and the other representing a member region. Interestingly, the three existing joint working groups have come into being through different processes, and there does not seem to be any single criterion for the establishment of joint working groups: the Joint Working Group on Education and Research evolved from a merger of a programme board (which had completed its original task) and a regional working group. The Joint Working Group on Energy became 'joint' after Norway proposed to include the regions in an existing Barents Council working group. And finally, the Joint Working Group on Health and Related Social Issues was an entirely new creation.

Three reasons spring to mind as the rationale for the creation of such joint working groups. An official reason, given as justification for the launch of the Joint Working Group on Energy, is the inclusion of both levels in the work of the Barents cooperation. There are both democratic and practical reasons for this; moreover, the inclusion of the regional level in international cooperation is one of the distinguishing features and underlying ideals of the Barents cooperation. A second reason for setting up joint working groups would be the cost aspect. By reducing the total number of working groups in this way, the associated costs can be significantly reduced. In fact, most of the regional working groups were dissolved for cost reasons in 1999 and only re-established in 2001 thanks to EU funding.[26] Finally, joint working groups eliminate the duplication and overlapping that unavoidably take place when parallel groups exist.

Proposed organisational changes

The Barents Regional Committee established an ad-hoc group on organisational changes in June 2005. So far, two of the group's recommendations have been partly realised. At the 2007 meeting of the Barents Council in Rovaniemi, a decision was made to set up an International Barents Secretariat. Its primary responsibilities will be to provide administrative and organisational support to participants, maintain databases and other records, and assist the working groups in obtaining financial support. Geographically, the international secretariat will be co-located with the existing Norwegian Barents Secretariat in Kirkenes.

A Finnish Barents Secretariat has also been founded recently to serve a similar function as the Norwegian one. With the creation of the international secretariat, it is hoped that the national and international secretariats will fill a network function, ensuring continuity and momentum within the Barents cooperation between meetings. The new secretariats are potentially the greatest organisational change in the history of the Barents cooperation, although it remains to be seen what the practical consequences will be.

Further changes to the organisational structure can be expected as a result of the completion of the Barents 2010 project. This was a large research project initiated by the Barents Council and partly funded by the Interreg IIIB Baltic Sea Programme to develop a strategy and action plan for future cooperation within the Barents region. Among its clearest recommendations was the creation of several sector programmes to facilitate economic cooperation. The sector programmes essentially consist of smaller packages of specific goals and projects, supervised by a single region throughout the programme period. As the Barents 2010 project itself was completed only a few months prior to the writing of this chapter, the extent to which the recommendations will be implemented is still unclear.

---

[26] See Stokke, Hønneland and Schei (2007), op. cit., pp. 78–112.

6.   Lessons learned

What lessons can be drawn from 15 years of collaboration among the Nordic countries and Russia within the framework of the Barents cooperation? We have especially looked for those lessons along two dimensions: changes in the actual content of cooperation and organisational development.

There is broad agreement that the Barents cooperation has been a mixed success: there are notable accomplishments in the realm of health and somewhat fewer in economic cooperation.

An overall lesson seems to be that this kind of cooperation is not one that produces quick results – results are better measured over decades than years – especially since the overarching goals of the cooperation concern long-term positive development in the region rather than specific short-term objectives. This outcome, of course, also requires long-term political commitment.

As an example of such long-term positive development, several observers have pointed to the valuable but frequently overlooked effects of the emergence of professional networks across the national and regional borders. This point is for instance highlighted in a 2005 evaluation of the Barents cooperation. In particular, improved cross-border contacts among officials at the regional level were here described as a tremendous advantage when dealing with regional issues, both within and outside the framework of the Barents cooperation. From this perspective, the primary significance of the Barents cooperation is not so much in the immediate effects of the various projects, as in the creation of common fora for debate and improved relations with – and access to – officials in the participating counties. These contacts, in turn, improve conditions for collaboration on substantive issues of common interest.

Cooperation partners have also frequently mentioned the importance of developing mutual trust and understanding in a region where cultural differences are significant, yet not always sufficiently recognised.[27] In fact, the underestimation of cultural, structural and even legal differences has marred many Barents cooperation projects. Maintaining channels for communication and creating cross-border networks on the other hand reduces tensions and facilitates further cooperation.

---

[27] See Fløtten (2005), op. cit.

The same lesson is highlighted in the area of health cooperation. While the Barents Health Programme certainly achieved many positive, concrete results, the improved communication and collaboration among health professionals within Russia as well as throughout the region is often considered one of its most important accomplishments – and indeed something of a requirement for further progress.

Experiences from the health cooperation also suggest that well-defined projects with clearly specified, short-term goals have been relatively effective (e.g. the introduction of the DOTS strategy in north-west Russian health care). It is important, however, to note several other factors that have contributed to success. First, the objectives have been mutually understood, and more crucially, shared by all participants, something that has often not been the case in other projects: objectives and methods have frequently been specified by the Western partners, and Russian agreement and understanding been taken for granted. Yet in reality, these objectives have not been shared or they have even seemed meaningless and incomprehensible to the Russian participants. Second, health cooperation has generally taken place among medical workers with relatively similar educational backgrounds and outlooks despite some differences in methodology and priorities. Cooperation among professionals is often easier to implement than among actors seeking political gains or economic profit from the collaboration.

In short, it seems that the basic requirement of mutual trust, understanding and shared objectives has been essential for ensuring successes in the Barents cooperation. That this requirement has not been met in many projects is perhaps primarily a result of the novelty of East–West cooperation at the time the Barents cooperation was established. It is to be hoped that this problem will become less prominent as Nordic–Russian interaction develops further – and indeed, there are signs that this problem is less acute today.

Moving on to the recent changes in organisational structure, these are intended to address lack of coordination – an issue that for a long time has been voiced by a number of Barents cooperation participants. With the exception of the Norwegian Barents Secretariat, the Barents cooperation has always lacked permanent coordinating institutions. Many have argued that this has hindered multilateral cooperation and made work between meetings more complicated than necessary.

Another frequently mentioned problem is the lack of funds managed independently by a Barents cooperation institution. The dependence on unpredictable and occasionally less than enthusiastic national governments for funding has reduced the attraction of the Barents cooperation for many project entrepreneurs.

The establishment of the joint working groups seems to be the result of a long period of uncertainty as to what the priorities of the Barents cooperation should be, and perhaps more significantly, to its ability to deliver on promises. Over time, areas in which cooperation appeared most successful have also tended to receive the most attention and funds. The economic cooperation, a cornerstone of the early days, has now been relegated to a secondary role. The most important lesson to be learned from these developments is perhaps, superficial though it may sound, that to retain public support for a large international cooperative arrangement like the Barents cooperation, it is necessary to have some safe bets.

The health cooperation has a strong standing in the public; its effects are perceived as mutually advantageous, and almost indisputably so, whether this is true or not. In Norway, certainly, the impression that the government is acting to stop the spread of diseases that might otherwise cross borders, while at the same time showing solidarity with our Russian neighbours, has done much to improve the public image of the Barents cooperation. Organising the structure of the cooperation in ways that emphasise successes may thus be advantageous, even necessary, to maintain public support, which in turn is a requirement for large and long-term investments in international collaboration.

The Barents cooperation has been around for 15 years. Mistakes and miscalculations have been made, some of which have been corrected. There have also been successes. Both failures and successes provide valuable lessons for future cooperation in the northernmost reaches of Europe. It can only be hoped that these lessons will be taken to heart in the further development of the Barents cooperation, as well as in other cooperative efforts spanning the former East/West divide in the High North, such as the Northern Dimension.

7. References

Averre, D. (2007), "'Sovereign Democracy' and Russia's Relations with the European Union", *Demokratizatsiya*, Vol. 15, No. 3, pp. 173–90.

Fløtten, E. (2005), *Barentssamarbeidet – hva nå? En kortfattet evaluering som tar for seg utfordringer og videre veivalg* (retrieved from www.aksjonsprogrammet.no/vedlegg/barentssamarbeid.pdf).

Hønneland, G. (2005), *Barentsbrytninger: norsk nordområdepolitikk etter den kalde krigen*, Kristiansand, Høyskoleforlaget.

Nielsen, J.-P. (2001), "Russian–Norwegian Relations in Arctic Europe: The History of the 'Barents Euro-Arctic Region'", *East European Quarterly*, Vol. 35, No. 2, pp. 163–81.

Norwegian Barents Secretariat (2006), *Project Catalogue 2006*, Norwegian Barents Secretariat, Kirkenes (retrieved from www.barents.no/getfile.php/403095.900.eswstrbvqs/Prosjektkatalog+2006.doc).

Norwegian Ministry of Foreign Affairs (2007), "Agreement on an International Barents Secretariat in Kirkenes", Press Release No. 135/07, Oslo (retrieved from www.regjeringen.no/en/dep/ud/Press_Contacts/News/2007/international_barents-secretariat.html?id=490271).

Rowe, L. and G. Hønneland (2007), "Communicable Disease Control", in O.S. Stokke and G. Hønneland (eds), *International Cooperation and Arctic Governance: Regime Effectiveness and Northern Region Building*, London: Routledge, p. 54.

Stokke, O.S., G. Hønneland and P.J. Schei (2007), "Pollution and Conservation", in O.S. Stokke and G. Hønneland (eds), *International Cooperation and Arctic Governance: Regime Effectiveness and Northern Region Building*, London: Routledge, pp. 78–112.

4. BEST PRACTICES IN FISHERIES MANAGEMENT: EXPERIENCES FROM NORWEGIAN–RUSSIAN COOPERATION

ALF HÅKON HOEL[*]

1. Introduction

To the north of Norway and north-west Russia lies the Barents Sea, an ocean area of some 1.4 million km². Because of favourable climatic and oceanographic conditions, the Barents Sea sustains productive ecosystems and major commercial fisheries that are among the most important in the world. Each year, millions of tonnes of fish are taken here by vessels from Norway, Russia and several other countries.

Since the mid-1970s, Norway and Russia have developed a joint management regime for these fisheries, entailing extensive bilateral cooperation on scientific as well as management-related issues. This cooperation has been able to function in the context of the security concerns of the cold war as well as in the post-cold war period. The joint management regime is considered relatively effective, in the sense that most major fisheries in the area are carried out at sustainable levels.

This chapter reviews and discusses experiences from this cooperation, with a view to identifying potential best practices in cooperation on fisheries management. Such experiences may have interest

[*] For crucial support while working on this research, Alf Håkon Hoel would like to thank his institution, the Department of Political Science at the University of Tromsø, Norway.

outside the realm of fisheries as well, as an example of bilateral cooperation on the management of joint problems and issues. In the context of the Northern Dimension, the experience and lessons learned from a successful bilateral cooperation over an extended period are certainly of relevance.

2.   The fisheries and their context

The Barents Sea is home to a number of major fish stocks that spend some or all of their life cycle there. Central here is north-east Arctic cod, which sustains a major fishery that in recent years has been in the range of 400–500,000 tonnes annually. Other important fisheries include haddock, capelin, saithe, shrimp, red king crab and redfish.[1] Of marine mammals, harp seals and minke whales are harvested. Also, Norwegian spring spawning herring, which sustains one of the world's largest fisheries, spends its juvenile years here, although it is fished further south along the Norwegian coast and in the Norwegian Sea. Altogether, this makes the Barents Sea a fishing ground of global significance.

The stocks of cod, haddock and capelin are shared between Norway and Russia, in the sense that these stocks have a geographical distribution spanning the waters of both countries. Other stocks are exclusive, in the sense that they are viewed as being under the jurisdiction of one of the two. Saithe, for example, is exclusively a Norwegian stock.

In addition to vessels from Norway and Russia, vessels from several other countries, such as the EU member states, the Faroes and Iceland, enjoy fishing rights in the Barents Sea. Most of the catch, however, as well as the actual management of the fisheries, is done by the two coastal states.

The management regime for the fisheries in the Barents Sea is premised on recent developments in international ocean law. Particularly important here is the extension of coastal state jurisdiction over waters off their coasts, codified in the United Nations Law of the Sea Convention (in force since 1994).[2] The Convention states that coastal states have sovereign rights over the natural resources in their exclusive economic zones (EEZs),

---

[1] See Havforskningsinstituttet [Institute of Marine Research], *Havets ressurser og miljø 2008: Fisken og havet* 1, 2008.

[2] See S.E. Ebbin, A.H. Hoel and A. Sydnes, *A Sea Change: The Exclusive Economic Zone and Governance Institutions for Living Marine Resources*, Dordrecht: Springer, 2005.

which extend seawards to 200 nautical miles (370 km). It also specifies that coastal states have obligations to conserve and utilise living marine resources optimally, as well as cooperate with other countries on their management where the resources are transboundary. This regime implies, on the one hand, an ownership of resources and a right to manage them; on the other, these rights are to be exercised in a sustainable manner and through international cooperation when necessary.

Norway and Russia established EEZs in 1977 and 1978, respectively. In drawing the boundaries between the two EEZs in the Barents Sea, the two countries based their claimed boundary line on different principles, so there remains a large, wedge-shaped disputed area of 175,000 km² for which the two states are still negotiating a final boundary line.[3] In the middle of this area is a smaller area, which is beyond national jurisdiction and therefore has the status of international waters, known as 'the Loophole' (Figure 4.1).

An additional jurisdictional complexity arises in the Svalbard archipelago. The 1920 Svalbard Treaty, which applies to the islands and the territorial waters, establishes that Norway has "full and absolute" sovereignty over Svalbard. Yet, the Treaty restricts the way Norway can exercise its sovereignty. Among other things, citizens of all Treaty parties are to be treated equally with regard to industrial activities. With the introduction of EEZs, Norway established a 200-mile non-discriminatory Fishery Protection Zone around the archipelago in 1977. This arrangement was contested by the then Soviet Union, and several countries have reserved their rights under the Treaty. The dispute today concerns how Norway can exercise its jurisdiction in the waters beyond the 12-mile territorial waters off Svalbard.

---

[3] Norway claims that the boundary is to be based on an equidistance principle, with the boundary running along a line equidistant from the land territories of the two states. Russia's claim is based on a sector principle, according to which the boundary is to follow a straight line from the northernmost point of the land boundary on the continent and onwards to the North Pole.

Figure 4.1 Barents Sea maritime zones

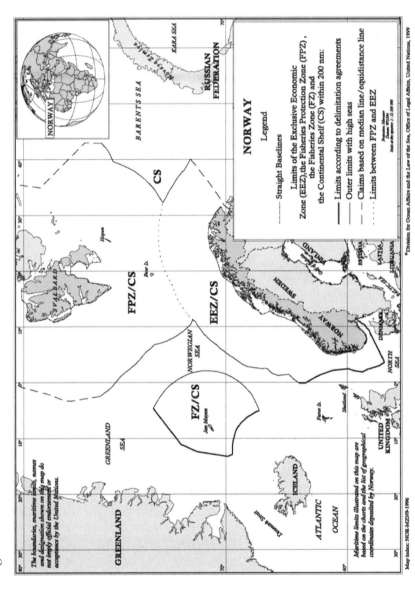

Source: UN Division for Ocean Affairs and the Law of the Sea, Office of Legal Affairs, 1999.

3.   The organisation and evolution of cooperation

Norwegian–Russian cooperation in the management of the fisheries in the north is based on several bilateral agreements: a 1975 agreement establishes the Joint Fisheries Commission, a 1976 agreement covers joint management of shared fish stocks as well as related issues and a 1978 agreement clarifies responsibilities in the enforcement of fisheries regulations in a 'Grey Zone' (see Figure 4.1), which covers some of the area where jurisdiction is contested. Prior to these arrangements, coastal state jurisdiction extended to only 12 nautical miles, and the area beyond was high seas. The fisheries in these areas were in principle managed by the Northeast Atlantic Fisheries Commission, although not very successfully.

The Joint Fisheries Commission meets annually. Based on scientific advice from the International Council for the Exploration of the Sea (ICES) on catch levels and management strategies, it sets total allowable catches for the three shared stocks – cod, haddock and capelin. In addition, the Commission also provides for quota swaps of various other species, including seals.[4] The actual management measures for implementing the catch limits set by the Commission are established by the two countries, each regulating fishing activities in the waters under its jurisdiction and enforcing regulations in its own waters.

Scientific cooperation under the Commission is substantial, with several working groups addressing a range of issues. The cooperation between Norway and Russia in fisheries science goes back more than 50 years. Following the establishment of the Joint Fisheries Commission, scientific cooperation has become a major undertaking, with annual joint surveys and workshops. This work feeds into the ICES process, and forms the basis for the scientific advice on management provided by that body. In recent years, a particular problem for the scientific cooperation has been that Norwegian research vessels have been denied access to Russian waters, as well as lack of funding for Russian marine science.[5] Since 2007,

---

[4] See G. Hønneland, *Kvotekamp og kystsolidaritet: Norsk-russisk fiskeriforvaltning gjennom 30 år*, Bergen: Fagbokforlaget, 2006.

[5] See Riksrevisjonen, *Riksrevisjonens undersøkelse av forvaltningen og kontrollen av fiskeressursene i Barentshavet og Norskehavet – en parallell revisjon mellom norsk og russisk riksrevisjon*, Document 3:2 (2007–2008), Oslo, 2007, p. 9.

however, Norwegian research vessels have again been admitted to Russian waters; moreover, the growth of the Russian economy has also benefited Russian science.

Increasingly, the Commission has also engaged in issues beyond science and the setting of total allowable catches (TACs). Following the growth in illegal fishing, for instance, the Commission has discussed enforcement measures in fisheries and has launched a separate committee to pursue cooperation in that regard (see below).

When the cooperation was established in the 1970s, understanding of the need to manage fisheries by restricting access and catches was generally not very well developed. A notable change over time has been the greater recognition of the need for management to ensure that resources are used in a sustainable manner. A major issue has been overfishing. Until the 1980s, this was mainly a Norwegian problem, since, by reference to a provision in the 1976 agreement, its coastal fleet was permitted to overfish the Norwegian share of the TAC. At the insistence of the then Soviet Union, this practice was discontinued by the mid-1980s. On the Soviet side, there was no incentive to overfish, as there were no gains to be had from taking more than the allotted quota.

Following the fall of the Iron Curtain and the introduction of a market economy in Russia, the incentives of the Russian fishing industry changed. The cash flow rose with the quantity of fish caught. Incomes were significantly boosted when catches were landed in Norway, where payment was in the form of hard currency. An additional incentive to land fish abroad came from the cumbersome and expensive procedures for landing fish in Russia. Especially since 2000, the Russian fleet has been overfishing its share of the TAC substantially, although at declining rates for the past two years. A recent report from the Norwegian fisheries authorities indicates that overfishing halved from 2006 to 2007.[6] The Russian side has contested the figures calculated by Norway, although agreeing that IUU (illegal, unregulated and unreported) fishing is going on.

Another period of overfishing the TAC for cod took place in the Loophole in the central Barents Sea for some years in the 1990s. As mentioned above, the Loophole is beyond national jurisdiction, and was

---

[6] See "Overfisket i Barentshavet halvert", Fiskeridirektoratet, 2008 (retrieved from www.fiskeridir.no/fiskeridir/aktuelt/fiskets_gang/fiske/2008/0308/overfisket_i _barentshavet_halvert).

subject to substantial overfishing by third-country vessels. By the end of the 1990s, cod had largely disappeared from the area, and since then very little fishing activity has taken place in the Loophole. Moreover, in 1999 Norway and Russia entered into an agreement with Iceland to make certain that in the future the Icelandic fishing fleet would refrain from fishing there.[7] Similar arrangements have been made with other countries as well.

Following the increase in fishing on the high seas globally, the UN General Assembly in 1995 adopted an agreement that requires states to apply a precautionary approach to the management of their fisheries.[8] In practice, this means that states are to develop management strategies for their fisheries that make sure that the reproductive capacity of fish stocks is not threatened. Following work by ICES to operationalise the concept, the Joint Fisheries Commission adopted a management strategy for cod in 2002. The management strategy has a catch control rule that seeks to ensure that the quotas set are in accordance with the precautionary approach. Such management strategies have now been established for most fisheries.

For the Barents Sea fisheries, in recent years the quotas have largely been set according to the adopted management strategies.[9] But because of overfishing by the Russian fleet, the real catch has been substantially higher than the TAC. Over time, this increases the risk of depletion of stocks.

The substantial overfishing notwithstanding, the management regime, together with serendipity in terms of nature – especially in relation to the cod stock as well as to other stocks (herring, saithe) – has produced fairly good results. The most important fish stocks are currently in reasonably good shape.[10] An indicator of this is that the total spawning stock biomass of the major fish stocks in the north has been increasing over the last two decades, as shown in Figure 4.2. This tendency has continued in the years after 2006, with growing prognoses for spawning stock size.

---

[7] See O.S. Stokke, "The Loophole of the Barents Sea Fisheries Regime", in O.S. Stokke (ed.), *Governing High Seas Fisheries*, Oxford: Oxford University Press, 2002.

[8] See the UN Fish Stocks Agreement (New York, September 1995) (retrieved from www.un.org/Depts/los/fish_stocks_conference/fish_stocks_conference.htm).

[9] See Riksrevisjonen (2007), op. cit., p. 9.

[10] See Havforskningsinstituttet [Institute of Marine Research] (2008), op. cit., p. 10.

Figure 4.2 Spawning stock biomass for important groundfish species in the north

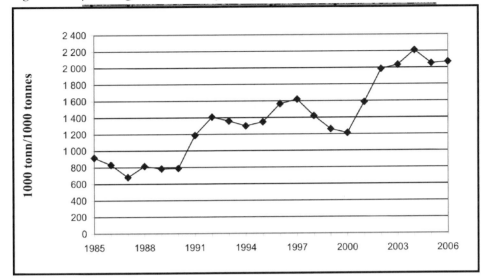

Source: Fiskeridirektoratet, *Nøkkeltall fiskeri 2007* (retrieved from www.fiskeridir.no/ fiskeridir/fiskeri/statistikk/noekkeltall).

In the EEZs, the enforcement of fisheries regulations is the prerogative of coastal states. In Norwegian waters, Norwegian authorities enforce regulations against vessels from all states, as do the Russian authorities in Russian waters. On the high seas, beyond the areas under national jurisdiction, responsibility for enforcement resides with the flag state. Several issues that arise in the context of enforcement do benefit from inter-state cooperation, however; under the Joint Fisheries Commission cooperation on enforcement issues has gradually developed since 1992. A working group to address enforcement issues was established that year, later replaced with a permanent body. There is also regular direct contact between the enforcement authorities of the two countries. A Memorandum of Understanding on cooperation on control issues was adopted by the Commission in 2000, addressing among other things exchange of routine information relating to satellite data and landings of catches, exchange of information about control activities, operational measures such as meetings between control agencies and exchange of inspectors and observers, and exchange of experiences at regular seminars.[11]

---

[11] See Riksrevisjonen (2007), op. cit.

In the last decade, the management of red king crab has emerged as a major issue in the bilateral cooperation. Introduced into the Barents Sea in the 1960s, the crab stock started to grow very rapidly during the 1990s and began appearing on the Norwegian side of the Barents Sea, where it interfered with coastal fisheries. A substantial crab fishery has developed in Finnmark, and it is now one of the most important in the north. King crab is managed separately by the two countries, each within their jurisdiction. Norway sets a quota of around 300,000 crabs for its fisheries (2007), while Russia sets its quota about 10 times higher.[12]

A significant share of the total fisheries in the Barents Sea is in the Fishery Protection Zone around Svalbard. While all fisheries in the Barents Sea are counted against the total quotas, Norway sets and enforces regulations for the Fisheries Protection Zone. The management regime here has become more comprehensive over time. In practice, most countries observe the fisheries regulations established by Norway, based on the recognition that the fisheries have to be managed.

4.   Experiences and lessons: Towards best practices

The ultimate test of any resource management regime is that it achieves the objective of resource conservation. Contrary to the situation in many other regions and fisheries management regimes, the bilateral cooperation in the Barents Sea has been essentially successful in this regard,[13] and is therefore also particularly interesting from the point of view of 'best practices'. A best practice can be understood as a "method, process, activity, incentive or reward that is more effective at delivering a particular outcome than any other technique, method, process, etc."[14]

What lessons, then, can be learned from the bilateral cooperation between Norway and Russia in fisheries management? There are at least five factors or best practices that stand out as important to the success of the cooperation:

---

[12] See the Protocol, 35th Session in the Joint Norwegian–Russian Fisheries Commission, Ministry of Fisheries and Coastal Affairs, Oslo, 2007 (retrieved from www.regjeringen.no/nb/dep/fkd/tema/Internasjonalt_samarbeid_om_fiskeri/Fi skerisamarbeidet-med-Russland.html?id=376440).

[13] See Havforskningsinstituttet [Institute of Marine Research] (2008), op. cit., p. 10.

[14] Refer to the Wikipedia discussion on "Best practice" (retrieved from http://en.wikipedia.org/wiki/Best_practices).

- a robust but flexible legal basis,
- mutual learning over time,
- joint science to develop common frameworks of understanding,
- the isolation of particularly intractable problems from the rest of the cooperation, and
- the ability and willingness to modernise and expand the cooperation.

Ultimately, the rationale for international cooperation is that countries gain benefits from cooperation that outweigh the costs.[15] In fisheries, this logic manifests itself in the need for those who have access to the resource to agree on limits to exploitation. If the use of fish resources is not limited, a 'tragedy of the commons' logic may play out: the fisheries will be overexploited and may eventually collapse.[16] Cooperation thus brings the potential mutual benefit of sustainable fisheries with associated economic outcomes for the cooperating parties. For such outcomes to materialise, a basic precondition is that access to resources is restricted. At the domestic level, this requires states to develop and implement legislation along with regulatory and enforcement measures that close access to fisheries and restrict participation to a delimited group. At the international level, this requires that states agree on regulatory measures for shared fish stocks and for fisheries on the high seas.

As regards the management of fisheries in the Barents Sea, the cooperation is first *based on a set of legal agreements* specifying the rights and obligations of the two parties. The agreements of 1975, 1976 and 1977 outlined objectives for the cooperation and addressed the need for joint management of joint resources. Each country is to regulate fisheries in its own zone, based on the recommendations of the Joint Fisheries Commission. And each party is to enforce these regulations in its own zone. The 1978 Grey Zone agreement resolves the issue of how enforcement of fisheries regulations is to be handled in the area where

---

[15] See R. Hilborn, A.E. Punt and J. Orensanz, "Beyond Band-aids in Fisheries Management: Fixing World Fisheries", *Bulletin of Marine Science*, Vol. 74, No. 3, 2004, pp. 493–507.

[16] See G. Hardin, "The tragedy of the commons", *Science*, Vol. 162, No. 3859, 1968, pp. 1243–48.

jurisdiction has not been agreed.[17] This framework has provided a robust basis for cooperation, while also proving sufficiently flexible to allow the cooperation to evolve to take account of relevant developments in international fisheries law and politics. A significant factor here is that the parties at a very early stage agreed on a fixed allocation key for the shared stocks (50–50 in the case of cod and haddock, and 60–40 in favour of Norway for capelin), and how to relate to third countries in this regard. Resolving distributional issues is critical to achieving sustainable management practices.[18]

Moreover, the above-mentioned agreements are in turn grounded in international ocean law, to which both parties subscribe. The existence of the 1982 Law of the Sea Convention and the 1995 UN Fish Stocks Agreement, and the two countries' shared interpretation of these agreements in relation to fisheries management, has been important in fending off external threats like the substantial fishing in the Loophole in the Barents Sea in the 1990s.

Second, the cooperation has been *underway for a long time*. Over the course of more than 30 years, activities under the Commission have been gradually expanded, and the cooperation has developed as a series of 'repeated games', wherein mutual understanding has evolved of each other's fisheries and the political context in which decisions on management are taken. This factor has undoubtedly been central in maintaining and developing cooperation in the face of difficult issues such as Russia's overfishing of its quota in recent years and skirmishes over enforcement in the Fisheries Protection Zone around Svalbard.[19]

An important step in the evolution of the bilateral cooperation has been the development and adoption of management strategies for the shared stocks. Such strategies essentially commit the parties to follow a

---

[17] This arrangement was contested in Norway at the time of its negotiation, because it also covers substantial areas that are under undisputed Norwegian and Russian jurisdiction, and the area that is under undisputed Norwegian jurisdiction is larger than that under Russian.

[18] See A.H. Hoel and I. Kvalvik, "The Allocation of Scarce Natural Resources: The Case of Fisheries", *Marine Policy*, Vol. 30, No. 4, 2006, pp. 347–56.

[19] Most of these concerns have involved issues relating to logbooks and so forth. A few larger incidents have involved arrests or attempts to arrest vessels operating in breach of regulations.

precautionary course of action over time in the management of any given fish stock. Such a strategy was first adopted by the Commission for cod in 2003, which has been evaluated by ICES as being in conformity with the precautionary approach.

A milestone in the cooperation was the decision by the authorities of the two countries in 2005 to initiate a parallel audit of the performance of the bilateral cooperation. Spurred by the overfishing in the Barents Sea, the analyses were to be carried out by the auditors-general of the two countries, rather than by the fisheries authorities. The audit proved a very difficult exercise, involving fundamental disagreements over data and ways of interpreting them. On the other hand, it also brought important lessons for both countries in how the other party views central issues in the cooperation. The reports from the audit indicated a number of areas where management could be improved.[20] It has been decided to follow up on the audit on both sides at regular intervals.

A third factor in explaining the functioning of the regime is the *scientific cooperation* between Norwegian and Russian scientists. As mentioned, Norwegian and Russian scientists have cooperated regularly at least since the 1950s. Following the establishment of the Joint Fisheries Commission, scientific cooperation became more structured, with the adoption of research plans in which joint surveys and the development of assessment methods were central elements. Today, this scientific cooperation on fisheries management is a major undertaking involving a large number of scientists as well as a huge infrastructure of research vessels, the production of joint reports,[21] etc.

An important aspect of the scientific cooperation is also that it is embedded in the broader framework of ICES, in which scientists from all countries around the North Atlantic participate. This arrangement has contributed to the development of a joint frame of reference for Norwegian and Russian scientists. Their common perception of and agreement on

---

[20] See Riksrevisjonen (2007), op. cit.

[21] See, for example J.E. Stiansen and A.A. Filin (eds), *Joint PINRO/IMR Report on the State of the Barents Sea Ecosystem in 2006 with Expected Situation and Consideration for Management*, IMR/PINRO Joint Report Series No. 7/2007, Bergen and Murmansk, 2007 (retrieved from www.imr.no/__data/page/7709/Nr.2_2007_Joint_PINROIMR_report.pdf).

scientific advice through the ICES advisory committees has been central to the status of scientific advice in the Commission.

Scientific agreement on issues relating to resource management is a major precondition for effective management,[22] and in this case the agreement among scientists from the two countries has provided an important basis for the decision-making. This is not to say that scientists from the two countries agree on all issues all the time. There can be substantial and long-lasting disagreement, but in the broader picture and in relation to the major questions, comprehensive scientific cooperation is an important best practice.

A fourth and significant factor is that the cooperation on fisheries management has largely been retained as a fundamentally sectoral issue. This means that most of the time it has been *insulated from the more controversial issues* relating to boundary delimitation and security politics. Talks on a boundary in the Barents Sea have been underway since 1974, and while some progress has been made, the issue remains essentially unresolved.[23] Although the question of the 50–50 share of cod and haddock and the 60–40 share of capelin has been raised in the context of these talks, it has not been a major issue. In terms of security politics, the Barents Sea was a global hotspot during the cold war, but even then fisheries management was not significantly impacted by security concerns. For example, Norwegian fisheries research vessels were admitted to Soviet waters and the port of Murmansk.

The one area where fisheries occasionally become entrenched in high politics is in relation to the issue of jurisdiction in the waters beyond the territorial waters around Svalbard. Here, Norway has gradually developed a regulatory regime that encompasses more fish species, and the enforcement of regulations has become stricter over time. The 2001 arrest of a Russian vessel at sea by the Norwegian Coast Guard for breaches of

---

[22] See S. Andresen, T. Skodvin, A. Underdal and J. Wettestad, *Science and Politics in International Environmental Regimes*, Manchester: University of Manchester Press, 2000.

[23] While the waters of the Barents Sea extend beyond the areas under national jurisdiction, thereby creating an area of international waters (the Loophole), all of the Barents Sea is continental shelf and therefore under the jurisdiction of the two states.

regulations resulted in a serious controversy with Russia, but it was quickly resolved.[24]

An important reason for this relative calm and isolation from high politics is probably that both parties have a strong interest in keeping the cooperation in fisheries management going. The cost of a breakdown could be severe, as both countries would then have to set unilateral quotas that would probably be far higher than are those dictated by management strategies aimed at ensuring the long-term sustainability of the fisheries. Another important factor in keeping fisheries issues isolated from the question of boundary delimitation is the Grey Zone arrangement. By specifying rights and obligations as to which country can enforce regulations against which vessels in that area, disturbing episodes can be avoided. This is probably why the agreement has been renewed annually for 30 years.

Finally, a factor not to be overlooked is that the bilateral Joint Fisheries Commission has been *able to adapt* to changing circumstances and adopt new and modern principles for management. In the context of global fisheries management, the Commission has been a forerunner in terms of establishing catch control rules and management strategies that seek to ensure compliance with the precautionary approach. This capacity to modernise and adapt to new principles and concerns is an important factor in explaining the relative success of the Commission in maintaining stocks at a healthy level. To a great extent, the past two years' reduction in overfishing stems from the systematic work to extend the reach of the enforcement system to include port state controls, thereby blocking market outlets in Europe and Northern Africa for illegally caught fish. In these achievements, the work in the Northeast Atlantic Fisheries Commission, in which both Norway and Russia participate, has been instrumental.

5. Conclusions regarding best practices

The bilateral cooperation between Norway and Russia in fisheries management in the Barents Sea has evolved over more than 30 years, a period that has witnessed major changes in both the political context and the understanding of how to manage fisheries. Although difficult and at times controversial, the cooperation has been relatively successful in terms

---

[24] This was the 'Chernigov incident'.

of the status of important fish stocks, in particular when compared with the situation off north-east Canada or in the North Sea.

We have pointed to some factors – best practices – that can help to explain this relative success. The grounding of the cooperation in a set of legal agreements that in turn are based on global agreements is certainly one important factor. Another is the long history of the cooperation, in which each of the parties has become acquainted with the other's situation and policy contexts, thereby developing an understanding of what the other party's issues are. A third is the joint scientific cooperation embedded in the broader framework of ICES. This helps to ensure that the parties have a common perception of the science underlying management. Fourth, it has generally been possible to isolate fisheries management from the high politics of the region. And finally, there is the capacity to adapt to changing circumstances and modernise management, extending its reach beyond conventional resource management to impact on trade as well.

Do these observations have relevance beyond the Barents Sea and fisheries? They probably do. For the Northern Dimension cooperation, for instance, the lessons relating to the importance of basing cooperation on firm legal commitments and common scientific understandings are significant. Also, it is well known from the international literature on resource management that a firm legal basis is beneficial,[25] and that agreement on scientific knowledge is important.[26] Furthermore, isolating the substance of cooperation from high politics can prevent cooperation from being contaminated by controversies on other issues.

Another question is how the fisheries regime will face up to new and emerging challenges – like the impact of climate change. Increasing ocean temperatures may well affect the geographical distribution of fish stocks in the ocean.[27] This may bring questions of distributional keys in important fisheries to the table in a more forceful way than seen up to now. A major task facing the two parties is the introduction of ecosystems-based

---

[25] See R.R. Churchill and A.W. Lowe, *The Law of the Sea*, Manchester: Manchester University Press, 1999.

[26] See Andresen et al. (2000), op. cit.

[27] See Artic Climate Impact Assessment (ACIA), *The Arctic Climate Impact Assessment*, Cambridge: Cambridge University Press, 2005; see also A.H. Hoel, "Jurisdictional Issues in the Arctic – An Overview", *Oslo Files on Defence and Security*, No. 2, 2008.

management of the marine ecosystems. In Norway, a management plan for the Norwegian part of the Barents Sea and the areas north of Lofoten is being implemented, basically as a response to the emergence of commercial-scale petroleum production in the region. If the Barents Sea ecosystem as a whole is to be covered, Russia will have to adopt a similar arrangement. As this step will necessarily have an impact on Russia's main breadwinner – the petroleum industry – it will constitute an important test of the bilateral cooperation.

6. References

Andresen, S., T. Skodvin, A. Underdal and J. Wettestad (2000), *Science and Politics in International Environmental Regimes*, Manchester: University of Manchester Press.

Artic Climate Impact Assessment (ACIA) (2005), *The Arctic Climate Impact Assessment*, Cambridge: Cambridge University Press.

Churchill, R.R. and A.W. Lowe (1999), *The Law of the Sea*, Manchester: Manchester University Press.

Ebbin, S.E., A.H. Hoel and A. Sydnes (2005), *A Sea Change: The Exclusive Economic Zone and Governance Institutions for Living Marine Resources*, Dordrecht: Springer.

Hardin, G. (1968), "The Tragedy of the Commons", *Science*, Vol. 162, No. 3859, pp. 1243–48.

Havforskningsinstituttet [Institute of Marine Research] (2008), *Havets ressurser og miljø 2008: Fisken og havet* 1.

Hilborn, R., A.E. Punt and J. Orensanz (2004), "Beyond Band-aids in Fisheries Management: Fixing World Fisheries", *Bulletin of Marine Science*, Vol. 74, No. 3, pp. 493–507.

Hoel, A.H. (2008), "Jurisdictional Issues in the Arctic – An Overview", *Oslo Files on Defence and Security*, 2/2008.

Hoel, A.H. and I. Kvalvik (2006), "The Allocation of Scarce Natural Resources: The Case of Fisheries", *Marine Policy*, Vol. 30, No. 4, pp. 347–56.

Hønneland, G. (2006), *Kvotekamp og kystsolidaritet: Norsk-russisk fiskeriforvaltning gjennom 30 år*, Bergen: Fagbokforlaget.

Riksrevisjonen (2007), *Riksrevisjonens undersøkelse av forvaltningen og kontrollen av fiskeressursene i Barentshavet og Norskehavet – en parallel revisjon mellom norsk og russisk riksrevisjon*, Document 3:2 (2007–2008), Oslo, p. 9.

Stiansen, J.E. and A.A. Filin (eds) (2007), *Joint PINRO/IMR Report on the State of the Barents Sea Ecosystem in 2006 with Expected Situation and Consideration for Management*, IMR/PINRO Joint Report Series No. 7/2007, Bergen and Murmansk.

Stokke, O.S. (2002), "The Loophole of the Barents Sea Fisheries Regime", in O.S. Stokke (ed.), *Governing High Seas Fisheries*, Oxford: Oxford University Press.

5. EXPERIENCES OF ENVIRONMENTAL COOPERATION BETWEEN THE NORDIC COUNTRIES AND RUSSIA: LESSONS LEARNED AND THE WAY FORWARD
NINA TYNKKYNEN

1. Introduction

Northern Europe has a rich history of environmental cooperation. Multilateral environmental collaboration started back in the 1970s in the context of the Baltic Sea area, aided by scientific and other cooperation between Finland and the Soviet Union. Since the early 1990s, several other states and actors in the region have developed bilateral and regional environmental partnerships with Russia. The record of these initiatives includes both success stories and problematic ones.

This chapter examines case studies of environmental cooperation between the Nordic countries and Russia. The aim is to analyse drivers of and barriers to success in these experiences with Russia to enable lessons to be drawn for future collaboration in this sphere under the new Northern Dimension. The new documents of the Northern Dimension policy, which were adopted in Helsinki in November 2006, underline that experience gained from existing forms of cooperation at the regional, sub-regional and local levels should be utilised in the development of the Northern

Dimension.[1] The focus of this chapter is therefore on existing forms of regional cooperation. The analysis centres on 'conventional' environmental initiatives rather than cooperation on issues of nuclear safety (see chapter 2). The latter has only recently taken off on a larger scale; moreover, the conditions for nuclear safety cooperation also differ fairly significantly from those of more conventional environmental efforts. This has been taken into consideration in the policy's main funding instrument for environmental collaboration, the Northern Dimension Environmental Partnership (NDEP), which is divided into nuclear and non-nuclear windows. The flagship NDEP project, the St. Petersburg water sector, is one of the concrete examples examined in this chapter. The other examples discussed are not, however, included in the NDEP project pipeline, as most projects in the pipeline are still in an initial phase or under construction, which makes assessment premature.

In many of the cases covered in this chapter, there is a strong emphasis on Finnish–Russian collaboration. This partly stems from Finland's longstanding record in this sphere, its eagerness to intensify the former Finnish–Soviet environmental cooperation with Russia in the early 1990s and its present status as one of Russia's main partners in environmental projects.[2] The main criteria for Finnish assistance are that projects should help to control transboundary pollution in Finland and should promote the use of Finnish environmental technology. In addition, the assisted counterpart is to cover at least half of the expenses. These are not drastically different priorities from those of Russia's other partners in regional environmental cooperation. The data used in the analysis consist of interviews,[3] reports and other documents, along with previous research.[4]

---

[1] See the "Political Declaration on the Northern Dimension Policy" (Helsinki, 24 November 2006) (retrieved from http://ec.europa.eu/external_relations/north_dim/doc/pol_dec_1106.pdf); see also the Northern Dimension Policy Framework Document (Helsinki, 24 November 2006) (retrieved from http://ec.europa.eu/external_relations/north_dim/doc/frame_pol_1106.pdf).

[2] Since 1990, Finland has provided a total of €38 million for environmental investments in Russia and €17 million for technical assistance projects; see K. Eloheimo, *Suomen alueelle Venäjältä kohdistuvat rajat ylittävät ympäristöuhat*, 36/2007, Finnish Ministry of the Environment, Helsinki, 2007.

[3] The interviews were conducted with Russian and Finnish stakeholders as part of the author's doctoral research; see N. Tynkkynen, *Constructing the Environmental Regime between Russia and Europe: Conditions for Social Learning*, Tampere: Acta

2.   The environment in the new Northern Dimension

The environment is one of the key areas of collaboration between the EU and Russia. Activities are naturally concentrated in the European part of Russia and particularly Russia's north-western territories, which have a long border with the EU. Owing to the historical legacies of the Soviet era, the lack of local resources and institutional capacity, and the fragile ecology, there is an urgent need for environmental investment in this region. Consequently, the NDEP was developed in 2001 to address environmental problems in north-west Russia. Now that the environmental dialogue between the EU and Russia is emerging as part of the work of establishing a 'common economic space', the NDEP will be implementing some of its specified activities within the geographical boundaries of the Northern Dimension area.

The NDEP support fund, as the main instrument of the NDEP, awards grants to environmental projects. As of spring 2007, several EU member states, the European Commission, the Russian Federation, Norway and Canada had contributed a total of €243.4 million to the fund (Table 5.1). Two-thirds of the total sum is tied to nuclear safety projects, with the remainder for other environmental projects.

Universitatis Tamperensis, 2008(a). Information is also derived from interviews with a representative of the Finnish Ministry of the Environment and a representative of the Nordic Environment Finance Corporation (Nefco). In some of the interviews, as well as the study undertaken by Monica Tennberg from which the analysis draws, environmental cooperation between Finland/the Nordic countries and Russia was discussed at a more general level. See M. Tennberg, "Trust in International Environmental Cooperation in North-western Russia", *Cooperation and Conflict*, Vol. 42, No. 3, 2007, pp. 321–35.

[4] See Tennberg (2007), op. cit.; G. Hønneland, *Russia and the West: Environmental Cooperation and Conflict*, London: Routledge, 2003; P. Nikula and V.-P. Tynkkynen, "Risks in Oil Transportation in the Gulf of Finland: Not a Question of If – But When", in C. Pursiainen (ed.), *Towards a Baltic Sea Region Strategy in Critical Infrastructure Protection*, Stockholm: Nordregio, 2007, pp. 141–64.

Table 5.1 Contributors to the NDEP support fund

Contributor	Non-earmarked (in € million)	Nuclear window (in € million)	Total (€ million)
EU	20	40	60
Denmark	10	1	11
Finland	16	2	18
Norway	0.4	10	10.4
Sweden	16 + 1.3*	–	17.3
Belgium	–	0.5	0.5
France	–	40	40
Germany	10	10	20
Netherlands	–	10	10
United Kingdom	–	16.2	16.2
Russia	20	–	20
Canada	–	20	20
Total	93.7	149.7	243.4

* New contributions received after the Assembly of Contributors in November 2007.

Source: NDEP, "Pledges and Contributors to the NDEP Support Fund" (retrieved from www.ndep.org/partners.asp?type=nh&pageid=2).

With conventional environmental projects, NDEP grants cover some of the total costs, while the majority of funding is provided through normal project finance from other sources. Accordingly, the main aim of the grants is to act as a catalyst, promoting further investments in environmental initiatives in the region. The list of non-nuclear projects approved by the Assembly of Contributors in November 2007 includes 12 projects altogether (see Table 5.2). Some have already been completed whereas others are still in the planning phase.

Table 5.2 NDEP non-nuclear projects approved by the Assembly of Contributors (November 2007)

No.	Project	Lead intl. financial institution	Project cost (€ million)	NDEP grant (€ million)	Status	Completion date
1)	St. Petersburg WTP	NIB	194	5.8	Completed	2005
2)	St. Petersburg Flood Protection Barrier	EBRD	2,000	1	Under construction	2010
3)	St. Petersburg Northern Incinerator	EBRD	90.4	6.35	Plant inaugurated	2007
4)	Leningrad Oblast Programme	NIB	20.3	4	Under construction	2009
5)	Komi Syktyvar municipal services	EBRD	29.5	6.04	Under construction	2009
6)	Kaliningrad district heating	EBRD	21.8	7.3	Grant yet to be signed	2012
7)	Arkhangelsk municipal services	EBRD	25.3	8.2	Under construction	2012
8)	Murmansk district heating	NIB	29.6	5	Grant yet to be signed	2012
9)	Kaliningrad water services	EBRD	106.8	10	Under construction	2012
10)	Kaliningrad PIU	EBRD	3.8	3	In operation	2012
11)	Vologda water services	EBRD	18.4	3.5	Under construction	2012
12)	Novgorod	NIB	16.1	2	Under construction	2012
	Total (€ million)	–	2,556	62.19	–	–

Notes: EBRD refers to the European Bank of Reconstruction and Development; NIB refers to the Nordic Investment Bank.

Source: NDEP, "Approved Projects in the NDEP Non Nuclear Window" (retrieved from www.ndep.org/projects.asp?type=nh&cont=prjh&pageid=4).

We now move on to discuss six concrete cases of regional environmental cooperation to illustrate existing activities in this sphere of Northern Dimension and Nordic–Russian cooperation in greater detail. The survey of the six cases forms the basis for analysing barriers to and drivers of successful cooperation on a more general level.

3. Examples of cooperation

1) The St. Petersburg water sector. The water sector of the city of St. Petersburg has been the focus of joint environmental activities between Russia and Finland since the early 1990s. Cooperation has centred on the technical improvement of the water supply and wastewater management system, and on the institutional development of the city's water and sewage utility Vodokanal. For example, about 40 km of sewers in the city centre and wastewater pumping stations have been reconstructed as part of the joint efforts.[5] Up until 2003, about one-fifth of the grant assistance given by Finland to the development of the St. Petersburg water sector was directed at 'twinning activities' between Helsinki Water and Vodokanal of St. Petersburg, initiated in 1995.[6] The main idea of twinning is to become familiar with practices and functions of a twin utility abroad so that solutions might be replicated or modified for application at home. In addition, the Finnish Ministry of the Environment has been subsidising activities of a private Finnish foundation, the John Nurminen Foundation, which, through its Clean Sea project, seeks to use chemical phosphorous removal at one medium-sized and three small wastewater treatment plants in St. Petersburg.[7] This project involves close coordination between Vodokanal, the city of St. Petersburg and the foundation to which private donors and companies have contributed.[8]

---

[5] See the Finnish Ministry of the Environment, *Evaluation and Strategy Study of the Cooperation Between the Ministry of the Environment, Finland, and Vodokanal of St. Petersburg, Russia,* Ministry of the Environment, Helsinki, 2002. Altogether, Finland assisted almost 100 projects in the St. Petersburg water sector by providing €28 million; see Finnish Ministry of the Environment, "St. Petersburg Wastewater Treatment Boosted: Cooperation to Improve the State of the Gulf of Finland Continues", press release, Ministry of the Environment, Helsinki, 1 October 2007.

[6] See Finnish Ministry of the Environment, *Cooperation Between Vodokanal of St. Petersburg and the Ministry of the Environment of Finland, Framework Programme 2004–2007,* WaterPro Partners Ltd., Helsinki, 2003.

[7] For more information on the project, see the Clean Baltic Sea website (www.cleanbalticsea.fi).

[8] See Finnish Ministry of the Environment, *From Co-operation in Central and Eastern Europe to European Union Partnership,* Ministry of the Environment, Helsinki, 2006.

Sweden, Denmark and the UK, as well as international financial institutions have also made an important contribution to the development of the St. Petersburg water sector. Nevertheless, the leading financier has been the European Bank for Reconstruction and Development (EBRD). The largest single project has been the construction of the St. Petersburg Southwest Wastewater Treatment Plant, with total costs amounting to €200 million. This project has also been included on the list of the NDEP support fund. The plant, which was completed in 2005, was financed through a combination of international loans, grant aid, venture capital and local investment.[9]

With the help of these concerted efforts, the water sector of St. Petersburg has developed significantly, especially in institutional terms, over the past 10 years. In 2000, St. Petersburg Vodokanal was recognised as the leading water utility in Russia and the leading public utility in St. Petersburg. In 2005, it won the Swedish Baltic Sea Water Award.[10] Cooperation has also had an immediate impact on the state of the environment: the new wastewater treatment plant is able to process the sewage of 700,000 residents, thereby cutting the city's discharges of untreated sewage to the Gulf of Finland by about one-third. Still, many problems remain, in both water supply and wastewater management. The next major investment will be the main sewer in the north of the city, the construction of which is estimated to cost nearly €500 million.[11]

2) *Pechenganikel mining industry.* The Nordic countries have been active in attempting to reduce mining-related pollution in the Murmansk

[9] See N. Tynkkynen, "Environmental Cooperation and Learning: The St. Petersburg Water Sector", in D. Lehrer and A. Korhonen (eds), *Western Aid in Post-communism: Effects and Side effects*, Basingstoke: Palgrave Macmillan, 2008(b), forthcoming.

[10] See Vodokanal St. Petersburg, *Final Report of the Corporate Development Support Programme*, St. Petersburg, 2001; Helcom, "As Driving Forces Behind New Treatment Plan, St. Petersburg's Water Authority and its Director Win the 2005 Swedish Baltic Sea Water Award", Helcom, Helsinki, 21 June 2005 (retrieved from www.helcom.fi/press_office/news_baltic/en_GB/StPetersburg).

[11] For a more detailed analysis of the cooperation, see Tynkkynen (2008b), op. cit.; O. Salmi and N. Tynkkynen, "Environmental Governance in Russia: Changing Conditions for International Environmental Cooperation in the Case of the Murmansk Region Mining Industry and the St. Petersburg Water Sector", submitted draft article, 2008.

region through collaborative work.[12] The restructuring project of Pechenganikel, a subsidiary of Norilsk Nikel operating cupro-nickel smelters in the cities of Nikel and Zapolyarnyi, has been the largest single project in this respect. The project started in 1993 when a Scandinavian consortium consisting of Norwegian, Finnish and Swedish governments, private companies and intra-governmental agencies won a tender for the reconstruction of Pechenganikel with a budget of $300 million. The project was soon halted because of lack of funding from the Russian side and the process of privatisation of the company, which made the division of responsibilities unclear. In 1997, negotiations with Norilsk Nikel were resumed by the Nordic Investment Bank (NIB). In the course of the negotiations, the differing expectations of the NIB and the Norilsk Nikel management came up. Simply put, more environmentally-motivated Nordic expectations clashed with Russian expectations that emphasised the economic side.[13] The Russian party did not consider the emissions of 150,000 tonnes of sulphur dioxide as significant for the environment. Therefore, the company called for extensive restructuring at a cost of $300 million that would double the production capacity and simultaneously reduce per-tonne environmental emissions.

This conflict of goals and different motivations brought the restructuring project to a standstill on several occasions between 1997 and 2003. By 2005, however, the project was again advancing smoothly. It appears that Pechenganikel is finally making progress in its environmental

---

[12] Although lower than before, the level of sulphur dioxide and heavy metals emissions from smelting and enrichment of electrolytic and carbonyl nickel and electrolytic copper by Norilsk Nikel still exceeds the corresponding levels in Western Europe. In 2003, sulphur was emitted from the region's cupro-nickel smelters in amounts exceeding the national sulphur emissions of the whole of Finland; see O. Salmi, "Eco-Efficiency and Industrial Symbiosis – A Counterfactual Analysis of a Mining Community", *Journal of Cleaner Production*, Vol. 15, No. 17, 2007, pp. 1696–05. The effects of sulphur dioxide on local ecosystems are significant, even though they do not travel very far from the source; see Artic Monitoring and Assessment Programme (AMAP), *AMAP Assessment Report: Arctic Pollution Issues*, Arctic Council, Oslo, 1998.

[13] Derived from an interview with a representative of the Nordic Investment Bank, 2005.

profile, which is likely to improve the state of the environment of the entire Murmansk region.[14]

3) *The hazardous waste facility Krasnyi Bor.* The hazardous waste incinerator and storage facility Krasnyi Bor near St. Petersburg, built in 1969, has been a source of concern for local politicians and environmental organisations.[15] The facility contains over 1.5 million tonnes of hazardous waste. The site is in poor condition and poses a serious environmental risk to the region as well as to the Gulf of Finland. The capacity of the facility to store and process waste is limited, and in case of heavy flooding, 700,000 tonnes of liquid toxic waste threaten to flow into the River Neva, poisoning the city's main source of drinking water.

Krasnyi Bor is managed by the Environmental Committee of the city of St. Petersburg. It has been included on the priority list of Finnish environmental cooperation with Russia. During the 1990s, the Finnish government financed several studies on possibilities for developing the facility. These studies did not lead to investments, however. During 1998–2000, a French consulting company conducted a TACIS project, resulting in recommendations to build a semi-mobile incinerator to process hazardous waste at Krasnyi Bor. In 2000, the EBRD began preparing a new project, and the following year, the city of St. Petersburg and international financial organisations signed a funding agreement for $10 million for rehabilitation of the facility.[16] In this rehabilitation programme, Finland and Denmark were to fund the construction of a chemico-biological treatment facility. But in 2007, the Environmental Committee of the city of St. Petersburg announced that the project would be halted and that Russia would make its own decisions on the problem of hazardous waste. Uncertainty concerning the future ownership of the facility, changes in the composition of project participants, a multitude of financiers, Russian suspicion towards the chemico-biological treatment process designed by the Danish partner, the

---

[14] For a more detailed analysis of the cooperation, see Salmi and Tynkkynen (2008), op. cit.

[15] See Eloheimo (2007), op. cit.

[16] Derived from an interview with a representative of the EBRD, 2002, and an interview with a representative of the Finnish Ministry of the Environment in St. Petersburg, 2002.

lack of common understanding and an insufficient cost estimation, all hindered implementation of the project.[17]

4) The Gulf of Finland Mandatory Ship Reporting System. Oil transport in the Baltic Sea is growing rapidly. The volume of oil transport in the Baltic Sea is at present seven times higher than it was 10 years ago, and the VTT Technical Research Centre of Finland estimates that it will increase to about 250 million tonnes a year by 2015.[18] Russia is currently building more port infrastructure in the Gulf of Finland, where navigation is challenging owing to the low water levels, narrow navigation routes and icy conditions in wintertime.

The Gulf of Finland Mandatory Ship Reporting System (GOFREP), which was developed to improve the safety of the rapidly growing shipping traffic in the Gulf of Finland, went into operation in 2004. The GOFREP system gathers information on ships, their cargo and routes for the authorities responsible for vessel traffic control. One recent evaluation notes that the GOFREP system has improved risk management (oil transportation safety) by 80%.[19] According to Piia Nikula and Veli-Pekka Tynkkynen, the core of the safety-enhancing system resulted from intense cooperation among the maritime authorities, although the adoption of the GOFREP system itself was mandated by the International Maritime Organisation (IMO). As the traffic is still growing and GOFREP has certain deficiencies, the Estonian, Finnish and Russian maritime authorities are currently trying to bolster the GOFREP system. There are high hopes, based on the very good experience of the previous joint work, that this upgrade could become operational in 2008.

5) Energy-saving projects in north-west Russia. The Nordic Environment Finance Corporation (Nefco) has implemented more than 45 small-scale projects for saving energy in north-west Russian municipalities, through its Facility for Energy Saving. The projects have been targeted at the social infrastructure, such as schools, kindergartens, hospitals, sports facilities and street lighting. Repayment of the loans is directly tied to the savings resulting from the investment. Project activities have focused on renovating

---

[17] See Eloheimo (2007), op. cit., pp. 19–21.

[18] See J. Rytkönen, "Latest Development of Oil and Chemical Transportation on the Baltic Sea", presentation at the Conference on "Dangerous Goods Transportation" in St. Petersburg, 26 October 2006.

[19] See Nikula and Tynkkynen (2007), op. cit., pp. 141–64.

and glazing windows, upgrading heating sub-stations, insulating pipelines, optimising hot water supply systems and installing thermostatic radiator valves. For example, at several schools in Kirovsk, some 200 km south of Murmansk, the heating system was upgraded and energy consumption was reduced significantly after the installation of new equipment. In the city of Segezha in northern Karelia, 1,660 mercury lamps for street illumination were replaced with new energy-saving sodium lamps in 2008. The city of Onega in Arkhangelsk Oblast will move from coal to biomass in its heating production. The phasing-out of coal-fired boilers in the town will improve the air quality considerably. These projects have been proceeding smoothly, with the local stakeholders as active participants. Cooperation among the local authorities and with energy-efficiency centres has also been successful.[20]

6) City twinning activities. The Environmental Committee of the city of St. Petersburg and the Finnish Ministry of the Environment are engaged in a programme that aims at reinforcing environmental management, improving management and control of hazardous waste, and increasing environmental awareness in St. Petersburg. In addition, it seeks to support city twinning for joint environmental efforts. Under the city twinning programme, a project carried out between Turku in Finland and St. Petersburg has compared environmental monitoring practices at industrial plants. The project has included study tours for supervisors from St. Petersburg to Turku to familiarise them with the practices and working methods of the Finnish partner and vice versa. These exchange visits have provided new perspectives for both parties, with a multiplier effect in terms of environmental awareness-raising and better management.[21] In addition, St. Petersburg and Tampere in Finland are engaged in a project to improve air quality monitoring, which includes studying the air quality

---

[20] See the *Nefco Newsletter*, November 2007 (retrieved from www.nefco.org/documents/NEFCO.NEWS.NOV2007.pdf); information also derived from a communication with a representative of Nefco, October 2007.

[21] See Finnish Ministry of the Environment (2006), op. cit.; information also derived from an interview with a representative of the St. Petersburg Environmental Committee, 2003.

systems in both cities, developing a monitoring network, finding locations for measuring stations and comparing modelling procedures (Table 5.3).[22]

Table 5.3 Summary of the six cases of environmental cooperation with Russia

Case	Activities	Main foreign partner	Timeframe	Scope of funding
St. Petersburg water sector	Technical and institutional development	Finland, EBRD, others	1991–	Loans and grants
Pechenganikel mining industry	Emissions reduction, modernisation	Norway, Finland, Sweden, NIB	1993– (with interruptions)	Loans and grants
Hazardous waste facility at Krasnyi Bor	Modernisation	Finland, Denmark, TACIS, EBRD	Plans, pilots and evaluations since the mid-1990s; halted in 2007	Some evaluations funded, large-scale loans and grants planned
GOFREP	Maritime safety improvement	Maritime authorities of Russia, Estonia and Finland	System put into use in 2004	No special grants or loans
Nefco energy-saving projects	Energy saving	Nefco	Ongoing	Loans
City twinning	Institutional development of environmental administration	8 cities in Finland	2003–	Small grants

Source: Author's compilation.

4. Drivers of and barriers to success in environmental cooperation

Environmental cooperation is difficult to evaluate in terms of its effectiveness, not least because of the many intervening factors and time lags. Its success should instead be evaluated in terms of institutional development and changes in the meanings attached to the environment

---

[22] See the St. Petersburg City Twinning Programme website (www3.turku.fi/ctw/index.shtml); Finnish Ministry of the Environment (2006), op. cit.

rather than in terms of direct improvements in the state of the environment, which will often be problematic to measure and isolate from other events.[23]

Successful cooperation is here defined mainly on the basis of the experience of the participants in and observers of the joint work in the six cases described above – whether the participants themselves have defined the process as successful or not. Based on these assessments and literature, the next section analyses the drivers of and barriers to successful cooperation.

Drivers of success

The recognition of a *common interest* – that is, a *shared understanding of goals and means of cooperation* – was identified as a key driver of success by the Nordic and Russian parties to regional environmental coordination. In the case of the St. Petersburg water sector, the partners – the management of the utility, foreign partners and the authorities – shared the central idea of the initiative. The partners were also allowed to negotiate and define its content without much steering from above. Relative *financial and administrative independence from the Russian authorities* has allowed the St. Petersburg water utility, at least in recent years, to act independently of federal, local and regional authorities and without having to think about subsidies.

Furthermore, Russians in particular emphasise *trust* as an important driver of success in environmental cooperation. Trust is connected to other factors of success: the long association of partners and having the right persons in the right places with good and stable relationships.[24] Personal relations that have time to evolve through long-term cooperation, as well as individual skills, are very important in working together with Russians. Nikula and Tynkkynen (2007) note that in the case of GOFREP, many potential barriers to collaboration have been avoided thanks to good and personal contacts with the Russian authorities.[25]

Achieving relationships of trust presupposes negotiation and action on an *equal intellectual and financial basis* among the partners. The material basis of cooperation is a crucial element here. Russians widely share the

---

[23] See Tynkkynen (2008a), op. cit.; cf. Tennberg (2007), op. cit., pp. 321–35.

[24] See Tennberg (2007), op. cit., p. 327; Tynkkynen (2008b), op. cit.

[25] See Nikula and Tynkkynen (2007), op. cit., pp. 141–64.

view that more Russian material resources should be used in joint activities. Equality is encouraged by applying partnership and *learning-by-doing* methods. Russian partners in particular have emphasised the importance of a "long-term partnership that aims at concrete results".[26] In this respect, twinning activities seem a particularly fruitful form of collaboration.

Russians notably praise cooperation that can proceed among experts, without much involvement from the authorities – as exemplified by the GOFREP work. The EU and the IMO set the legal framework, but the working procedures related to traffic surveillance and control adopted by marine safety authorities in all three countries have been developed through day-to-day cooperation at the level of professional practitioners – the maritime safety authorities of Estonia, Finland and Russia (Box 5.1).

Box 5.1 Drivers of success in Nordic–Russian environmental cooperation

- Common interests
- Shared understanding of goals and means
- Independence/autonomy from the authorities
- Trust, personal relations and individual skills (long association of partners)
- Financial and intellectual equality of the partners
- Partnerships and a learning-by-doing approach
- Expert-level interaction

Barriers to success

When asked to list the various problems of environmental coordination in Russia, the following were stressed by project partners: *intricate negotiation processes, lack of commitment, funding insecurity, information problems* and *prolonged project schedules.*[27] These problems apply to political cooperation ('environmental diplomacy') in particular, but they have also been encountered at the level of joint practical work in projects.

---

[26] See Tennberg (2007), op. cit., p. 327; Tynkkynen (2008b), op. cit..

[27] See in particular Tennberg (2007), op. cit., pp. 321–35.

Most problems stem from the way in which environmental policy itself has evolved in the hierarchy of Russian political priorities.[28] The unclear administrative status of environmental policy is reflected in *continuous administrative and legal reforms* and in *insufficient domestic environmental expenditure*, resulting in a loss of environmental expertise and awareness in the Russian administration. Confusion over the allocation of responsibilities, decision-making power and ineffective communication between the federal and regional authorities in Russia has formed barriers to cooperation. Administrative turbulence has caused constant replacement of Russian participants and a lack of active Russian participation in cooperative processes. In the Pechenganikel case, for example, the problems partly originated in the unclear status of the roles of the federal and regional governments. Moreover, the decentralisation of responsibilities in environmental administration has not been compensated by adequate financial resources, leading to difficulties in funding the Russian share of the project.

In some cases, however, changes in environmental governance have actually enhanced the autonomy of local actors in solving practical problems and improved the possibilities for local stakeholders to participate in environmental projects. This has enabled direct cross-border contacts, but has also made the success of cooperation highly dependent on the interests and commitment of local actors.

The lack of economic incentives for making environmentally sound investments in Russia, and the insecurities inherent in Russia's economy in general and the property rights system in particular, are also listed among the barriers to success in environmental partnerships. These factors lead to situations characterised by diverging interests between the Russian and Nordic partners. As the Pechenganikel case demonstrates, there is often tension between environmental and other goals, such as industrial modernisation and greater profitability. The *conflict of interests* appears in diverging views over the goals and means of cooperation, which significantly reduces the potential for successful collaboration. The *financial imbalance* means that Russian participants often perceive the arrangements

---

[28] See D.J. Peterson and E.K. Bielke, "The Reorganisation of Russia's Environmental Bureaucracy: Implications and Prospects", *Post-Soviet Geography and Economics*, Vol. 42, No. 1, 2001, pp. 65–76; J. Oldfield, *Russian Nature: Exploring the Environmental Consequences of Societal Change*, Aldershot: Ashgate, 2005.

as 'unequal'. The material imbalance may form barriers, mental ones not least, to open communication and interaction. This was, for instance, the case with the St. Petersburg water-sector projects, until the water and sewage utility Vodokanal, the Russian partner in the projects, became more viable in financial terms. In addition, many Russian project managers complain that their knowledge and expertise are not effectively put to use in such efforts, and that priority lists, evaluations and briefings are usually made by non-Russians. A related problem is that Russian participants often have financial difficulties in attending meetings and in obtaining clearance to travel.

In some cases *cultural disparities*, such as differing conceptions concerning time and place, the role of authorities, the bureaucratic system and the hierarchy of problems add to the financial issues, causing misunderstandings and frustration. Geir Hønneland, who has studied Russian–Norwegian environmental cooperation, distinguishes between a Russian "techno-centric meta-discourse" and the Norwegian "eco-centric meta-discourse" – which effectively crystallises the basic differences produced by alternative cultural and historical contexts. The former discourse emphasises the positive effects of polluting industrial activities, viewed as contributing primarily to regional development and wealth, whereas the latter focuses on the degradation of the environment and health (Box 5.2).[29]

Box 5.2 Barriers to success in Nordic–Russian environmental cooperation

- Intricate negotiation processes
- Lack of commitment
- Insecurity of funding
- Information problems
- Prolonged project schedules
- Instabilities in Russian environmental administration and funding
- Conflicting interests and goals
- Financial imbalances among partners (also leading to imbalances in the use of intellectual capacity)
- Cultural traits: differing hierarchies of problems, differing discourses

---

[29] See Hønneland (2003), op. cit.

5. Lessons and conclusions

These cases of environmental cooperation between the Nordic countries and Russia show that the main barriers to success in such efforts chiefly stem from economic, political and administrative instabilities in Russia. That in turn should indicate that the barriers would be temporary in character. With the resurgence of the economy, more Russian intellectual and material resources should gradually become available for addressing environmental concerns and investing in joint environmental projects. The NDEP is a showcase of such positive developments. Russian interest in and commitment to the support fund has increased significantly since 2006.[30] In the future, it is crucial to maintain this strong commitment at all levels of the administration to ensure a clear sense of ownership and to attract new funds from international partners.[31]

One way to strengthen commitment and avoid misunderstandings is to make the intentions of Nordic and other Western partners as explicit as possible for the Russians, and to make motivations more transparent.[32] This effort will require joint project preparation involving all partners. The long association of partners, in addition to a practical orientation, will help in this respect. Gradually, partners become familiar with each other's views and learn to appreciate each other's priorities. Contacts from regional cooperation are valuable and could be capitalised upon systematically in activities under the new Northern Dimension.

In many instances, matters that may hinder cooperation at the highest political level – such as sovereignty questions or other political problems – do not interfere with cooperation at the practical level or the expert level in particular. Here it is easier to identify the relevant stakeholders, negotiate over the goals and means, and find stronger personal interest and commitment. Emerging forms of such partnerships, such as that of the John Nurminen Foundation and Vodokanal, represent a positive development and are worth encouraging. In project-level work, flexible, small-scale,

---

[30] See Tennberg (2007), op. cit., p. 330; information also derived from an interview with a representative of the Finnish Ministry of the Environment, 2007.

[31] See J. Henttonen, "The New Northern Dimension. Case: Environment"', presentation at the seminar on "The New Northern Dimension: Regional Co-operation, Business and Energy", St. Petersburg, 17 January 2008.

[32] See Hønneland (2003), op. cit., p. 140.

interactive and relatively informal forms of cooperation, such as twinning and other day-to-day joint activities, seem to drive success. On the whole, local stakeholders represent an underutilised resource. They are usually highly motivated to participate in environmental projects because they stand to benefit directly from the improved state of the environment.

Seen from this perspective, small-scale projects and the long association of partners can also prove productive and may even have greater impact than large-scale projects determined on the basis of competitive bidding. At the moment, the NDEP support fund's environmental window includes only large-scale projects, although there are many smaller sub-projects. Still, it might be a good idea to include more small-scale activities as well in the NDEP project pipeline. These can serve as important means of environmental capacity-building and may carry multiplier effects, possibly leading to more fundamental changes than direct investments.

The environmental sphere is not the easiest context for cooperation. For one thing, environmental problems are highly heterogeneous and context-specific. In different economic and political settings, physically similar environmental changes may lead to quite different societal effects. Lessons learned affirm this and indicate that differentiation and specification of forms of cooperation is necessary, depending on the issue and circumstances. Accordingly, in environmental cooperation 'form should follow function': the best form of cooperation will depend on the situation at hand. Experience has shown that one size does not fit all – there is no general model of collaboration that would suit every case. Therefore, it is important to consider carefully the most suitable level and form of cooperation on a case-by-case basis, which also applies in the framework of the Northern Dimension.

6.   References

Artic Monitoring and Assessment Programme (AMAP) (1998), *AMAP Assessment Report: Arctic Pollution Issues*, Arctic Council, Oslo.

Eloheimo, K. (2007), *Suomen alueelle Venäjältä kohdistuvat rajat ylittävät ympäristöuhat*, Finnish Ministry of the Environment, Helsinki.

Finnish Ministry of the Environment (2002), *Evaluation and Strategy Study of the Cooperation Between the Ministry of the Environment, Finland, and Vodokanal of St. Petersburg, Russia*, Ministry of the Environment, Helsinki.

——————— (2003), *Cooperation Between Vodokanal of St. Petersburg and the Ministry of the Environment of Finland, Framework Programme 2004–2007*, WaterPro Partners Ltd., Helsinki.

——————— (2006), *From Cooperation in Central and Eastern Europe to European Union Partnership*, Ministry of the Environment, Helsinki.

——————— (2007), "St. Petersburg Wastewater Treatment Boosted: Cooperation to Improve the State of the Gulf of Finland Continues", press release, Ministry of the Environment, Helsinki, 1 October.

Helcom (2005), "As Driving Forces Behind New Treatment Plan, St. Petersburg's Water Authority and its Director Win the 2005 Swedish Baltic Sea Water Award", Helcom, Helsinki, 21 June (retrieved from www.helcom.fi/press_office/news_baltic/en_GB/StPetersburg).

Henttonen, J. (2008), "The New Northern Dimension. Case: Environment"', presentation at the seminar on "The New Northern Dimension: Regional Co-operation, Business and Energy", St. Petersburg, 17 January.

Hønneland, G. (2003), *Russia and the West: Environmental Cooperation and Conflict*, London: Routledge.

Nikula, P. and V.-P. Tynkkynen (2007), "Risks in Oil Transportation in the Gulf of Finland: Not a Question of If – But When", in C. Pursiainen (ed.), *Towards a Baltic Sea Region Strategy in Critical Infrastructure Protection*, Stockholm: Nordregio, pp. 141–64.

Oldfield, J. (2005), *Russian Nature: Exploring the Environmental Consequences of Societal Change*, Aldershot: Ashgate.

Peterson, D.J. and E.K. Bielke (2001), "The Reorganisation of Russia's Environmental Bureaucracy: Implications and Prospects", *Post-Soviet Geography and Economics*, Vol. 42, No. 1, pp. 65–76.

Rytkönen, J. (2006), "Latest Development of Oil and Chemical Transportation on the Baltic Sea", presentation at the Conference on "Dangerous Goods Transportation" in St. Petersburg, 26 October.

Salmi, O. (2007), "Eco-Efficiency and Industrial Symbiosis – A Counterfactual Analysis of a Mining Community", *Journal of Cleaner Production*, Vol. 15, No. 17, pp. 1696–05.

Salmi, O. and N. Tynkkynen (2008), "Environmental Governance in Russia: Changing Conditions for International Environmental Cooperation in the Case of the Murmansk Region Mining Industry and the St. Petersburg Water Sector", submitted draft article.

Tennberg, M. (2007), "Trust in International Environmental Cooperation in North-western Russia", *Cooperation and Conflict*, Vol. 42, No. 3, pp. 321–35.

Tynkkynen, N. (2008a), *Constructing the Environmental Regime between Russia and Europe: Conditions for Social Learning*, Tampere: Acta Universitatis Tamperensis.

————— (2008b), "Environmental Cooperation and Learning: The St. Petersburg Water Sector", in D. Lehrer and A. Korhonen (eds), *Western Aid in Post-communism: Effects and Side effects*, Basingstoke: Palgrave Macmillan, forthcoming.

Vodokanal of St. Petersburg (2001), *Final Report of the Corporate Development Support Programme*, St. Petersburg.

Interviews and communications

Communication with a representative of Nefco, October 2007

Interview with a representative of the European Bank for Reconstruction and Development, 2002

Interview with a representative of the Finnish Ministry of the Environment in St. Petersburg, 2002

Interview with a representative of the Finnish Ministry of the Environment, 2007

Interview with a representative of the Nordic Investment Bank, 2005

Interview with a representative of the St. Petersburg Environmental Committee, 2003

6. ASSESSING THE NORTHERN DIMENSION PARTNERSHIP IN PUBLIC HEALTH AND SOCIAL WELL-BEING

*AADNE AASLAND**

1. Introduction

The "Declaration concerning the establishment of a Northern Dimension Partnership in Public Health and Social Well-being" (NDPHS) was signed in Oslo on 27 October 2003.[1] The idea of a social and health care partnership in the Northern Dimension had been put forward in 2000. A Working Group was then established to prepare a proposal on the focus, structures and procedures of the partnership, and this proposal was approved at the high-level meeting in Oslo. Since 2003, the structures have been set up, plans for collaboration agreed and concerted action initiated. The partnership represents an umbrella for activities on the regional, sub-regional and local levels, serving as a forum for coordination and synergies among the various actors. Today, the partnership involves thirteen governments, the European Commission and eight international

---

* The author would like to thank Helge Blakkisrud, Jørn Holm-Hansen and Bernd Treichel for comments on a draft version of this chapter.

[1] See the Oslo Declaration, adopted at the ministerial meeting in Oslo on 27 October 2003 (retrieved from www.ndphs.org/internalfiles/File/About_NDPHS/Oslo_Declaration.pdf).

organisations.[2] The inclusion of social welfare and health among the seven priority sectors of the Northern Dimension policy and the explicit mention of the NDPHS have established it as an important part of Northern Dimension cooperation.[3]

After presenting the background of the NDPHS, its objectives and structure, this chapter discusses some potential challenges facing the partnership. A first challenge lies in the disparities in health and social problems in the Northern Dimension area and their implications for the geographical focus. A second one is the variation in the level of commitment among the partners and the implications for ensuring 'fair' and adequate funding. A third concerns dissemination of information about the partnership among key policy-makers and other stakeholders. In the Second Northern Dimension Action Plan for 2004–06,[4] HIV/AIDS and tuberculosis were singled out as priority health issues in the Northern Dimension area. To illustrate NDPHS collaboration in one of its priority areas, the chapter examines how the issue of HIV/AIDS prevention and treatment has been addressed in the Northern Dimension context. Throughout the chapter, lessons learned from the collaboration are noted and suggestions made for issues on which continued political efforts are needed.

2.   Background, objectives and structure

When the NDPHS was launched, it could build on already well-established joint initiatives and structures in the Northern Dimension area within the health and social sphere. The NDPHS not only followed up the tasks and

---

[2] Partner countries are Canada, Denmark, Estonia, Finland, France, Germany, Iceland, Latvia, Lithuania, Norway, Poland, Russia and Sweden. Partner organisations are the Barents Euro-Artic Council (BEAC), Baltic Sea States Sub-Regional Cooperation, the Council of the Baltic Sea States (CBSS), International Labour Organisation (ILO), International Organisation for Migration (IOM), Nordic Council of Ministers, Joint UN Programme on HIV/AIDS (UNAIDS) and World Health Organisation (WHO).

[3] See the list of priority sectors on the European Commission's website, Northern Dimension Basic Documents (retrieved from http://ec.europa.eu/external_relations/north_dim).

[4] The text of the Action Plan is available at the European Commission's website (retrieved from http://ec.europa.eu/external_relations/north_dim/ndap/ap2.pdf).

activities of the Task Force on Communicable Diseases in the Baltic Sea Region (henceforth, the Task Force),[5] but was also intended to constitute a framework for many other collaborative activities in the field, e.g. under the auspices of the BEAC, the Nordic Council of Ministers and bilateral programmes. Thus, the initiative was set up in a context in which coordination had already become institutionalised, a network had been established and actors at the professional and policy levels had been working together since the mid-1990s. Their concerted efforts had many positive achievements to show, in areas such as the development of personnel, professional knowledge, networks and inter-institutional cooperation.[6]

Why was the health and social sphere singled out as a priority area of Northern Dimension partnership? First, although motivations may have varied, all the countries involved share an interest in working together on health and social issues. The severity of the health situation in some of the Northern Dimension countries was seen as a hindrance to the general development of the region. In some countries, most notably Russia and the Baltic States, mortality rates were disturbingly high, and illnesses such as HIV/AIDS and tuberculosis were recognised as major threats to at least parts of the Northern Dimension area. The common understanding prevailed that these health and social problems would require joint action by the Northern Dimension partners.

Second, as noted above, many actors had been engaged in bilateral and multilateral activities in the health and social sphere since the mid-1990s. Establishing a formal partnership could improve the coordination of such activities by avoiding duplication, enabling the exchange of experiences, engaging policy-makers and increasing visibility. Also, the

---

[5] The Task Force was launched by the CBSS in 2000 to combat the emerging threat to public health caused by the sharp increase in communicable diseases, and to elaborate a joint plan to enhance disease control throughout the region. See L. Rowe and B. Rechel, "Fighting tuberculosis and HIV/AIDS in Northeast Europe: Sustainable collaboration or political rhetoric?", *European Journal of Public Health*, Vol. 16, 2006, pp. 609–14.

[6] See T. Bjørnkilde and A. Wynn, *Social and Health Sector Projects in Russia: Final Report*, Sida, Stockholm, 2004; G. Hønneland and A. Moe, *Evaluation of the Barents Health Programme – Project Selection and Implementation*, Fridtjof Nansen Institute, Oslo, 2004; J. Holm-Hansen, A. Aasland and L.S. Malik, *Health and Social Affairs in Norway and Russia: The Cooperation Evaluated*, NIBR, Oslo, 2007.

establishment of the partnership took place in a global setting in which health had gradually gained greater recognition as an issue in international relations. In their recent evaluation of the Task Force, Geir Hønneland and Lars Rowe stress the role of "health as international politics" by referring to communicable disease control as a "global public good".[7]

The overall efforts of the new partnership were directed towards achieving two major objectives:

- reducing major communicable diseases and preventing lifestyle-related non-communicable diseases, and

- enhancing and promoting healthy and socially rewarding lifestyles.

The NDPHS has largely concentrated on themes and issues that have ranked high on the agenda ever since the establishment of collaboration on health and social issues in the Northern Dimension area. More recently, it has begun to broaden its scope of activity, e.g. by introducing a new Partnership Strategy on Health at Work (2007)[8] aimed at reducing non-communicable diseases to benefit health and well-being in the work environment.

Eligible partners of the NDPHS are EU member states and Northern Dimension partner countries, the European Commission and other EU institutions, regional cooperation bodies, international organisations and financing institutions. In addition, interested sub-national administrative entities in the Northern Dimension area are eligible participants in the partnership.

The NDPHS has a rather complex organisational structure, which was put in place at the time of its establishment. The main decision-making body is the Partnership Annual Conference (PAC), which convenes once a year, with ministerial participation in alternating years. The PAC is

---

[7] See G. Hønneland and L. Rowe, *Health as International Politics*, Aldershot: Ashgate, 2004.

[8] The strategy can be found on the NDPHS website (retrieved from www.ndphs.org///documents/779/NDPHS_Strategy_on_Health_at_Work.pdf).

responsible for formulating NDPHS policies, reviewing the progress of the partnership and providing high-level guidance.[9]

The main coordinating body of the partnership is the Committee of Senior Representatives, consisting of senior-level representatives appointed by the partners. Its chief task is to make sure the decisions and recommendations of the PAC are followed up and implemented.

In accordance with the Oslo Declaration, the Committee of Senior Representatives may also establish expert groups to serve in an advisory capacity, providing professional input into the preparation and implementation of joint activities within the framework of the partnership. To date, four such expert groups have been established, covering the following topics: HIV/AIDS; prison health; primary health care; and on social inclusion, healthy lifestyles and work ability. In addition, there are two 'associated expert groups' working within the NDPHS framework: the CBSS Working Group for Cooperation on Children at Risk and the Baltic Sea Network on Occupational Health and Safety. All these expert groups consist of high-level experts from national ministries, research institutions, health institutions and other relevant bodies.

The NDPHS has a permanent Secretariat with a staff of two, based in Stockholm. The main task of the Secretariat is to provide support to the Committee of Senior Representatives. The Secretariat has developed a comprehensive website[10] with information not only about the partnership and its structure and tasks, but also about funding opportunities and the activities and projects underway concerning public health and social well-being. The Secretariat is furthermore responsible for implementation of the NDPHS pipeline and database project, as presented below.

3. Disparities in health and social problems

It is generally acknowledged that health problems and levels of welfare are far from evenly distributed in the Northern Dimension area. Indeed, the divide in life expectancy between Russia and its Nordic neighbours is

---

[9] Lithuania chaired the partnership November 2005–November 2007, with Norway as a co-chair. Norway has since taken over the chairmanship, with Russia in the co-chair position. The division of chair and co-chair between East and West appears to have been institutionalised.

[10] The NDPHS website address is www.ndphs.org.

larger than that of any other neighbouring countries of the world, which is a strong indication of health and social inequalities. While in 2005 life expectancy at birth for Russian men was only 59 years, the figures for Finland and Norway were 76 and 78 years respectively.[11] Even if the Russian economy has improved significantly in recent years, the overall health status of the population can still be characterised as critical.

Given the great disparities in health and social conditions among Northern Dimension countries, much of the focus of the NDPHS has centred on improving the situation in north-west Russia and (to a lesser degree) Estonia, Latvia and Lithuania. The NDPHS database of collaboration projects in the Northern Dimension area shows that the vast majority of projects deal with health issues in one or more of the regions of north-west Russia. The minutes of meetings of the NDPHS expert groups (also accessible from the NDPHS website) show a corresponding emphasis on issues involving the situation in north-west Russia, which most probably reflects an objective assessment of where health and social problems are the most acute.

The heavy emphasis of the NDPHS on social and health problems in north-west Russia may also cause some tension, however. A more self-assertive Russia is not necessarily interested in spreading the impression of a country in need of special attention, as the weakest partner dependent on outside assistance to solve its health and social problems. Although not trying to hide the seriousness of the health situation, Russian policy-makers have stressed that they give priority to NDPHS initiatives that deal with cross-border activities and issues relevant to the entire Northern Dimension area instead of just the situation in Russia.[12] For the future, it is likely that increased weight will be given to health challenges that are common to several or all the Northern Dimension countries.

---

[11] These figures are derived from the Statistical Division Database of the United Nations Economic Commission for Europe (retrieved from www.unece.org/stats). For women, the differences are somewhat less dramatic but still notable, with a 2005 life expectancy in the Russian Federation of 72 years, as against 82 in Finland and 83 in Norway.

[12] This point was stressed by the Russian participants during a series of expert seminars on the new Northern Dimension organised by the ministries of foreign affairs of Norway and Finland as part of the project "The New Northern Dimension and the Possibility of an Energy Partnership" (2007–08).

Health problems are unevenly spread not only among countries, but also within individual Northern Dimension countries. For example, in Oslo the difference in male life expectancy between the 'inner east' and 'outer west' is more than seven years.[13] North-west Russia is characterised by marked regional variations in the spread of HIV, and some north-west Russian regions have lower HIV prevalence than the Nordic average, at least according to official statistics.[14] In general, gaps in health among different social groups have been growing across the Northern Dimension area over the past decade.

The Northern Dimension countries also share many challenges, although these vary in acuteness. All the countries are in the process of reforming their health care systems. Additionally, several or all NDPHS countries must deal with the prevalence of communicable (and other) diseases, alcohol and drug abuse, institutional capacity, differences between the centre and periphery, information to citizens, the needs of vulnerable groups and institutionalisation of changes, to mention some pressing issues. Thus, there is an abundance of fields in which all countries may benefit from increased collaboration and exchange of experiences and best practices.

Nevertheless, Russia remains a special and separate case in the NDPHS collaboration – a point stressed in key NDPHS documents.[15] It has been argued, also within the NDPHS context, that the Russian health care system is not so much a system as a collection of fragmented elements.[16] Soviet traditions remain more firmly entrenched in Russia than in the Baltic States, for instance. The low life expectancy, high mortality rate among

---

[13] See K.E. Dybendal and H. Skiri, "Klare geografiske forskjeller i levealder mellom bydeler i Oslo", *Samfunnsspeilet*, Vol. 6, No. 19, 2005, pp. 18–27.

[14] Still, statistics are likely to underestimate the actual figures on HIV incidence in Russia. See H. Blystad, Ø. Nilsen and S. Andresen, "Hivsituasjonen i våre nærområder", *Tidsskrift for Den norske Legeforening*, Vol. 23, No. 106, 2006, pp. 3131–34.

[15] See M. Maciejowski, B. Treichel and M. Nachtigall, "The Northern Dimension Partnership in Public Health and Social Well-being", *Barents*, Vol. 10, No. 2, 2007, pp. 46–48.

[16] See for example the minutes of the first meeting of the NDPHS Primary Health Care Expert Group on 13 February 2005 (retrieved from www.ndphs.org/// documents/348/PHC_1_Meeting_Minutes.doc).

those of working age and the rate of the spread of communicable diseases are still serious challenges. Also, the difficulties in access to and the quality of health care services and social care represent a greater problem than is the case in other Northern Dimension countries. Therefore, improving health and welfare in north-west Russia is likely to remain high on the policy agenda of the NDPHS.

The emphasis on Russia in terms of interventions makes the inclusion and input of relevant actors (policy-makers, bureaucrats, professionals) from Russia an essential factor for success. Much of the practical project collaboration with north-west Russia has taken place without involving policy-makers at the federal level. In fact, it is not always necessary to engage the actors at the federal level in coordination that is so regionally-based and involves only a few of its federal subjects. The Russian health system is quite decentralised, and in many cases the federal districts, cities and municipalities are the pertinent levels of collaboration. It is, however, crucial to engage the Russian federal authorities when the issues relate to the overarching priorities of the partnership. For the partners, the federal level needs to be involved, for example, when large-scale multilateral projects are developed and implemented or when the area of joint work involves systemic reform. For visibility and dissemination of best practices among federal subjects, the coordination undertaken by federal authorities is also valuable. Although there is a Plenipotentiary Representative of the President of Russia in the Northwest Federal District with a head office in St. Petersburg, this office does not have a strong focus on health issues. Therefore, for NDPHS collaboration it is vital to involve also the federal Ministry of Health and Social Affairs and other federal agencies.

4.   Commitment and funding issues

Evaluations of projects under the NDPHS umbrella indicate a very high level of commitment of the professionals involved.[17] A potential difficulty, however, are the substantial disparities in the involvement of different partners and partner countries at the policy level. There can be many, and well-founded, reasons why not all countries enter the partnership with the same degree of interest and priority, but the continued dominance of a few

---

[17] See Bjørnkilde and Wynn (2004), op. cit.; Hønneland and Moe (2004), op. cit.; Holm-Hansen, Aasland and Malik (2007), op. cit.

(notably Norway and Finland) over others may in the longer run affect the partnership spirit.

The Partnership Secretariat has established an NDPHS Project Pipeline that seeks to act as a multi-agency on-line tool for coordinating project funding. The idea is to provide assistance from the inception of a project initiative through project application to project financing. On the NDPHS website, the pipeline is presented as a 'marketplace' for project proponents (organisations and individuals) and project financing agencies working for public health and social well-being in northern Europe.

Since the pipeline was launched in November 2007, two funding schemes have been announced through its website. First out was a funding scheme of the Ministry of Foreign Affairs of Finland for the period 2008–10, with €1.5 million to be allocated to health projects in north-west Russia. The second involves funding from the Norwegian Ministry of Health and Care Services for projects under the Barents Health and Social Programme. The latter is a funding scheme that has been in operation since 1999 and allocates approximately NOK 17 million (about €2.1 million) each year to projects aimed at preventing and combating communicable diseases; preventing lifestyle-related health and social problems, and promoting healthy lifestyles; and the development and integration of primary health care and social services.

The Swedish agency Sida is currently phasing out its programme of support for social and health sector projects in north-west Russia. None of the international organisations that are partners of the NDPHS has yet announced funding opportunities through the new pipeline. It should be stressed, however, that the international organisations that are NDPHS partners are not donor organisations as such.[18]

In the midst of Russian economic crises and needs for restructuring the health sector in the late 1990s, the other Northern Dimension countries did not object to paying the main bulk of the costs of the collaboration. With improvements in Russian living conditions and the national economy, the basis for Russian financial contributions to the collaboration on health and social issues has improved. Indeed, an increase in funding by Russian

---

[18] This does not imply that the organisations are not active in the partnership. Examples of dynamic participation include the collaboration of the WHO Health in Prisons Project with the Prison Health Expert Group, and the efforts of the ILO in helping to develop the NDPHS Strategy on Health at Work.

authorities for health and social issues has been observed in recent years. For example, one of the four national priority projects announced by President Vladimir Putin in 2005 to solve the most crucial problems of national development (by accumulating funds and resources for priority tasks) deals directly with health issues.[19] Considerable funding accompanies the project: the equivalent of €3.7 billion each year for the initial two years.[20] Moreover, the priorities under this national project largely correspond with those of the NDPHS, such as strengthening primary health care and preventive efforts.

The relatively strong diplomatic support for the NDPHS has not yet been accompanied by corresponding financial support from most partner countries or international organisations. There has not been a substantial rise in funding for collaborative activities in line with the establishment of the partnership. Previous experience from the Task Force revealed difficulties in raising additional funding for health-related cooperation in most donor countries, and it remains to be seen whether this will be the case with the NDPHS as well. On the other hand, the stronger inclination of the Russian side to allocate funding to health and social projects, together with the growing robustness of reform efforts, may boost Russian responsiveness to health and social projects under the NDPHS umbrella. In the long run, this will undoubtedly be much more important for improving the health and social conditions in north-west Russia than the necessarily limited financial support available from neighbouring countries.

To truly strengthen the partnership, the partners will need to pool more resources into multilateral programmes and institutions. As yet, there have been no indications of such pooling of resources on a large scale: instead, the partner countries seem to prefer bilateral programmes that permit more control of the funding. Moreover, the Russian side tends to earmark its funding for specific prioritised projects, whether bilateral or multilateral.

5. Dissemination and evaluation

Although the NDPHS enjoys high-level political support in all Northern Dimension countries, one may ask how familiar the key actors in the health

---

[19] The other national priority projects are in the housing, education and agricultural sectors.

[20] See Holm-Hansen, Aasland and Malik (2007), op. cit.

and social sphere are with the partnership and the NDPHS structure. Several stakeholders have indicated that awareness is rather weak in most partnership countries, and that many actors in the health and social sphere are not familiar with the partnership at all.[21] Thus, one priority of the NDPHS has been to increase the visibility of its continuing collaboration and activities.

In addition to a biannual e-newsletter issued by the NDPHS Secretariat, in November 2007 an NDPHS database was launched and integrated into the NDPHS website. The database features information about projects, organisations, persons and publications. This information has been gathered by manual input, from data gathered from the NDPHS Project Pipeline (see above) and from other databases available on the web. The intention is to make the NDPHS database the natural starting point for anyone wishing an overview of health-related project activities in the Northern Dimension area. At present, there is information on 500 projects, 235 organisations, 192 persons and 19 papers accessible in the database.[22]

The database is one example that shows the attention devoted to dissemination activities over the past few years. The partnership is also exemplary in its transparency concerning public access to meeting agendas, minutes of meetings, policy papers and other relevant information on the partnership website.

The large number of actors, diversity of activities, ambitious goals and complex structure all speak for continuous monitoring of developments and directions in the partnership. At the time of writing, an evaluation of the NDPHS is underway that will address, inter alia, the political dimension of the partnership, its overall structure and the progress and commitment of partners. It will additionally assess visibility and opinions outside the partnership structure. Such an evaluation should provide useful feedback to stakeholders and suggestions for improvement, as well as indicate new directions of relevance to the various actors involved. Still, to allow for learning processes and adjustments throughout

---

[21] Derived from the author's interviews and conversations with professionals and policy-makers in Russia and the Nordic countries in connection with health-related project work.

[22] The database project is financed by the EU within the framework of the Public Health Programme, in addition to funding from 10 NDPHS partners. The figures were accessed from the NDPHS database website on 24 April 2008.

the cycle of the collaboration, one might question whether a formative (ongoing) approach should have been preferred to an outcome (summative) one. Furthermore, given the strong focus on health and social issues in north-west Russia, Russian involvement in the evaluation team could have yielded additional insights as to the position of the partnership in political and professional arenas in the Russian Federation.

6.   HIV/AIDS and the NDPHS

One of the priority areas of the NDPHS is HIV and AIDS. Whereas most Western European and Nordic countries have largely succeeded in stabilising the situation, the social and economic impacts of HIV are far more severe in the eastern Northern Dimension area, particularly in north-west Russia, Estonia and Latvia. In north-west Russia, the number of reported cases rose rapidly from the mid-1990s until 2005, when there were more than 46,000 cases.[23] Actual figures are likely to be significantly higher owing to underreporting. Particularly hard hit are the city of St. Petersburg, Leningrad Oblast and Kaliningrad. The epidemic is still driven by infections among injecting drug users (IDUs). Yet, infections are increasingly reported by those who have received the virus through heterosexual transmission, and women make up a growing share of the infected. Among the Baltic countries, Estonia has been hardest hit, and new cases are rapidly appearing. Although the rate is declining, the disease burden is among the highest in Europe. Also, Latvia has a heavy burden of infections, while the situation in Lithuania is less severe. With the predominance of new cases among IDUs in north-west Russia and the Baltic States, the newly infected tend to be younger than in the Northern Dimension countries of Western Europe.

It was decided to establish an expert group on HIV/AIDS within the NDPHS partnership, consisting of professionals representing interested parties and other international experts. This expert group constitutes a direct continuation of the work initiated under the Task Force framework.

Most Northern Dimension countries are members of the EU, which, through its financing and political instruments, is able to shape and direct HIV-related activities within member states. But, there are not yet any new financing instruments in the EU that cover the costs of projects involving countries both within and outside the EU. Many HIV/AIDS projects are

---

[23] This figure is derived from national AIDS centres.

therefore covered by other financial sources, usually bilateral ones. The Barents Health and Social Programme is one such major source of funding for HIV/AIDS project collaboration involving north-west Russia.

The Barents HIV/AIDS Programme under the larger Barents Health and Social Programme is a joint effort of north-west Russia, Norway, Sweden and Finland to halt and better control the spread of HIV in the Barents region and to reduce the social and economic costs of HIV and AIDS. At a meeting of the NDPHS Committee of Senior Representatives in October 2005, it was decided that the Barents HIV/AIDS Programme would be expanded to the Northern Dimension area. The geographical scope of the programme would also be broadened to cover adjoining areas in north-west Russia not included in the Barents region. Furthermore, the partnership would initiate the planning process of a new but similar programme for Estonia, Latvia, Lithuania and Poland through the NDPHS Expert Group on HIV/AIDS.

One may ask whether it makes sense to operate with two rather parallel and partly overlapping groups of experts working on similar issues. The Barents HIV/AIDS Programme works under the umbrella of the NDPHS and has close contacts with the NDPHS HIV/AIDS Expert Group.[24] The international technical adviser of the NDPHS Expert Group is simultaneously the programme coordinator of the Barents HIV/AIDS Programme. Undoubtedly, as stated in a Barents HIV/AIDS Programme description, the initiative contributes to the NDPHS,[25] e.g. experience from projects under the Programme can be used as input to the NDPHS.

There have been discussions on merging the two groups. Some experts feel that the synergies between the two groups could have been stronger, and are calling for a clearer division of the roles of the two HIV/AIDS bodies. Other experts have expressed concern that the project-oriented and practical approach of the Barents collaboration in the field would be at risk if it were to be merged with the larger and allegedly less flexible structure of the NDPHS. Thus, while a merger is favoured by some stakeholders, the issue does not yet seem to figure on the policy agenda – neither of the NDPHS nor the Barents HIV/AIDS Programme.

---

[24] See O. Karvonen, "Barents HIV/AIDS Programme – Protection for Vulnerable Groups", *Barents*, Vol. 10, No. 2, 2007, pp. 52–54.

[25] See Maciejowski, Treichel and Nachtigall (2007), op. cit., pp. 46–48.

In Russia, HIV/AIDS was for many years branded as a 'Western' disease, surrounded by rejection and negative attitudes, linked to immoral behaviour and associated with the most criticised social groups – first homosexuals, and later drug addicts and sex workers. Although considerable social stigma remains,[26] in recent years the federal authorities have begun evincing a much higher commitment to combat the AIDS epidemic. In October 2006, a high-level, multi-sectoral governmental Commission on AIDS was established, tasked with coordinating general and regional authorities in implementation of the national AIDS policy. Federal funding of HIV/AIDS programmes increased twenty-fold in one year, from 2005 to 2006.

Russia's heightened focus on HIV and AIDS has facilitated the implementation of collaborative projects under the NDPHS umbrella in north-west Russian regions. Russian participants in the expert group have shown their commitment to the joint efforts from the very start. More recently, however, the greater emphasis on HIV/AIDS issues at the highest political level has made it easier to gain acceptance of projects among government structures where conservative attitudes, although still prevalent, have become less dominant. Some issues, such as drug substitution treatment among IDUs and other harm-reduction initiatives, remain controversial – but this is the case both within as well as between individual Northern Dimension countries. Despite differing views, such issues are discussed within the NDPHS context, and experiences from the various Northern Dimension countries are shared in relevant arenas. One example of an innovative project in Russia is the establishment of a low-threshold centre in Murmansk, where risk groups have access to free needle exchange and free fast-track tests for HIV, Hepatitis B and C, along with pregnancy tests, condoms and other materials. Such projects would not be feasible without the support of local authorities.

The literature and recommendations of organisations combating HIV/AIDS at every level around the world have stressed the importance of partnerships and multi-sectoral responses to the epidemic.[27] In Russia,

---

[26] See Y. Balabanova, R. Coker, R.A. Atun and F. Drobniewski, "Stigma and HIV infection in Russia", *AIDS Care*, Vol. 18, No. 7, 2006, pp. 846–52.

[27] One of the "Three Ones" key principles affirmed by UNAIDS and other international agencies and applicable to all stakeholders in national-level HIV/AIDS responses reads: "[o]ne national AIDS coordinating authority with a broad-based

there appears to be a consensus that such multi-sectoral involvement has traditionally been weak.[28] HIV/AIDS, however, represents one of the areas of NDPHS collaboration where cross-disciplinary and multi-sector action has been stimulated and strengthened. For instance, HIV/AIDS centres have been opened in all districts of the Russian Federation as part of government policy for combating HIV/AIDS. These centres are intended to coordinate with district and municipal health authorities, but there is great variation among regions in terms of the level and form of this collaboration.[29] The stress on and positive experience of cross-sectoral collaboration in the NDPHS is likely one reason such practices have become further developed in HIV/AIDS centres in north-western Russian regions in comparison with much of the rest of the country.

To what extent, then, are developments in the HIV/AIDS response in north-west Russia a result of NDPHS collaboration and activities? Domestic economic developments, political priorities, large-scale HIV/AIDS prevention and treatment projects supported by the Global Fund in recent years in Russia,[30] and naturally enough, the activities of Russian NGOs and other civil society actors are likely to be far more decisive than the admittedly modest contributions of the partnership. Nevertheless, there can be no doubt that NDPHS activities have had a positive impact on the HIV/AIDS response, which goes far beyond the rhetorical value. Support for developing cross-sectoral collaboration, harm-reduction initiatives (as previously mentioned, still controversial in Russia) and other preventive measures that have been important aspects of the NDPHS involvement are necessary to halt a further rapid spread of the virus in the region. It is in these spheres that stakeholders consider the exchange of experience,

---

multisectoral mandate"; see e.g. the related flyer on the UNAIDS website (retrieved from http://data.unaids.org/UNA-docs/three-ones_key principles-flyer_en.pdf).

[28] See E. Tkatchenko, M. McKee and A.D. Tsouros, "Public Health in Russia: The View from the Inside", *Health Policy and Planning*, Vol. 15, No. 2, 2000, pp. 164–69.

[29] Derived from author's interviews with representatives of Russian authorities, international and national non-governmental organisations (NGOs) in Moscow, 1–14 May 2008, as part of fieldwork on Russian HIV/AIDS policy.

[30] For an overview of projects that are supported by the Global Fund to Fight AIDS, Tuberculosis and Malaria in Russia, see the UNAIDS website (http://data.unaids.org/UNA-docs/three-ones_keyprinciples-flyer_en.pdf).

capacity building and learning from best practice through the NDPHS partnership activities to have been most beneficial.[31]

7. Conclusions: Instruments in place, but greater commitment needed

Motivations for entering and playing an active role in the NDPHS may have been mixed. Naturally, working to improve health and social conditions in one's own neighbourhood may be considered a sound political priority in itself. An underlying assumption is that many health challenges, such as infectious diseases, require joint efforts. Even so, it seems unlikely that the reasons for engaging in the partnership have been exclusively altruistic. An additional motivation may have been the perceived political benefits, both domestically and internationally. Working on health issues is regarded as uncontroversial, and a political commitment to improve health conditions is likely to find support among the general public at home. Internationally, collaboration on 'soft' issues may help to create a favourable climate for negotiations on 'harder' security issues.

Stakeholders from both the Nordic countries and Russia, however, aver that while differences in motivations were quite common at earlier stages of the collaboration, the continuous meetings and discussions among the partners and actors – at policy as well as project levels – have fostered a stronger sense of unity of motivations and goals for future activities, notably among those directly involved in the partnership. As the partners have become more familiar with each other's health systems, cultural codes and work methods, more efficient collaboration has developed.

Today's more self-assertive Russia is now in a position where it can be more openly critical of expertise offered by Western partners. Russia is mainly interested in supporting projects that are perceived as genuinely contributing to and supporting its national health priorities. The budget-line increase following the Russian national priority project on health may create a window of opportunity for bolstering the NDPHS partnership, and synergies with the NDPHS should be actively sought by the relevant actors both within and outside Russia.

---

[31] Derived from author's interviews and conversations with representatives of Russian federal and regional authorities, international and national NGOs, as part of fieldwork on Russian HIV/AIDS policy.

There is no longer a demand for material support to Russia and projects for which such support is the main focus are being phased out. These are developments that, by and large, should be welcomed. Still, it may become harder for Western project partners who wish to strengthen alternative ways of thinking, new methods and new focal areas in Russia, as they may encounter more reluctant counterparts. It is relatively easy to agree on projects on themes like child health, compared with issues that are more controversial like prison conditions, substitution therapy in HIV/AIDS prevention among IDUs or domestic violence.

The partners in the NDPHS have so far justified an emphasis on activities leading to tangible results. Scientific collaboration has therefore largely been written out by the NDPHS partners, and very few scientific projects have been initiated under the auspices of the partnership. Yet, in order to succeed, many of the objectives of the partnership depend on 'advocacy coalitions' consisting of sufficiently large and influential groups from various walks of life (e.g. public administration, politics, the voluntary sector and science), and here the scientific element can be highly relevant. A firmer focus on involving the research communities in the Northern Dimension area in the collaborative work of the NDPHS would therefore be recommended.

There is potential for the NDPHS to become the most important arena for collaboration on health and social issues in the Northern Dimension area, and to fulfil its ambition of serving as a framework for joint activities in the field. Many project-level actors who are involved in the field are still unaware of the NDPHS, however. As is also stressed in NDPHS strategic documents, the partners need to develop a stronger identity, not least through greater emphasis on disseminating information about the partnership to increase its visibility and impact. The possibilities for increased visibility are greater now than before thanks, inter alia, to the recently launched NDPHS Project Pipeline and database.

Having the instruments in place is one thing; but most crucial for future visibility and impact will still be the level of commitment of the partners. Political declarations will have to be matched by corresponding levels of funding and the willingness of partners to pool resources into multilateral and joint activities, as well as reinforced links between key committees and expert groups of the NDPHS on the one hand, and national (and EU) policy-making institutions on the other. Thus far, the diversity in health and social conditions in the Northern Dimension area appears to be matched by diversity in the commitment levels of its partners.

8. References

Balabanova, Y., R. Coker, R.A. Atun and F. Drobniewski (2006), "Stigma and HIV infection in Russia", *AIDS Care*, Vol. 18, No. 7, pp. 846–52.

Bjørnkilde, T. and A. Wynn (2004), *Social and Health Sector Projects in Russia: Final Report*, Sida, Stockholm.

Blystad, H., Ø. Nilsen and S. Andresen (2006), "Hivsituasjonen i våre nærområder", *Tidsskrift for Den norske Legeforening*, Vol. 23, No. 106, pp. 3131–34.

Dybendal, K.E. and H. Skiri (2005), "Klare geografiske forskjeller i levealder mellom bydeler i Oslo", *Samfunnsspeilet*, Vol. 6, No. 19, pp. 18–27.

Holm-Hansen, J., A. Aasland and L.S. Malik (2007), *Health and Social Affairs in Norway and Russia: The Cooperation Evaluated*, NIBR, Oslo.

Hønneland, G. and A. Moe (2004), *Evaluation of the Barents Health Programme – Project Selection and Implementation*, Fridtjof Nansen Institute, Lysaker.

Hønneland, G. and L. Rowe (2004), *Health as International Politics*, Aldershot: Ashgate.

Karvonen, O. (2007), "Barents HIV/AIDS Programme – Protection for Vulnerable Groups", *Barents*, Vol. 10, No. 2, pp. 52–54.

Maciejowski, M., B. Treichel and M. Nachtigall (2007), "The Northern Dimension Partnership in Public Health and Social Well-being", *Barents*, Vol. 10, No. 2, pp. 46–48.

Northern Dimension Partnership for Health and Social Well-being (2005), Primary Health Care Expert Group Planning Workshop (meeting minutes), in Helsinki, 3–5 February (retrieved from www.ndphs.org///documents/348/PHC_1_Meeting_Minutes.doc).

Rowe, L. and B. Rechel (2006), "Fighting tuberculosis and HIV/AIDS in Northeast Europe: Sustainable collaboration or political rhetoric?", *European Journal of Public Health*, Vol. 16, pp. 609–14.

Tkatchenko, E., M. McKee and A.D. Tsouros (2000), "Public Health in Russia: The View from the Inside", *Health Policy and Planning*, Vol. 15, No. 2, pp. 164–69.

Interviews

Interviews with representatives of Russian authorities, international and national NGOs in Moscow, 1–14 May 2008, as part of field work on Russian HIV/AIDS policy

7. EU–Russian cooperation on transport: Prospects for the Northern Dimension transport partnership

Katri Pynnöniemi

1. Introduction

The process that started with the collapse of the cold war order in Europe has led to the eastward enlargement of the EU, and eventually to the reorganisation of Europe's economic and political space. Far from being unidirectional, this process has given rise to multiple politico-economic orders – sometimes overlapping or complementary, at times conflicting. The integration of national transport networks into trans-European transport networks (TENs) has been an important part of the rearrangement of Europe's economic space. It is regarded as a means to "foster regional cooperation" within the EU and between the EU and its neighbours.[1] The improvement of transport infrastructure networks is also considered "vital to competitiveness, economic growth and employment

---

[1] See European Commission, *Networks for Peace and Development: Extension of the Major Trans-European Transport Axes to the Neighbouring Countries and Regions*, Report by the High-Level Group chaired by Loyola de Palacio, Directorate-General for Energy and Transport, European Commission, Brussels, November 2005 (retrieved from www.osce.org/documents/eea/2006/01/17793_en.pdf).

throughout Europe",[2] that is, for improving global competitiveness within the EU's economic space. The transport infrastructure provides, in a very concrete way, a common ground for an interface between Russia and the EU. But there is nothing self-evident in the way the integration of their respective transport infrastructures has been proceeding.

Cooperation between the EU and Russia on transport issues has evolved along two separate but parallel tracks. In the broader European context, Russia is seen as part of the new neighbourhood, with the cooperation institutionalised along the lines of the 10 pan-European corridors, and later the 5 transnational axes. At the same time, the general lines for EU–Russian cooperation on transport were set out in the Partnership and Cooperation Agreement (1997) and in subsequent declarations that are part of their evolving strategic partnership.[3] The objective of creating four 'common spaces', declared at the EU–Russia summit in St. Petersburg in May 2003, is the latest twist in a series of efforts to frame Russian–EU transport relations into a specific policy direction. Here reference is made to the "priority corridors of mutual interest" rather than "pan-European corridors" – a shift that reflects changes in the policies of both the EU and Russia on the development of transport infrastructures.[4]

Several studies have addressed the importance of transport and infrastructure development for the further improvement and continuing expansion of trade relations between EU member states and Russia. Both the evolution of the TENs and the improvement of the links to the EU's

---

[2] See United Nations Economic Commission for Europe (UNECE), Inland Transport Committee, "Evaluation of Inland Transport Infrastructure Projects: Transport Infrastructure Needs Assessment (TINA), Executive Summary and Conclusions", TRANS/WP.5/2000/5, UNECE, Geneva, 2000, p. 3.

[3] See the Agreement on Partnership and Cooperation between the European Communities and the Russian Federation (Corfu, 24 June 1994, entered into force 1 December 1997), Art. 70 (retrieved from http://ec.europa.eu/external_relations/ceeca/pca/pca_russia.pdf); see also the Common Strategy of the European Union on Russia, 4 June 1999, *Official Journal* L157, pp. 7, 24.

[4] On the common economic space and EU–Russian relations, see e.g. P. Sutela, "EU, Russia, and the Common Economic Space", *BOFIT Online*, p. 3, 2005 (retrieved from www.bof.fi/bofit); M. Emerson, *Four Common Spaces and the Proliferation of the Fuzzy*, CEPS Policy Brief No. 71, Centre for European Policy Studies, Brussels, 2005; K. Barysch, "Is the Common Economic Space Doomed?", *EU–Russia Review*, No. 2/2006.

eastern neighbours have been subjects of continuous examination.[5] In previous research, the redrawing of the communication networks within the EU, and between the EU and its neighbours, has been approached from the perspective of the economic competitiveness of a particular transport chain or country. Here it is suggested that the topic should also be studied as an important component of the emerging new politico-economic order in Europe. Consequently, the focus here is on cooperation between the EU and Russia on transport, and in particular the recent initiative to launch a Northern Dimension transport and logistics partnership.

To assess these prospects, we must first ask how cooperation between the EU and Russia on transport has proceeded so far. Although Russia has been active in reconceptualising how the transport and infrastructure development is addressed at the all-European level (e.g. within the framework of cooperation under the United Nations Economic Commission for Europe (UNECE)), cooperation in this field has been largely structured around Community initiatives. Therefore, it is useful to start the discussion by looking at relevant EU policies on transport network development and their evolution within the framework of the EU's eastern enlargement. We then move on to assess how Russia has responded to the EU's conceptualisation of EU–Russian cooperation on transport in terms of pan-European transport corridors (PECs). Scrutiny is directed towards the meaning of the concept of 'pan-European corridor' (if any) in the context of Russian transport policy. In this way, the chapter seeks to clarify whether the policy vocabularies of the two parties entail complementary or conflicting policy agendas and guidelines for action. We conclude with a discussion of the lessons learned from previous experiences and an evaluation of the prospects for cooperation in the transport sphere under the new Northern Dimension policy.

---

[5] See e.g. H. Hernesniemi, S. Auvinen and G. Dudarev, *Suomen ja Venäjän logistinen kumppanuus*, Liikenne- ja viestintäministeriön SVULO-projektin loppuraportti, ETLA, Helsinki, 2005; O.-P. Hilmola (ed.), *Third Research Meeting held at Kouvola – Value Adding Role of Logistics in Northern Europe*, Research Report 183, Lappeenranta University of Technology, Lappeenranta, 2005.

2. Redrawing Europe's economic borders: The trans-European transport network

The first steps towards the institutionalisation of transport network development as a part of Europe-wide integration were taken in the early 1980s in conjunction with the idea of a single market within the European Community (EC) and within the framework of the UNECE. Until then, the development of the transport infrastructure had remained the task of the EC member states. But after 1982, the Community started to allocate special subsidies for transport infrastructure development. The Maastricht Treaty introduced the concept of TENs and with that, the EU's involvement in infrastructure policy evolved from an objective pursued through other activities to a responsibility conferred upon it.[6]

A little earlier, the first pan-European transport conference held in Prague in October 1991 had marked a turning point. Here the need to formulate a common understanding on an all-European transport policy was promoted for the first time. The conference adopted a declaration calling for identification of "the most important major transport routes linking the European countries and regions" – a formal and concrete expression of the need to engage in building a transport infrastructure network for the new Europe.[7]

The subsequent creation of PECs was not merely a symbolic gesture. It also included practical dimensions. The prioritisation of nine corridors in 1994 was an act aimed at fostering a new spatial as well as temporal order for an enlarged Europe (a tenth corridor was added after the end of hostilities in former Yugoslavia). The PECs were the formal expression of a new order inasmuch as the set of road and rail connections, border-crossing points, seaports, airports and the like were in purposive relation to each other. PEC secretariats were created for policy implementation at the transnational level, but their role has varied considerably as a function of

---

[6] See the "Special Report N1 on the Financing of Transport Infrastructure Accompanied by the Replies of the Commission", *Official Journal* C069, 11 March 1993; European Parliament, *Financing of Trans-European Transport Networks*, Working Document, Transport Series E4/5, Directorate-General for Research, 1997, pp. 9–12 (www.europarl.eu.int/dg4/wkdocs/tran/e4/en/fulltext.htm).

[7] See the "Prague Declaration on an All–European Transport Policy" (Prague, 31 October 1991) (retrieved from www.internationaltransportforum.org/europe/ecmt/paneurop/pdf/DeclPrag91.pdf).

the interests of the member states involved. As the former Director General for Transport, Robert Coleman, has emphasised,

> [t]he map [of the PECs] has no binding authority, much less any magic power. Its real value lies in it defining the priorities which are shared by the countries concerned so that they can focus their efforts, technical and financial, on the developments which are in their common interest.[8]

During the subsequent 10-year period, the EU policy on eastern enlargement provided a frame through which the European Commission could commit the EU to financing the development of the PECs within the territory of the new member states. Thus, the PECs formed a backbone network for the development of the TENs on the territory of accession countries. In 1996, guidelines for the TENs were adopted.[9] These outline plans for the land transport networks and criteria for network nodes such as airports or seaports.[10]

The conceptualisation of the TENs was a declaration of intent to restructure national networks into a single market. It also provided an institutional framework for Community funding for transport infrastructure projects through the structural funds and PHARE in accession countries. Between 1996 and 2003, total investment in the TEN-T (Trans-European Network for Transport) programme was in the order of €225 billion. The bulk of investments in the TEN-T programme comes from national budgets and private sources.[11] Yet, in the EU-15 only 3 of the 14 so-called 'Essen priority projects' defined in 1994 have been completed.

The accession of 10 new EU member states in 2004 led to a conceptual reshuffling of the overall framework. In June 2004, a High-Level Group headed by former Commission Vice President Loyola de Palacio was commissioned to redraw priorities for the development of transport connections between the enlarged EU and its neighbouring partner

---

[8] See R. Coleman, "On Trans-European Networks and Transport Infrastructure", presented at the "Third Pan-European Transport Conference", Helsinki, June 1997.

[9] The TEN-T consists of 75,200 km of roads, 78,000 km of rail tracks, 330 airports, 270 international sea ports, 210 inland ports and traffic management systems.

[10] See UNECE, Inland Transport Committee (2000), op. cit., p. 3.

[11] See M. Schwarz, "Developing the Trans-European Transport Networks (TEN-T) and the Role of the Corridors", Vienna, 22 May 2007 (retrieved from www.ceinet.org/download/sdf_2007/MR%20MICHAEL%20SCHWARZ.pdf).

countries. Based on its work, five trans-European transport axes were identified as an extension of the concept of the European Neighbourhood Policy into the sphere of transport:[12]

- *Motorways of the Seas*, to connect the Baltic, Barents, Atlantic (including outermost regions),[13] Mediterranean, Black and Caspian Sea areas as well as the littoral countries and with an extension through the Suez Canal towards the Red Sea;

- *Northern Axis*, to join the northern EU with Norway to the north and with Belarus and Russia to the east. A tie to the Barents region linking Norway through Sweden and Finland with Russia is foreseen;

- *Central Axis*, to link the centre of the EU to Ukraine and the Black Sea and via an inland waterway to the Caspian Sea. A direct connection from Ukraine to the Trans-Siberian railway and a link from the Don/Volga inland waterway to the Baltic Sea are also included;

- *South-eastern Axis*, to connect the EU with the Balkans and Turkey and further with the southern Caucasus and the Caspian Sea as well as with the Middle East up to Egypt and the Red Sea; and

- *South-western Axis*, to link the south-western EU with Switzerland and Morocco, including the trans-Maghrebin link that spans Morocco, Algeria and Tunisia and its extension to Egypt.[14]

The geographical scope of the five transnational axes indicates the scale of the exercise. Although actualised as policy frameworks for funding by the Community and international financing institutions, the transnational axes also represent examples of 'mental mapping' within the EU: possible, probable and planned conjunction points between the enlarged EU and its immediate neighbours. Of the five axes, the Northern Axis directly involves regions of Norway, Finland and Russia, while the Motorways of the Seas also pertain to the rest of northern Europe (see Figure 7.1). In EU spatial planning, the axes substituted the previous pan-European transport corridors and areas.

---

[12] See European Commission, Communication on the Extension of the Major Trans-European Transport Axes to the Neighbouring Countries: Guidelines for Transport in Europe and Neighbouring Regions, COM(2007) 32 final, European Commission, Brussels, 31 January 2007(a).

[13] These include the Canary Islands, the Azores and Madeira.

[14] See European Commission (2007a), op. cit.

Figure 7.1 The northern part of the Motorways of the Seas programme and the Northern Axis

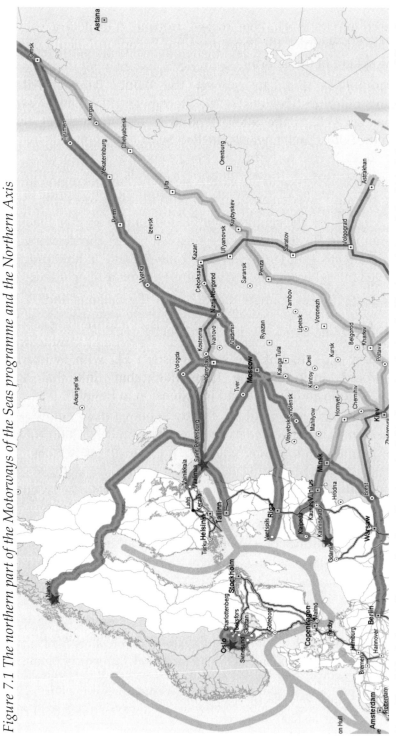

Note: The thick, dark grey line running from Russia to the Baltic Sea region depicts the Northern Axis and the thick, lighter grey line straddling the sea areas shows the northern parts of the Motorway of the Seas programme.

Source: Adapted from European Commission, "Communication: Guidelines for transport in Europe and the neighbouring countries" (presentation), European Commission, Brussels, November 2007(b) (retrieved from http://www.crpm.org/pub/agenda/483_jean_trestour_session_4.pdf).

3.   Russian responses towards the Northern Axis

The map of transnational transport axes reflects the growing demand for improved communication linkages between EU member states and their eastern neighbours. Nevertheless, from the viewpoint of the Russian authorities, the current constellation of five transnational axes raises questions. Even if the problems associated with integrating transport networks are usually of a technical and administrative nature, the importance of undisturbed transportation of goods, especially energy products, adds an element of domestic and international politics to the picture. In Russia, the importance of transport infrastructure as a strategic asset and foreign policy resource has been recognised, and increasingly *used* in the country's relations with its neighbours – especially those in Central Asia and the Caucasus. At the same time, competing interests concerning Russia's energy export routes influence and at times hamper its relations with neighbours in the Baltic Sea area.

In terms of scope and situational context, Russia and the EU share the same problem: how to restructure the existing 'intransigent infrastructures'[15] to meet the requirements of their respective polities and the growing competition among major economic regions in the world. A glance at trade statistics shows the extent of the change. With the disintegration of the former Soviet bloc, the trade between the countries of Central and Eastern Europe (CEE) and the Commonwealth of Independent States (CIS) decreased considerably.[16] At the same time, the pattern of trade between CEE countries and the EU (after 2004, the EU-25) changed both qualitatively and quantitatively. A recent study that scrutinised changes in the quantity, variety and quality of exports shows that, in general, CEE states have been more successful than CIS countries in changing the pattern of their trade flows (product differentiation and product quality).[17]

---

[15] See S.J. Collier, "Pipes", in S. Harrison, S. Pile and N. Thrift (eds), *Patterned Ground: Entanglements of Nature and Culture*, London: Reaktion Books, 2006, p. 52.

[16] See L. Ojala, T. Naula and C. Queiroz, "Transport Sector Restructuring in the Baltic States Toward EU Accession", Turku School of Economics and Business Administration, 2004, pp. 70–71 and 148–49.

[17] Yener Kandogan concludes that this is partly a consequence of the liberalisation agreements that forced the CEE states to compete with market economies. These states have also received higher amounts of foreign direct investment accompanied

By the year 2020, however, trade between the EU-25 and the CIS countries is expected to almost triple.[18]

A major part of the trade between Russia and Europe currently passes through Russian ports in the Gulf of Finland. Even if the current constellation of freight flows is not expected to change considerably in the foreseeable future, the estimated rapid increase of freight volumes between the EU, Russia and other major economic regions is one of the reasons for intensified talks between the EU and Russia on trade facilitation, including the development of efficient 'transport corridors', and later, 'axes'. A closer study reveals that the vocabularies with which the integration of transport networks is addressed are complementary in the EU and Russia. Nonetheless, merely using the same words – such as transport corridor, competitiveness, hubs, logistics chains – does not on its own translate into similar policy actions. Former transport minister Sergei Frank summed up the Russian debate on corridors in 2003 by saying that it had evolved

> from an idea of enlarging the system of pan-European transport corridors into Russia to the development of our own system of international and domestic transport corridors, on the basis of which the main transport infrastructure projects will be realized.[19]

---

by the technology transfers required to push through qualitative changes in their industries. The CIS customs union, however, lacks similar incentives since it does not encourage trade with market economies; see Y. Kandogan, "The Reorientation of Transition Countries' Exports: Changes in Quantity, Quality and Variety", *Intereconomics*, Vol. 4, 2006, pp. 216–29.

[18] See K. Lautso, K. Hietala, E. Jaakkola, H. Lehto, M. Miettinen, W. Segercrantz and P. Venäläinen, *EU:n ja Venäjän välisten liikenneyhteyksien nykytila ja kehitysnäkymät*, Liikenne- ja Viestintäministeriön julkaisuja 4, Helsinki: Edita, 2005, p. 41.

[19] See the speech by Sergei Frank at the scientific-practical Conference on "The Transport Strategy of Russia", Novosibirsk, Russia, 13 May 2003 (retrieved from www.mintrans.ru/Pressa/Novosty_030516_1.htm). The same idea is expressed in the first official document that defines the priorities of the development of Russian international transport corridors; see Government of the Russian Federation, "Osnovnye napravleniia formirovaniia i razvitiia mezhdunarodnykh transportnykh koridorov na territorii RF", press release N663, Moscow, 7 September 2000 (retrieved from www.government.ru/data/news_text.html?he_id=103& news_id=1032).

Frank thus suggests a shift from the idea of 'pan-European corridors' to the notion of 'international transport corridors' (*Mezhdunarodnye transportnye koridory, MTK*). Subsequently, this concept became the basis for reconceptualising the Russian policy on transport infrastructure modernisation.

Over the past eight years, the concept of international transport corridors has been almost synonymous with Russia's most important export article: energy. The majority of Russia's exports to the EU are transported via pipelines crossing the countries in between, whereas imports to Russia mostly involve manufactured goods carried by trucks or by railway transport, also passing through transit countries.[20] When it comes to imports, the share going to Russian ports is expected to increase, while transit through Finland is expected to decrease from the current 7% to 3%.[21]

The negative expectations regarding Finland's future share in Russian transit exemplifies the objective of the Russian policy of securing the export-oriented transport flows through the country's own ports, thereby lessening Russia's dependency on the infrastructures of neighbouring states. This policy has brought about a clear shift in Russian export flows. While in the 1990s, 46% of exports of oil and oil products were transported through Baltic and Ukrainian ports, in recent years their share of overall export volumes has decreased to 20%, and is expected to drop to a mere 5% by 2010. The announcement to build a new oil port at Ust-Luga, comparable in size to the Primorsk port, is a further sign of Russia's determination to build facilities to support export flows through the country's own ports.

---

[20] In 2003, Russia's energy exports to Europe amounted to 163 million tonnes and other exports to 74 million tonnes. More than half (54%) of other exports were transported via Russian ports in the Gulf of Finland (including Kaliningrad), 36% went through the Baltic ports, 5% through Finland and another 5% through Corridor 2 (from Russia via Belarus, Poland and Germany). In 2003, imports from Europe to Russia totalled 26 million tonnes distributed as follows: Russian ports (43%), Baltic ports (39%), Corridor 2 (11%) and Finland (7%).

[21] The scenario is based on the TEN-STAC 2020 scenario and on estimates formulated specifically to forecast changes in transit through Finland; see K. Lautso et al. (2005), op. cit., pp. 39–44; see also e.g. S.-E. Ollus and S. Heli, *Russia in the Finnish Economy*, Sitra Reports 66, Sitra, Helsinki, 2006 (retrieved from www.sitra.fi/julkaisut).

Accordingly, investments in infrastructure development have been targeted at the development of oil terminals (especially by the Gulf of Finland and the Black Sea) and at linkages between ports and the main transport network. Emphasis is also on the development of pipeline infrastructure and the railway network. The recently approved development plan of the Russian Railways (until 2030) reflects this general trend. In the first phase (2008–15), the focus will be on modernising the existing network. Phase two (2016–30) foresees the construction of more than 20,000 km of strategically important lines.[22]

Another equally important meaning of the term 'international transport corridor' is the reference made to Russia as an important 'transit bridge' between European consumers and Asian manufacturers. Investments are concentrated on the development of air transport hubs (St. Petersburg, Moscow and Krasnoyarsk) as well as port facilities and other infrastructure for general cargo and container transport in Russia. Still, investments in infrastructure will not bring the hoped-for results unless the reliability of transit through Russia can be improved at the same pace. Disagreements between the EU and Russia on Siberian over-flights and the queues of trucks at the EU–Russian border are recent examples of issues that need to be solved (see below).

The third aspect of the notion of an international transport corridor is a reference to infrastructure investments in general. A widely accepted view in Russia is that the country's transport infrastructure network is largely obsolete, hampering economic development and even the integrity of the state. Tellingly, during the 2008 presidential election campaign, when Dmitry Medvedev listed the key tasks of Russia's long-term development, infrastructure was among the top three priorities. The other two were the diversification of the economy and the development of human capital – both closely linked to the improvement of the transport and infrastructure system.

It will take more than campaign declarations to set things right, however. Without systemic improvement in the basic infrastructure, especially the roads, railways, inland waterways and domestic air transport, the Russian economy will be beset by serious problems. The country needs a better-integrated and more efficient transport system to

---

[22] See S. Zhuravlev, "Obkhodia rify", *Ekspert*, No. 2, 14–20 January 2008; V. Milov, "Uzkie mesta rossiiskoi ekonomiki", *Pro et Kontra*, July–October 2007, pp. 135–46.

improve the competitiveness of manufactured products in international markets and ensure a stable flow of raw materials to its foreign customers.

With improvements in the Russian economy, investments targeted at infrastructure modernisation have grown. In 2007, real investments in transport infrastructure amounted to 770 billion roubles (€21.4 billion), almost twice as much as in 2002. But the required investments in the transport and infrastructure system are enormous. For example, the investments necessary for the development of the rail system by 2030 will amount to 13 trillion roubles (€361 billion). Moreover, it has been estimated that developing the transport system up to 2015 alone would require up to 21 trillion roubles (€583 billion). The latter figure is comparable with the estimated total cost of €600 billion for the TEN in the EU area.[23] Yet, unlike the case during the past few years, the projected improvement in the investment capability of the Russian state is now taking place against the backdrop of rising inflation, global economic turmoil and lack of administrative improvement in the management of large-scale state projects.

4.   The EU–Russian dialogue on transport and the north

From the viewpoint of the EU, the five trans-European axes represent a spatial–functional expression of the Community commitment to improving communication linkages between the EU and its neighbouring areas. As shown above, Russia views the axes from a different perspective. Cooperation is further complicated by the current and prospective asymmetry of EU–Russian trade, and thus the structure of transport flows between the EU and Russia. Among the most visible symptoms of the latter are the problems with border crossings, which have led to the growing queues of lorries along the eastbound highways in countries neighbouring Russia.

In the case of Finland, for example, the queue of lorries at the Finnish side of the border has gradually grown from a few kilometres in the mid-1990s to almost a hundred in late 2007. Rapidly growing demand for manufactured goods and most recently the transport of imported cars through Finland is the simplest reason for these long queues. The use of

---

[23] See V. Yakunin, "Tematicheskoe prilozhenie: Zheleznodorozhnyi transport: O strategii razvitiia zheleznodorozhnogo transporta RF do 2030 goda", *Izvestiia*, 12 November 2007.

'grey schemes' in trade with Russia, an inadequate infrastructure base, and perhaps most importantly, lack of compatibility in administrative and customs practices between the EU and Russia, add to the obstacles. Negotiations to improve the situation at the EU–Russian and multilateral levels have stepped up, however, along with the number of lorries waiting at the border.

In the aftermath of the EU–Russia Partnership and Cooperation meeting in Lappeenranta, Finland, in September 2006, an ad hoc working group was formed to examine the situation at the borders of the EU and Russia. This has been one of the most active working groups within the framework of the transport dialogue between the EU and Russia (see below). In June 2007, the working group published its recommendations, which will be implemented by the permanent working groups under the dialogue.[24]

At the same time, negotiations at the bilateral level have not succeeded in easing the border traffic. On the contrary, both Russia and Finland have sought to solve the problem by unilateral actions. Russia has limited certain types of heavy-transport traffic at the busiest border-crossing point (Vaalimaa) and is also in the process of reorganising the customs and border administration into a single authority for border infrastructure (to be completed by the end of 2008). On the Finnish side, debate on the possibility of charging fees on Russian lorries intensified during spring 2008. Practical actions have focused on improving the existing road infrastructure, including parking spaces for queuing lorries, and efforts to streamline cooperation with the Russian customs authorities. The expanding role of consumption as an important component of economic growth in Russia should lead, at least in theory, to solving import flow problems. Improving storage facilities in the Moscow region, as well as shifting the mode of transport of the imported cars from lorries to railways, are among the pragmatic solutions available.

The initiative to establish a transport dialogue between Russia and the EU was made within the framework of the road maps for the four common spaces adopted at the Moscow summit in May 2005. The dialogue

---

[24] See European Commission, Directorate-General for Energy and Transport and the Ministry of Transport of the Russian Federation (2007), *Final Report of the Ad-hoc Working Group on EU–Russia Transport Logistics Problems: Joint Recommendations*, European Commission, Brussels, version 25 June 2007.

was launched in October 2005, institutionalising cooperation in the sphere of transport and infrastructure development. The dialogue consists of five working groups that deal, respectively, with transport strategies and infrastructure; transport security; air transport; maritime, sea, river and inland waterway transport; and road and rail transport. Parties in the dialogue have agreed to promote cooperation in areas such as maritime and aviation safety standards and interoperability in the rail sector.[25] Ideally, the transport dialogue – with its emphasis on "harmonisation and complementary evolution"[26] of the strategies on transport and infrastructure development – should contribute to the work already undertaken within the framework of corridor cooperation, and help to address gaps in the existing collaborative framework.

The main impact of EU policies in this sphere has been to provide dynamism and an institutional framework for joint action. In spring 2007, the Commission launched a new set of guidelines[27] and initiated exploratory talks with the neighbouring countries to assess the current situation and to formulate a new format and content for the cooperation structure. As a result, a common understanding exists on the usefulness of the axis approach, on the need to bring transport corridor development and overall policy discussion closer together, and on the necessity of a strong and binding coordination framework based on the existing regional structures and technical secretariats.[28]

Apart from official phraseology focusing on the revision of the institutional framework of cooperation, one major question on its cooperation agenda has been the row over Siberian over-flight fees for European aircraft. The EU regards the fees, amounting to €330 million in 2005 alone, as violating the 1944 Chicago Convention on International Civil Aviation, and the EU has linked the issue to implementation of Russia's WTO accession. Russia, on the other hand, holds that no such link exists,

---

[25] See "Transport Dialogue 2005: Terms of Reference", final consolidated draft 27 September 2005.

[26] Ibid.

[27] See European Commission (2007a), op. cit.

[28] See European Commission, Communication concerning the Progress of Explanatory Talks regarding Cooperation in the Field of Transport with the Neighbouring Countries, COM(2008), European Commission, Brussels, 5 March 2008.

and has instead claimed that the EU demands are "exorbitant".[29] The row led to the cancellation of the aviation summit in November 2007 and the forcing of Lufthansa's cargo services to move from the regional hub in Astana, Kazakhstan, to Krasnoyarsk in Russia.

Differences in interests and objectives concerning cooperation are related to the structural imbalance of EU–Russian economic relations and to diverging expectations. The initiative to create a Northern Dimension Partnership on Transport and Logistics that emerged at the Northern Dimension summit in November 2006 has been suggested as a model for future cooperation at the regional level.

5.   Prospects for the Northern Dimension transport and logistics partnership

The new Northern Dimension has been launched against a background in which Russia and the EU are both rethinking their transport and infrastructure policies. In the EU, this has taken the form of the new 'axes of cooperation' fashioned along the lines of the PECs. As the administrative structures for the corridors were rather weak, the new proposal made by the Commission to strengthen their institutional standing must be seen as a positive step.

A challenge for the proposed partnership on transport and logistics is to find a way of collaborating that would incorporate the Northern Dimension area in its totality, rather than merely some of its regional components. This means that the Commission and other agencies involved in redrawing the policy framework for the Northern Axis cooperation should clarify the relations between the axis cooperation and the proposed new partnership – especially regarding the role of the proposed secretariat. What is the role of the partnership vis-à-vis the axis policy and the transport dialogue? Would it be primarily a managing structure for large international projects? And if so, how could one ensure adequate levels of public consultation on policies adopted at the multinational level as well as by particular countries?

---

[29] Quotation derived from Dmitry Suslov, Director of Research at the Council on Foreign and Defence Policy, cited in T. Forsberg and A. Seppo, "Power Without Influence? The EU and Trade Disputes with Russia", paper presented at the "Fourth Pan-European Conference of the ECPR Standing Group on the European Union", Riga, 25–27 September 2008.

Permanent Secretary of the Ministry of Transport and Communications of Finland, Harri Pursiainen, has emphasised the role of international financial institutions, particularly the Nordic Investment Bank, the European Bank for Reconstruction and Development, the European Investment Bank and the World Bank, as "the driving forces of the Partnership".[30] In his definition, the Transport and Logistics Partnership

> would be an innovative joint effort for coordinated and concerted action. Its aim would be to provide a strong international framework, backed by the financial resources of governments, financial institutions, the private sector and all other parties working for sustainable transport and logistics solutions and for the promotion of public–private partnership.[31]

Pursiainen has noted that the main challenge involved in this innovative undertaking is to reach agreement on top priority projects that "clearly improve transport links and the effectiveness of logistics in the whole area".[32] Given the competing interests of participating countries in attracting transit transport to their territories and conflicting views on what is considered 'effective' management of transport flows, we should, however, remain cautious about raising expectations of the new partnership model.

The initial Russian reaction to reformulating the existing cooperation structure has been positive. At the practical policy-making level, Russia is more inclined to talk about specific infrastructure projects than 'horizontal measures', i.e. harmonisation of customs administration and the long-term development strategies of both sides. This underlines Russia's reluctance to see the proposed partnership and the Northern Axis cooperation in the wider perspective. Indeed, the concept of a 'Northern Axis' is not used in the Russian debate on infrastructure and transport modernisation, except in the immediate EU–Russian context.

---

[30] See H. Pursiainen, "Transport and logistics, a possible new Northern Dimension partnership", presentation at the Conference "The Renewed Northern Dimension: A Tool for Enhanced Regional and Cross-Border Cooperation", Tallinn, 9 June 2006 (retrieved from http://web-static.vm.ee/static/failid/037/Pursiainen.pdf).

[31] Ibid.

[32] Ibid.

This focus on "projects rather than policies", as it was formulated by a Russian representative at a seminar on Northern Dimension policies in 2008, is in line with Russia's objective of speeding up the restructuring of the infrastructure base in north-west Russia and in the Urals region. Investments are targeted at the development of port infrastructure in the Gulf of Finland and in the Murmansk region, and at new railway sections serving the ports and the regional economies in the Baltic Sea and in the Urals. For example, the Belkomur railway project, connecting the Komi Republic and the Archangelsk region, is listed among prioritised investment projects in the strategy of the Russian Railways until 2030. It is competing for financing from the newly created investment fund.[33] The case of the Belkomur railway is a marker of the improving financial means of the Russian state and private actors to commence and complete major infrastructure projects in the region.[34]

International financial institutions have been involved in the modernisation of Russia's infrastructure. In the road sector, for example, the World Bank has provided loans for major federal road projects in north-west Russia as well as in Siberia. Since the emphasis in the current plan for infrastructure modernisation is on the road sector, it can be expected that this previous experience can be used in formulating rules for the participation of foreign investors. Yet the Transport and Logistics Partnership is more ambitious than that. It is hoped it will provide a forum for establishing common guidelines for infrastructure investments in the area and identifying the most viable projects. The negotiations are driven mostly, although not solely, by the commercial interests of future investors and players in East–West-oriented transport markets.

The debate about the partnership initiative reflects a more general dilemma that foreign investors face. Economic growth in Russia is expected to continue even in the midst of the present global economic crisis. Nevertheless, the economic and political risks of investing in Russia are

---

[33] See V. Buldakov, "Magistral nad provalom", *Argumenti Nedeli*, 6 March 2008, p. 27.

[34] The building of the Belkomur (Beloe More–Komi–Ural) railway has been on the agenda of regional governments since the early 1990s. Negotiations on investments have been conducted mainly between regional governments and private businesses interested in extracting forest resources in the area. Until recently, the federal government has been reluctant to commit to the project.

increasing rather than decreasing. The political risk comes in the form of the state's "strategic interest" (see chapter 11). Although the formulation of this interest in the transport and infrastructure sphere has a rather well-defined conceptual basis, at the practical level it is often applied in an arbitrary and ad hoc manner. This remains the principal challenge for the EU and other agencies involved in cooperation with Russia.

Finally, we should take note of the delicate balance between continuous economic growth and the stability of Russia's current regime. To keep the wheels rolling, the Vladimir Putin/Dmitry Medvedev team will have to focus more attention on tough structural reforms – from pensions to health care and education – at a time when this has become politically much more challenging. The challenge does not stem from a well-organised political opposition, but rather from the expectations for inching the country onto the path of 'innovative development'. Few Russians would set much store by politicians' declarations of a 'brighter future', but there is simply less and less room for the government to fail in modernising the country.

Real investments in infrastructure are among the key objectives of the government's development strategy until 2020. The costs of infrastructure investments are already high and are expected to increase owing to the volatile situation in the world markets and inefficient management of investments within the country. Given this background, Russia can be expected to be more open to calls for cooperation in this sphere. Despite the strong rhetoric emphasising the country's independence from others, Russia is still likely to be inclined to cooperate, especially in concrete development projects.

What is required now is an open and critical debate on the principles guiding infrastructure investments in the Northern Dimension area. If the proposed Northern Dimension Transport and Logistics Partnership can become a forum for such discussions, and eventually decision-making, then it can be considered a success.

6.   References

Barysch, K. (2006), "Is the Common Economic Space Doomed?", *EU–Russia Review*, No. 2/2006.

Buldakov, V. (2008), "Magistral nad provalom", *Argumenti Nedeli*, 6 March, p. 27.

Coleman, R. (1997), "On Trans-European Networks and Transport Infrastructure", presented at the "Third Pan-European Transport Conference", Helsinki, June.

Collier, S.J. (2006), "Pipes", in S. Harrison, S. Pile and N. Thrift (eds), *Patterned Ground: Entanglements of Nature and Culture*, London: Reaktion Books, p. 52.

Emerson, M. (2005), *Four Common Spaces and the Proliferation of the Fuzzy*, CEPS Policy Brief No. 71, Centre for European Policy Studies, Brussels.

European Commission (2005), *Networks for Peace and Development: Extension of the Major trans-European Transport Axes to the Neighbouring Countries and Regions*, Report by the High-Level Group chaired by Loyola de Palacio, Directorate-General for Energy and Transport, European Commission, Brussels, November (retrieved from www.osce.org/ documents/eea/2006/01/17793_en.pdf).

————— (2007a), Communication on the Extension of the Major Trans-European Transport Axes to the Neighbouring Countries: Guidelines for Transport in Europe and Neighbouring Regions, COM(2007) 32 final, European Commission, Brussels, 31 January.

————— (2007b), "Communication: Guidelines for Transport in Europe and the Neighbouring Countries" (presentation), European Commission, Brussels, November.

————— (2008), Communication concerning the Progress of Explanatory Talks regarding Cooperation in the Field of Transport with the Neighbouring Countries, COM(2008), European Commission, Brussels, 5 March.

European Commission, Directorate-General for Energy and Transport and the Ministry of Transport of the Russian Federation (2007), *Final Report of the Ad-hoc Working Group on EU–Russia Transport Logistics Problems: Joint Recommendations*, version 25 June.

European Parliament (1997), *Financing of Trans-European Transport Networks*, Working Document, Transport Series E4/5, Directorate-General for Research, pp. 9–12 (retrieved from www.europarl.eu.int/dg4/ wkdocs/tran/e4/en/fulltext.htm).

Forsberg, T. and A. Seppo (2008), "Power without Influence? The EU and Trade Disputes with Russia", paper presented at the "Fourth Pan-European Conference of the ECPR Standing Group on the European Union", Riga, 25–27 September.

Frank, S. (2003), Speech given at the scientific-practical Conference on "The Transport Strategy of Russia", 13 May, Novosibirsk, Russia (retrieved from www.mintrans.ru/Pressa/Novosty_030516_1.htm).

Government of the Russian Federation (2000), "Osnovnye napravleniia formirovaniia i razvitiia mezhdunarodnyh transportnyh koridorov na territorii RF", press release, N663, Moscow, 7 September (retrieved from www.government.ru/data/news_text.html?he_id=103&news_id=1032).

Hernesniemi, H., S. Auvinen and G. Dudarev (2005), *Suomen ja Venäjän logistinen kumppanuus*, Liikenne- ja viestintäministeriön SVULO-projektin loppuraportti, ETLA, Helsinki.

Hilmola, O.-P. (ed.) (2005), *Third Research Meeting held at Kouvola – Value Adding Role of Logistics in Northern Europe*, Research Report 183, Lappeenranta University of Technology, Lappeenranta.

Kandogan, Y. (2006), "The Reorientation of Transition Countries' Exports: Changes in Quantity, Quality and Variety", *Intereconomics*, Vol. 4, pp. 216–29.

Lautso, K., K. Hietala, E. Jaakkola, H. Lehto, M. Miettinen, W. Segercrantz and P. Venäläinen (2005), *EU:n ja Venäjän välisten liikenneyhteyksien nykytila ja kehitysnäkymät*, Liikenne- ja Viestintäministeriön julkaisuja 4, Helsinki: Edita, pp. 39–44.

Milov, V. (2007), "Uzkie mesta rossiiskoi ekonomiki", *Pro et Kontra*, July–October, pp. 135–46.

Ojala, L., T. Naula and C. Queiroz (2004), "Transport Sector Restructuring in the Baltic States Toward EU Accession", Turku School of Economics and Business Administration, pp. 70–71 and 148–49.

Ollus, S.-E. and S. Heli (2006), *Russia in the Finnish Economy*, Sitra Reports 66, Sitra, Helsinki (retrieved from www.sitra.fi/julkaisut).

Pursiainen, H. (2006), "Transport and logistics, a possible new Northern Dimension partnership", presentation at the Conference "The Renewed Northern Dimension: A Tool for Enhanced Regional and Cross-Border Cooperation", Tallinn, 9 June (retrieved from http://web-static.vm.ee/static/failid/037/Pursiainen.pdf).

Schwarz, M. (2007), "Developing the Trans-European Transport Networks (TEN-T) and the Role of the Corridors", Vienna, 22 May (retrieved from www.ceinet.org/download/sdf_2007/MR%20MICHAEL%20SCHWARZ.pdf).

Sutela, P. (2005), "EU, Russia, and the Common Economic Space", *BOFIT Online*, p. 3 (retrieved from www.bof.fi/bofit).

United Nations Economic Commission for Europe (UNECE), Inland Transport Committee (2000), "Evaluation of Inland Transport Infrastructure Projects, Transport Infrastructure Needs Assessment (TINA): Executive Summary and Conclusions", TRANS/WP.5/2000/5, UNECE, Geneva, p. 3.

Yakunin, V. (2007), "Tematicheskoe prilozhenie: Zheleznodorozhnyi transport: O strategii razvitiia zheleznodorozhnogo transporta RF do 2030 goda", *Izvestiia*, 12 November.

Zhuravlev, S. (2008), "Obkhodia rify", *Ekspert*, No. 2, 14–20 January.

PART II.
PROSPECTS FOR NEW ENERGY AND PUBLIC–PRIVATE PARTNERSHIPS

8. NATURAL GAS PROJECTS IN THE RUSSIAN NORTH: IMPLICATIONS FOR NORTHERN EUROPEAN COOPERATION
INDRA ØVERLAND

1. Introduction

Europe has a pressing need to develop new sources of natural gas to respond to concerns about supply shortages. Natural gas production in the traditional major sites in the North Sea and in Russia's western Siberia is set to decline. At the same time, the demand for gas is increasing, in many EU member states and in Russia. These developments are giving a northward push to the Russian gas giant Gazprom and many of its partner and competitor companies, as well as their patron states and other interested parties.

Two key Arctic projects could become the new mainstays for Gazprom and Russia, as well as for their European and other Western partners and customers: the Shtokman and Yamal gas fields. Yet, realistic timescales, cost frames and sources of financing for these two projects remain deeply unclear. It is also unclear whether the projects will be developed in parallel or sequentially. So far, there has been much more organisational stir surrounding the Shtokman field. It is located close to the Norwegian border in the Barents Sea, and the Norwegian oil major StatoilHydro and the French firm Total have been selected as the two main foreign partners for the project. The development of Shtokman and Yamal will have wide-ranging implications for cooperation between Russia and Norway, and for the character of overall European cooperation – both within the geographical scope of the Northern Dimension and beyond.

2.   Russian gas production and the Eurasian energy balance

Events in Ukraine in January 2006 and Belarus in January 2007 fuelled worries (largely unfounded) in some circles about Russia's reliability as a supplier to European markets. More recently, fears have shifted to the more serious concern of whether Russia will be physically and organisationally able to supply its customers, even if it wants to. The supply crunch is envisaged as occurring sometime between 2010 and 2012. These fears revolve around western Siberia's Nadym Pur Taz region and its three super-giant fields: Medvezhe, Urengoy and Yamburg. Over 90% of Russia's natural gas is extracted from Nadym Pur Taz, but production in the region is falling fast. The fields have all been producing for over 20 years (37 in the case of Medvezhe), and injection techniques applied during the Soviet period to boost output have shortened their lifespan and steepened the production decline.[1] At the same time, the Russian economy is expanding, while natural gas remains massively under-prized. As a consequence, domestic consumption is increasing. Foreign customers and Russian pundits are left wondering where the gas is going to come from in the future, and the simplest answer is Shtokman or Yamal (or both).

In a widely cited US Geological Survey, it is estimated that up to 25% of the world's undiscovered oil and gas may be located in the Arctic.[2] What is less often noted is that a large proportion of these resources are located in the Russian part of the Arctic. This is not just because almost half of the Arctic littoral is Russian, but also because the seabed along Russia's Arctic coast includes some of the largest finds ever in the Arctic, some of the most promising areas and some of the least explored ones.

Thus, Shtokman and Yamal are the gateways to an Arctic Russian adventure that could satisfy a substantial share of the world's future oil and gas demand, and provide business opportunities for European companies for many decades. In the Northern Dimension area, they will be important not only because of their capacity to provide the region with hydrocarbons, but also to generate economic activity, bolster employment

---

[1] See J. Stern, *The Future of Russian Gas and Gazprom*, Oxford: Oxford University Press, 2005.

[2] See US Geological Survey (USGS) World Assessment Team, *US Geological Survey World Petroleum Assessment 2000*, USGS, Reston, VA, 2000.

and potentially promote regional cooperation. The scale of these projects will also shape the way in which external actors relate to the region.

3.   Shtokman versus Yamal

The Shtokman field is located in the Barents Sea, off the coast of north-western Russia in the relative proximity of the Nordic countries. Yamal, by contrast, is a peninsula located further east in the Yamal-Nenets Autonomous District in the northern Urals (see Figure 8.1). Choosing between the two projects will have implications not only for Russia's internal economic geography, but also for the linkages to be developed with the Nordic countries and with the EU more widely, as well as for overseas markets (through exports of liquefied natural gas (LNG)).

Figure 8.1 Shtokman and Yamal

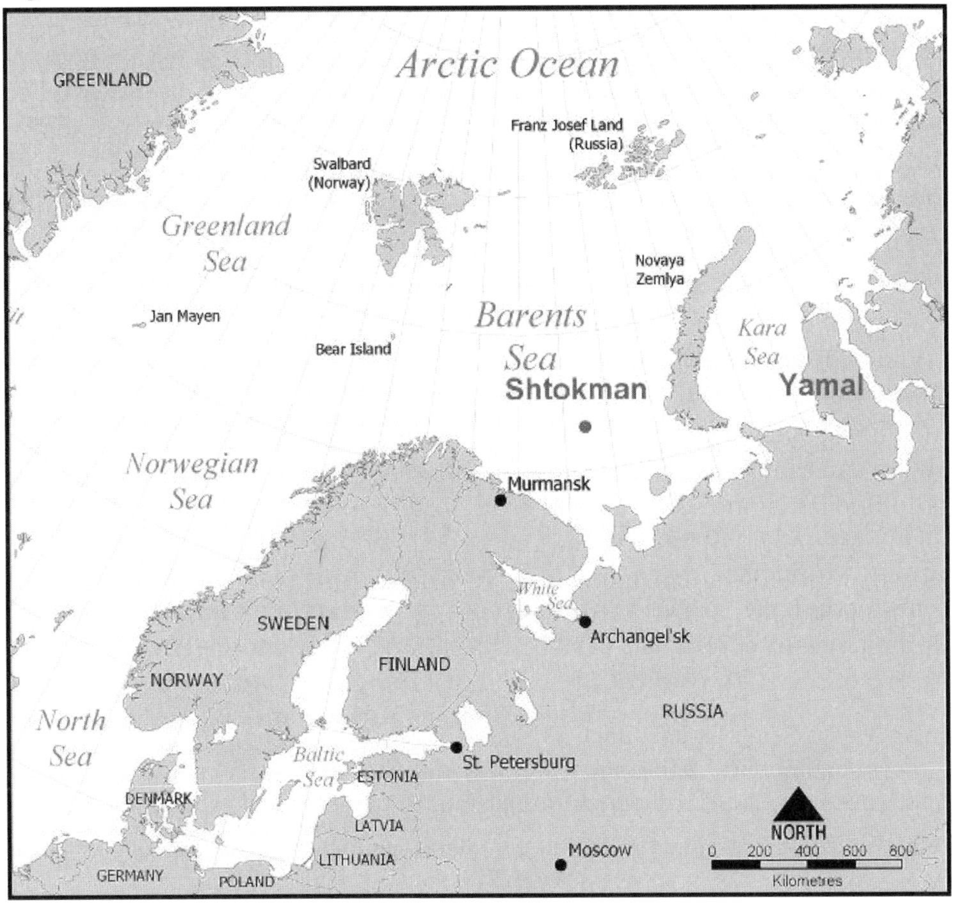

Source: Adapted from Wikipedia.

A commonly held perception of the Russian natural gas industry is that it is relatively well equipped to build pipelines and carry out other operations onshore, which were the main tasks of its predecessor during the Soviet period. It is also thought that, whether Russian actors admit it or not, the industry is woefully inexperienced and incompetent when it comes to offshore operations. This shortcoming has occasionally been cited as a reason why Russian industrial actors would prefer the onshore resources of Yamal to be given priority over the offshore Shtokman.

Arild Moe casts the choice between Shtokman and Yamal as a battle between different groups within Russia's petroleum sector and within Gazprom. A couple of years ago, it appeared that the western Siberian lobby had won in pushing for Yamal, and that it was unlikely that any Western companies would be invited to participate in the project at all.[3] Shtokman's current advantage over Yamal, however tenuous, probably does not indicate that the western Siberian lobby has been defeated irrevocably, nor does it reflect a particular urge to cooperate with Nordic or Western European countries in general. Rather, it could be an implicit recognition that it is better to go for a project where the capital, technology and (not least) organisational skills of Western companies can play a central role. Bringing in Western partners may help the project move forward – and if it does not, there will be more companies to share the blame.

Yamal

The Yamal Peninsula, along with the Kara Sea, into which the peninsula juts, probably holds over 30 trillion cubic metres of gas, enough to supply the whole world for a decade. Like Shtokman, however, Yamal involves daunting challenges. Railways and proper roads are non-existent. The melting and refreezing of the ground on the peninsula pose even greater challenges, since these changes may literally undermine the transport infrastructure, gas extraction and treatment facilities, as well as living quarters built for workers. Any onshore gas extraction would also infringe on the large-scale reindeer herding operations of the indigenous peoples of the region. Finally, the cost of fully developing the Yamal fields would be in the order of hundreds of billions of dollars and could take up to 50 years.

---

[3] See A. Moe, "Sjtokman-beslutningen: Forklaringer og implikasjoner", *Nordisk Østforum*, Vol. 20, No. 4, 2006, pp. 389–403.

On the other hand, Yamal is relatively conveniently located in relation to Russia's existing pipelines from Nadym Pur Taz to its domestic and foreign markets. The accelerated ice melting currently observed in the Arctic Ocean, which far outpaces the estimates of the relatively conservative International Panel on Climate Change, also opens interesting opportunities for LNG/marine transportation and for the offshore fields.

It has been estimated that developing Yamal will require 50,000 workers, many of whom will be foreigners. There are already more than 19,900 non-Russian workers in Yamal, mostly engaged in the construction sector.[4] One possibility that has been aired by Gazprom is to carry out the Yamal project along the same lines as Shtokman, with a shortlist of foreign companies competing for minority shares in the project.[5]

Gazprom officially plans that the largest field in Yamal, Bovanenko, will be in production by 2011.[6] That is optimistic. A decision has not been made on how to move gas from Yamal to consumers – by pipeline or LNG. If pipelines are chosen, this will entail an expansion of Russia's existent pipeline grid and most probably not involve significant new international cooperation. If LNG is chosen, this will presumably necessitate the large-scale involvement of foreign companies, making Yamal a driver for international cooperation. It is not unlikely that the pipeline and LNG solutions will be pursued simultaneously.

While Yamal is more extensive and in many ways more attractive to Russian actors than Shtokman, it is the latter that seems to be progressing fastest at the moment – however unpredictable that progress is – and that holds the greatest promise for northern European and wider cooperation in the energy sector. The rest of this chapter therefore focuses on Shtokman and on Russian–Norwegian cooperation in particular, since this will be by far the most substantial Nordic–Russian joint project in the coming decade and the largest collaborative energy project in northern Europe overall.

---

[4] See "Neftyanye novosti Murmana", *Murmanchanin.ru* [OffshoreSeis News] (retrieved from www.murmanchanin.ru).

[5] See the RIA Novosti website (retrieved from www.rian.ru/economy/20080618/111051855).

[6] See the article, "Gazprom upgrades production estimates", *Barents Observer.com*, 16 June 2008 (retrieved from www.barentsobserver.com/index.php?id=4492380&xxforceredir=1&noredir=1).

Shtokman

The Shtokman gas and condensate field was discovered in 1988. It was recently re-estimated by Gazprom to contain 3.8 trillion cubic metres of gas and 31 million tonnes of condensate (previous estimates had usually been in the order of 3.2 trillion cubic metres of gas). It is located 555 km north of the Kola Peninsula, in the Russian part of the Barents Sea. It is commonly referred to as the world's largest offshore gas field, but is in fact less than a tenth of the size of the South Pars/Northern Dome field shared by Iran and Qatar. Although Shtokman is not the world's largest offshore gas field and is smaller than the Yamal deposits, it contains more than twice as much natural gas as Canada's total known reserves and it will play a major role in European energy supplies.[7]

For several years, the US oil companies Chevron and ConocoPhillips, Norway's Hydro and Statoil and France's Total, all on a Gazprom shortlist, vied to acquire ownership stakes in the Shtokman field. In Norway, where the project received considerable attention, the result was a rollercoaster of rising expectations and subsequent disappointment as uncoordinated statements and accidental signals from the Russian side fuelled rumours and media speculation on the Norwegian side. There were variously expectations that a decision was imminent, that one or both of the Norwegian companies might be awarded a significant stake or that the game was over and no foreign companies would be included. In their endeavour to join the project, the two Norwegian companies had extensive support from the Norwegian government and diplomatic apparatus.

In July 2007, it was announced that Total had been awarded a 25% stake in the joint company that is to develop the first phase of Shtokman. The Russians have not given a clear explanation for why Total was selected first. Total's prowess in cold-climate offshore technology must have played an important role. In addition, this decision could be interpreted as a Russian attempt to enhance the relatively good relations with France. Germany obtained the Nord Stream pipeline (to be built from Russia's Vyborg across the Baltic Sea to the German port of Greifswald), whereas France's Total got a role in Shtokman.

---

[7] See A. Kramer, "French Oil Giant Agrees to Work on Russian Natural Gas Project", *New York Times*, 13 July 2007.

It had long been apparent that Gazprom would retain 51% ownership, so the final competition for the remaining 24% was between StatoilHydro and ConocoPhillips. To some extent, this was a competition between Norwegian technology and good-neighbourly relations in the north on the one hand, and US markets and big-power partnership on the other. Finally, on 24 October 2007, StatoilHydro was granted the final 24% of the field (see also chapters 9 and 10).

It is widely believed that the merger between Statoil and Hydro in October 2007 facilitated Norway's relative success in the Shtokman competition. Russian actors had several times noted that it was complicated to not only have to choose between Norwegian, French and US companies, but to also have to deal with two separate but rather similar Norwegian firms: Statoil and Hydro. And the main reason cited for the merger was precisely the aim of strengthening the position of Norway's petroleum sector in foreign arenas, including the Russian one. In the case of Shtokman this seems to have succeeded.

It is important to understand the nature of the legal solution chosen for the inclusion of foreign companies in the Shtokman project. Total and StatoilHydro have not been awarded ownership of the field itself, but of parts of the company that is to develop the field. This has resulted in a discussion about whether the two companies can count Shtokman as part of their reserves. The difficulties of replacing reserves is the main driver for Western companies to become involved in the Russian petroleum sector – despite the difficulties already experienced by foreign companies in projects such as Sakhalin II in the Far East, Kovykta in Siberia and Kharyaga in the Yamal-Nenets Autonomous District. Therefore, Total and StatoilHydro are fighting hard to get Shtokman fully recognised as part of their reserves by international financial markets and on international stock exchanges.

Another important aspect of the deals made so far is that they are more like options than ownership stakes. During the coming year or two, Gazprom and the two foreign companies will attempt to hammer out the technical and financial details of the Shtokman project, which are far from clear at the moment. In 2009, Total and StatoilHydro are to decide whether they want to make use of their right to a quarter each of the project under conditions still to be negotiated with Gazprom. Despite the symbolic and political weight of the project and its significance for international cooperation and European energy security, this will ultimately have to be a business decision. It is worth remembering that perhaps the most disruptive point in the bumpy negotiations leading up to the decision to allow Total and StatoilHydro to participate was the distribution of the financial burden and risks between the Russian and Western sides. In the autumn of 2006, Gazprom announced that no foreign companies would be involved in the Shtokman project after all, causing major disappointment in Norway. At the time, the main reason cited was lack of financially interesting offers from the Western suitors. Although Gazprom reversed this decision shortly after, there is no guarantee that Total and StatoilHydro will find the terms offered sufficiently attractive when a decision is to be made in 2009.

4.   The importance of the Shtokman field

The Shtokman field is now officially slated for production in 2013, although few believe it will be possible to stay within this timeframe or even near it. Should the project nonetheless develop according to schedule, it would be the biggest energy-related event and the chief international cooperation project in northern Europe in the decade 2010–20. There are several reasons for its importance:

1) In theory, the Shtokman field contains enough gas to satisfy the entire consumption of the EU for seven years.[8] In addition to Shtokman's direct significance for European energy supplies and security, it is valuable for Europe because it includes the French oil company Total, and because it involves cooperation between the EU's two largest external suppliers of natural gas – Russia and Norway (which jointly supply 65% of EU imports). Russia and Norway are also two of the world's largest oil and gas exporters, and from this perspective, the cooperation represents an interesting development in the global petroleum sector. It should not, however, be interpreted as a precursor to a Russian–Norwegian-led gas cartel, as all of Norway's main political parties seem firmly committed to avoiding any politicisation of Norwegian energy exports.

2) Shtokman has widely been seen as a driver of Russian–Norwegian cooperation across the border and of a joint Russian–Norwegian regional industrial boom in the 'High North', including northern Sweden and Finland. Expectations have run particularly high in northern Norway, where hopes for a petroleum boom centred on Shtokman have injected dynamism and optimism after decades of cold war confrontation and

---

[8] Ibid.

unemployment in fisheries. One of the most optimistic visions for the development of the region includes the 'Pomor Zone', a joint Norwegian–Russian industrial and economic cooperation zone-straddling the border near Kirkenes.[9]

3) Norwegian–Russian cooperation in the development of the Shtokman field has occasionally been cast as a possible precursor to a solution of the Norwegian–Russian border dispute in the Barents Sea. It is widely held that the disputed area may include large petroleum resources, although the two parties have agreed to place a moratorium on exploration in the area. Owing to the sensitivity of the topic, it is not possible to acquire reliable official information about the border negotiations, but several possible solutions have been discussed outside the negotiation process. One of these assumes that successful Norwegian–Russian cooperation on Shtokman could provide a precedent for a solution to the border dispute involving extensive collaboration in the formerly disputed area. According to this view, the parties would first have to agree on a new borderline in the disputed area. Once the border has been decided upon, the resources in the Norwegian part of the formerly disputed area could be owned 51% by Norway and 49% by Russia, whereas those in the Russian part of the formerly disputed area could be owned 51% by Russia and 49% by Norway. Obviously, such a solution would require a high degree of cooperation and coordination between the two countries, which could – it is thought – be demonstrated through successful partnership on Shtokman.

4) Developing the Shtokman field also involves making difficult choices about the marketing and transportation solution for the gas. The three main options are to a) build a liquefaction plant on the coast of the Kola Peninsula (most likely at the derelict fishing village of Teriberka) and export the gas as LNG by ship; b) build a pipeline from Murmansk to the St. Petersburg area and connect it to the Nord Stream pipeline going to Germany; or c) lay a pipeline southwards through the Norwegian part of the Barents Sea and halfway down the Norwegian coast, to connect with the Norwegian pipeline network.[10] To some extent, decision-making about Shtokman is thus also decision-making about whom Russia is going to

---

[9] See A. Johnsen, *Barents 2020: Et virkemiddel for en framtidsrettet nordområdepolitikk*, Ministry of Foreign Affairs, Oslo, 2006, p. 19.

[10] See J.P. Barlindhaug, *Petroleumsvirksomhet i Barentshavet: Utbyggingsperspektiver og ringvirkninger*, Tromsø: Barlindhaug Inc., 2005, pp. 14, 19, 20.

trade and cooperate with internationally. Option (a) – exporting the Shtokman gas as LNG – is often thought of as synonymous with exporting it to the US, but the LNG could also be shipped to Europe. One advantage of an LNG solution is thus that it would give some flexibility as far as the export market is concerned, although buyers would obviously need appropriate terminals for receiving the LNG. Currently, such facilities are in short supply in northern Europe. So far, the preferred solution seems to be (a) LNG, later to be combined with (b) a pipeline connection with Nord Stream. Solution (c), connecting Shtokman with the Norwegian pipeline network, may mostly be wishful Norwegian thinking. This solution might make sense in some practical respects, but it is hardly a politically or economically attractive option for Russia.

5.   Lessons learned from the Shtokman experience

Above all, the many phases of hope, ambition and disappointment in Western attempts to become involved in Shtokman illustrate the broader phenomenon of Western actors intensively debating cooperation with Russia on the basis of all kinds of assumptions and expectations – without engaging properly with significant Russian actors or being in touch with realities on the Russian side. In this regard, it is relevant to compare Shtokman with Norway's integrated management plan for the Barents Sea, which also involves great ambitions for involving Russian actors in environmental processes and solutions that rest on uniquely Norwegian perspectives and assumptions.[11] Clearly, climate change has not been viewed at all the same way in Russia as it has in the Western European countries participating in the Northern Dimension, and other environmental issues have ranked lower on the agenda in Russia than in the other states. Yet, the situation is not static and Russia's stance may change. It is important to continue the dialogue and to try to link energy and environmental issues, but also to be realistic about where the most influential Russian actors currently stand and to be aware of the difference between polite diplomacy and genuine dialogue.

As mentioned above, the official reason most often cited by Russian actors for the initial decision to exclude all foreign actors from the

---

[11] See the Ministry of the Environment of Norway, *Integrated Management of the Marine Environment of the Barents Sea and the Sea Areas off the Lofoten Islands*, Ministry of the Environment, Oslo, 2006.

Shtokman project was that none of the suitors had made offers that were attractive enough. That could indicate that, ultimately, financial considerations and profit may be the main driver for Russia in its energy cooperation with Western countries.

On the other hand, the politicisation of the Shtokman negotiations, with multiple meetings between Russian and foreign politicians along with high-level state functionaries, indicates that while business is important for the Russian side, business is controlled by politics. Western actors who want to be involved will need the backing of sufficiently influential politicians on the Russian side.

The development of the Shtokman field provides yet another illustration of the importance and sensitivity of strategic resources to the Kremlin (cf. chapter 11). These Kremlin priorities are also mirrored in other developments in Russian–Western energy cooperation, in which Russia has been taking back control from Western companies that bought into Russian fields in the 1990s. That being stated, because the legal–institutional infrastructure for the Shtokman field is being developed under the full control of a sober Kremlin from the outset, cooperative relations may prove more stable. Hence, it will be more difficult for the Russian authorities unilaterally to shift the blame for problems towards Western partners, although the pain of industrial delays and cost overruns may provide strong incentives to try to do so.

All discussion about Shtokman and other major petroleum developments in the north is generally disconnected from the Northern Dimension, the Barents cooperation, the Arctic Council and other multilateral frameworks for collaboration. One could get the impression that cuddly multilateral cooperation is acceptable – as long as it does not deal with the really big issues, which are to be handled in bilateral or narrow, ad hoc multilateral settings. This situation may in part stem from Russian preferences and Russia's image of itself on the international stage (not as one country among others, but as an exceptional case), or it may derive from hardcore Russian realism in international relations. If so, it is questionable whether the West in the short run can really lull Russia into full-hearted participation in a multilateral framework such as the Northern Dimension, the EU–Russia energy dialogue or the other available multilateral options, while buying its resources at bargain prices. At least a more innovative and realistic approach may be needed.

The acceptance of StatoilHydro as a partner in the Shtokman project shortly after Statoil and Hydro merged could be interpreted as indicating the importance of presenting Russian actors with a reasonably coherent set of interlocutors on the Western side. Indeed, trying to deal with the EU and its many member states and sub-components has often given rise to Russian complaints in this respect.

One aspect that remains to be exploited is the potential that follows from Gazprom's decision to include Total in the Shtokman project for mustering French support for the Northern Dimension within the EU. Indeed, the only potentially real connection between the EU and Shtokman is Total's involvement in the project, but again this seems to have more to do with markets (business) and bilateral relations with France than it does with anything politically multilateral.

On a pessimistic note, the Shtokman experience has shown that engaging Russia in serious cooperation, including large-scale investment from the Russian side, is a cumbersome and unpredictable endeavour, and that working through a multilateral channel can be difficult. On a more positive note, it shows that it *is* possible to engage Russia in serious cooperation on even the most significant issues, as long as it is of mutual benefit.

6.   Shtokman and the Northern Dimension: Mutual irrelevance

Energy has received relatively little attention in the Northern Dimension, despite early attempts to outline broad efforts in the energy sector since 1998 (see chapter 9).[12] The lack of a more elaborate energy focus is not solely the fault of the Northern Dimension. When it was initially launched in the 1990s, energy was not such a hot topic in Europe or in EU–Russian relations. To some extent, therefore, the Northern Dimension has simply been overtaken by events.

In the revamped version of the Northern Dimension launched in 2006, energy continued to be downplayed relative to its increasing significance in northern Europe's international politics in general. Efforts to improve energy efficiency and nuclear safety, mostly in north-western Russia, have been part of the policy, but hotter topics such as gas supplies, pipelines and the development of Arctic offshore petroleum are virgin territory for the Northern Dimension. More than a year after the new

---

[12] See also European Commission, Communication on Strengthening the Northern Dimension of European Energy Policy, European Commission, Brussels, 1999 (retrieved from http://ec.europa.eu/external_relations/north_dim/doc/energy.pdf).

Northern Dimension was launched, the EU's official website for the Northern Dimension still does not give any particular emphasis to energy. The website mentions seven priority sectors, one of which is "economic cooperation", which includes another 10 sub-topics, the very last of which is energy: "trade, investments, customs, SMEs, business, innovation, well-functioning labour markets, financial services, infrastructure and *energy*".[13] There is discussion of launching a Northern Dimension energy partnership covering energy efficiency, energy savings and renewable energy, but at least in terms of timing it is clear that this has either not been seen as urgent or feasible enough to be realised at this stage or to merit highlighting in the existing documents.

The absence of the big issues related to hydrocarbons in the Northern Dimension is striking given that

- Russia and Norway, which are both part of the Northern Dimension area, are respectively the largest and second-largest exporters of gas to the EU;

- almost all the EU's own oil and gas production is located in the northern part of the Union (the UK, Denmark and the Netherlands); and

- discussions about the supply of natural gas and selection of pipeline routes have been a critical issue in EU–Russian relations for several years now.

Part of the reason may be that such topics are already covered by the EU–Russia energy dialogue, but it still seems odd that the Northern Dimension with its grand ambitions for cooperation and integration across the north of Europe has failed to deal with the most important energy issues. One possibility would be to include the regional elements of the energy dialogue as an integral part of the Northern Dimension in the same spirit as the new policy is to function as a regional manifestation of the EU–Russia 'common spaces'. This step could increase coordination and coherence. At the same time, it might also make it possible to boost the issues of energy efficiency and renewable energy within the energy

---

[13] See European Commission, "Overview", Directorate-General for External Relations, European Commission, Brussels, October 2007 (retrieved from http://ec.europa.eu/external_relations/north_dim/#Objectives) (emphasis added).

dialogue, since these are two areas where the Northern Dimension does enjoy some clout, whereas so far they have mainly been window dressing in the energy dialogue.

For the moment, however, just as Shtokman has no place in the Northern Dimension, the Northern Dimension is not a topic that crops up when Shtokman is discussed. The result is a degree of somewhat surprising and unfortunate mutual irrelevance.

7. References

Barlindhaug, J.P. (2005), *Petroleumsvirksomhet i Barentshavet: Utbyggingsperspektiver og ringvirkninger*, Tromsø: Barlindhaug Inc., pp. 14, 19, 20.

European Commission (1999), Communication on Strengthening the Northern Dimension of European Energy Policy, European Commission, Brussels (retrieved from http://ec.europa.eu/external_relations/north_dim/doc/energy.pdf).

————— (2007), "Overview", Directorate-General for External Relations, European Commission, Brussels, October (retrieved from http://ec.europa.eu/external_relations/north_dim/#Objectives).

Johnsen, A. (2006), *Barents 2020: Et virkemiddel for en framtidsrettet nordområdepolitikk*, Ministry of Foreign Affairs, Oslo, p. 19.

Kramer, A. (2007), "French Oil Giant Agrees to Work on Russian Natural Gas Project", *New York Times*, 13 July.

Ministry of the Environment of Norway (2006), *Integrated Management of the Marine Environment of the Barents Sea and the Sea Areas off the Lofoten Islands*, Ministry of the Environment, Oslo.

Moe, A. (2006), "Sjtokman-beslutningen: Forklaringer og implikasjoner", *Nordisk Østforum*, Vol. 20, No. 4, pp. 389–403.

Stern, J. (2005), *The Future of Russian Gas and Gazprom*, Oxford: Oxford University Press.

US Geological Survey (USGS) World Assessment Team (2000), *US Geological Survey World Petroleum Assessment 2000*, USGS, Reston, VA.

9. Russia's Energy Strategy and Prospects for a Northern Dimension Energy Partnership

Jakub M. Godzimirski

1. Introduction

This chapter explores Russia's energy strategy and the impact of its implementation on energy sector cooperation in Northern Europe. Energy cooperation in this region is currently being pursued within several bilateral and multilateral contexts. One possible, further context is the new Northern Dimension: indeed, the founding documents of the new Northern Dimension mention the option of considering an energy partnership. In assessing the prospects for developing such a partnership, however, we must first examine the energy situation in northern Europe and the central role played by Russia.

Russia is by far the most important energy supplier in the Northern Dimension area. Of the other Northern Dimension countries, Finland and the Baltic republics receive all their gas supplies from Russia. Sweden buys oil from Russia but also receives small amounts of gas from Denmark. As for Germany, the high volumes of gas imported from Russia place Germany in a league of its own, even though Russian gas only accounts for a third of German consumption. Poland's import volumes from Russia are also sizable, although considerably smaller than Germany's. Nevertheless, Poland plays a crucial role as a transit country for Russian oil and gas. Denmark is self-sufficient because of its oil and gas fields in the North Sea. Norway is a major global exporter of oil and gas just like Russia, but within the Northern Dimension area it exports significant volumes only to Germany. The energy intensity of the economies in the region also varies considerably, with the post-Communist side being the least energy-efficient. The highest shares of renewable energy are found in the energy mix of the Nordic countries, and German and Danish companies are particularly strong in renewable energy technology.

Thus, we see that the countries of the region have very different energy relationships with Russia. Some have energy sectors that do not depend on Russian supplies at all, but instead compete with Russia for market shares (Norway and to an extent Denmark), whereas others have important energy ties with Russia (the Baltic States, Finland, Poland and Germany). Similar heterogeneity vis-à-vis Russia also prevails in the wider EU area. Overall, the situation in the energy-importing northern European states is similar to the average in the EU-27 (Table 9.1).

Table 9.1 Energy features in the Northern Dimension context

	Energy intensity (toe/€ mn 2000)[†]	Energy import dependency (%)	Oil import dependency (%)	Gas import dependency (%)	Import of gas from Russia (bcm/share of Russia in imports) [††]
EU-27	180	50.1	82.2	57.7	148/42
Denmark	111	–51.6	–104.8	–113.9	–
Finland	263	54.4	98.8	100	4.52/100
Germany	160	61.6	97.1	81.3	36.54/34
Iceland	314	28.8	102	–	–
Norway	142	–609.1	–854.3	–1,378.3	–
Sweden	186	37.2	103.8	100	–
Estonia	723	25.8	71.8	100	0.9/100
Latvia	404	56	101.8	105.6	1.7/100
Lithuania	549	58.4	92.7	100.6	2.9/100
Poland	444	18	96	69.7	7/70
Russia	2,552	–	–	–	–

[†] Tonnes of oil equivalent

[††] Billion cubic metres

Source: European Commission, "EU Energy in Figures 2007/2008", Directorate-General for Energy and Transport, Brussels, June 2008 (retrieved from http://ec.europa.eu/dgs/energy_transport/figures/pocketbook/doc/2007/2007_energy_en.pdf).

Russia's dominant position in the regional energy market has led some actors to fear that Russia may use their energy dependence for political leverage. Others are worried that the energy intensity of the Russian economy may cause future supply problems – i.e. that Russia will not be able to supply Europe with the agreed volumes of gas and oil. Such approaches to Russia add to the complexity of the energy picture in the region. To understand the potential for energy cooperation in the region, we therefore have to take into account not only statistical data, but also how mutual trust and mistrust may contribute to shaping energy sector cooperation: the less the field is politicised or securitised by the actors involved, the greater the potential for cooperation.

As Russia's energy policy choices will be the most critical single factor influencing development of transborder energy cooperation in the region, we need to understand the driving forces that mould Russian energy policy. We proceed by taking a closer look at the country's energy strategy and then assessing its potential impact on Europe in general and the Northern Dimension area in particular. In this analysis, Russia's energy strategy will be taken as an amalgam of policies expressing the country's new strategic thinking.

2.   Russia's energy strategy

One of the most striking features of Russian foreign policy under President Vladimir Putin (2000–08) was the use of energy resources as a political tool. Russia started labelling itself an 'energy superpower'. And as Putin started pursuing his short- to long-term objectives in the international arena in a much more coordinated and goal-oriented manner than his predecessor Boris Yeltsin ever did, Russia's energy resources became one of its most important strategic assets.

Putin recognised that Russia was vulnerable to shifts in energy prices on the international markets. For example, Russia's 1998 economic crisis had been prompted by a sharp drop in oil prices caused by the financial turmoil in Asia. Since the turn of the millennium, however, energy prices have skyrocketed. High international prices for energy have been a central factor underlying Russia's economic revival, and the crucial role of the energy sector has prompted the Kremlin to take a new approach to it, more in line with the views Putin himself expressed in his thesis.[1]

In 2003, Russia's official energy strategy until 2020 was adopted.[2] The document identifies the main challenges and measures to be taken to make the country a reliable and sustainable provider of energy on the domestic and international markets. To develop a full picture of how Russia's energy policy priorities and behaviour affect the Northern Dimension area, we also examine other policies and concepts of relevance for the energy strategy. Furthermore, the energy strategy (both the formal document and other strategy-relevant policies) must be understood as part of Russia's grand strategy of integrating its overall political, economic and military objectives to preserve the country's long-term interests.[3] Several important elements of Russia's overall energy strategy and its reflections in a Northern Dimension context can be identified.

1) Consolidation of the state's role in the energy sector. By 2007, the Russian state controlled approximately 30% of oil and 87% of natural gas production.[4] In the Northern Dimension context, one clear manifestation of the accent on state ownership is Gazprom's October 2006 decision to start developing the Shtokman gas field in the Barents Sea on its own. Even though it later was decided to include the French Total and Norwegian StatoilHydro firms in the Shtokman developing company (see chapters 8 and 10), Gazprom remains in charge. Although the Shtokman set-up is quite different from the old production sharing agreements, there is nevertheless a certain risk that the Western partners may be squeezed out once they have provided Gazprom with the needed technological solutions

---

[1] For more, see H. Balzer, "The Putin Thesis and Russian Energy Policy", *Post-Soviet Affairs*, Vol. 21, No. 3, 2005, pp. 210–25; H. Balzer, "Vladimir Putin's Academic Writings and Russian Natural Resource Policy", *Problems of Post-Communism*, Vol. 55, No. 1, 2006, pp. 48–54.

[2] See "Energeticheskaia strategiia Rossii na period do 2020 goda", adopted by the Russian government on 28 August 2003 (retrieved from www.mte.gov.ru/docs/32/103.html).

[3] See P. Kennedy (ed.), *Grand Strategies in War and Peace*, New Haven, CT: Yale University Press, 1991, p. ix.

[4] See Y. Pozzo di Borgo, *Union européenne – Russie: quelles relations?*, Rapport d'information 307 (2006–2007), Sénat, Paris, 2007 (retrieved from www.senat.fr/rap/r06-307/r06-30712.html).

and expertise. What seems certain is that the Russian state will retain complete control of the project in the foreseeable future and take a lion's share of the revenues generated by the field.

2) *Limiting the role of Western companies*. Several foreign companies – among them Shell, Mitsui, Mitsubishi and TNK-BP – have recently faced problems in the Russian energy sector. At the same time, there are few recent examples of the Russian state opening up the energy sector to Western companies. A litmus test in this regard will be the future of the cooperation between E.On, BASF and Gazprom in the development of the Yuzhno-russkoye gas field in western Siberia. Importantly, this cooperation is planned to provide gas to the Nord Stream pipeline, at least until the Shtokman field becomes operational (see chapter 8).

3) *Strengthening the link between the country's political and economic elite*. Putin has strengthened the links between the political and economic elite by placing his close aides and allies in key positions in the Russian energy sector. Aleksei Miller and Dmitry Medvedev were given key positions in Gazprom, Igor Sechin and Sergei Naryshkin in Rosneft, and Sergei Vainshtokh and Viktor Khristenko in Transneft. According to some sources, by the end of 2004, Putin's team controlled two-fifths of the country's GDP.[5] On the international scene, Putin also embarked on a policy of co-opting political decision-makers into the energy sector. The most notable example is former German Chancellor Gerhard Schröder, who became honorary chairman of the Nord Stream company. Schröder thereafter became one of the most vociferous advocates of closer energy cooperation between Russia and Germany, as well as Russia and the EU. Also, former Finnish Prime Minister Paavo Lipponen has been co-opted into the Nord Stream project, becoming a consultant for Nord Stream in the summer of 2008. Lipponen is to facilitate the company's contacts with decision-makers preparing the Finnish assessment of the project.

Putin's endorsement of Dmitry Medvedev, head of Gazprom's Board of Directors, as his successor is likely to make the link between the energy

---

[5] See M. Bruggman, "Uspeshnyi god AO Kreml", *Inosmi.ru*, 17 August 2005 (retrieved from www.inosmi.ru/translation/221590.html); N. Gevorkian, "Korporatsiia Rossiia", *Gazeta.ru*, 15 December 2005 (retrieved from www.gazeta.ru/column/gevorkyan/498063.shtml); P. Orekhin and E. Samedova, "Korporatsiia Kreml uspeshno porabotala", *Nezavisimaia gazeta*, 26 July 2005 (retrieved from www.ng.ru/economics/2005-07-26/1_corporation.html).

and political elites even stronger. Medvedev's experience from Gazprom will be an important element in his political toolbox. Moreover, the Medvedev–Putin tandem will ensure the continuation of Putin's line in the energy sector.

4) *Using energy as a political tool.* Russia has recently displayed a growing willingness to use energy as a political tool. This tendency has been seen in its relations with former Soviet republics, with new and old EU member states, and even with Norway, which, given its own energy resources, might have been expected to be more resistant.[6] This has given many Europeans second thoughts about Russia's reliability as a strategic energy partner. At the same time, there is a deep understanding that, because of its large reserves and geographical proximity, Russia cannot be replaced by any other actor as a long-term supplier of energy to Europe.

What can be called Europe's main 'energy challenge' with regard to Russia can hence be formulated as how to secure Russian supplies of energy to Europe without making Europe more exposed to Russia's political use of energy resources. Is there a way of getting Russia to pursue a depoliticised energy policy based on purely economic cost/benefit calculations? Although Russia – like the former Soviet Union – has a good track record as far as reliability of energy supplies is concerned, its recent politicisation of energy makes forecasting difficult. The treatment of energy-related issues as having strategic importance by both the EU and Russia raises the political stakes, moving them from the sphere of low politics to the strategic level of high politics.

The current situation may turn into a vicious circle of politicisation and securitisation, which may also cause considerable harm to energy cooperation in the Northern Dimension context.

---

[6] For example, both Ukraine and Belarus were exposed to Russian energy pressure in 2006 and 2007 when Russia decided to raise prices, and Moldova experienced a full stop in gas supplies in 2006 when it refused to agree to a higher price for Russian gas. Among the new EU member states, Lithuania experienced a cut in oil supplies to its Mazeikiu refinery when the facility was sold to a Polish and not to a Russian company in 2006, and Latvia lost its role as an important transit area for Russian oil owing to the Russian strategy of transit avoidance. As for old EU member states, Russia's political relations with Germany, France and Italy are largely driven by economic interests in the field of energy. Finally, Russia has treated Norway's interest in entering into partnership in the Shtokman development as an efficient political carrot.

5) State control of the export routes and transit avoidance. Clear examples of these core features of Russia's energy strategy are the fate of the proposed private oil pipeline to the Murmansk region and the current construction of the Nord Stream pipeline. The former project was planned in 2003 by a private consortium. Once realised, the Murmansk pipeline would have eased shipments of oil to global markets and transformed Murmansk into an international oil hub. The project was interpreted, however, as a challenge to the state's monopoly on the transport of oil. The subsequent dismantling of Yukos, a key actor behind the project, led to the project being abandoned.

Regardless of the different fates of the state-controlled Nord Stream and the private Murmansk pipeline project, they both represent the strategy of transit avoidance, which will also guide the realisation of similar strategic energy projects in the region. This means that Russia will probably choose to ship gas and oil to customers directly from the Murmansk area – thereby dramatically increasing maritime traffic along the Norwegian coast – or through a system of pipelines going exclusively through Russian territory, to avoid the political and economic risks linked with transit. This preference for transit avoidance will also most likely preclude the option of shipping Russian gas and oil through the existing Norwegian pipeline networks.

6) Preventing other suppliers' access to markets. Russia has frequently sought to prevent other energy suppliers' access to profitable markets where they would compete with Russian suppliers. The extent to which this policy will be applied in the Northern Dimension area remains to be seen. Yet, bearing in mind Russia's capacity to export three to four times more gas to the Finnish market through the Finnish connector than what is piped today, any additional gas supplies to Finland – for instance from Norway – would probably be viewed as a strategic challenge. Also, gas deliveries to other countries traditionally seen as exclusive Russian markets in the gas trade will be interpreted by Gazprom as contradicting Russia's long-term interests. All such projects may therefore have negative consequences for Russia's willingness to cooperate on energy issues. Above all this concerns Norway, which is the sole, viable alternative source of energy imports for the Northern Dimension area.

7) Downstream investments. Russia has shown increasing interest in downstream investments in the energy sector. In the EU, however, there is currently a debate on adopting measures that would limit Russian access to strategic assets in the European energy sector, unless Russia agrees to open up its own energy sector, particularly that for natural gas, to foreign investments. This EU reluctance towards Russian downstream investments is partly a result of Gazprom's market influence. More importantly, Gazprom is seen as an economic instrument of the Russian state whose long-term political intentions remain unclear. As Russian energy policy has become not only politicised but also securitised in many European countries, Gazprom's interest in downstream investments is interpreted as being driven by more than purely economic motives, and at least partly by political ones. Additionally, Gazprom's investment policy, and the lack of sufficient investments in existing and future fields as well as transport infrastructure, is seen as increasing the potential for a gas supply crunch.[7] At the same time, Russian actors complain about being discriminated against.

Both Russia and the EU thus wait for the other side to take the first step regarding market access. This standoff raises tensions and sours energy relations between Russia and Europe. Even though the main elements of Russia's energy strategy paint a somewhat bleak picture of the prospects for a possible energy partnership within the Northern Dimension, we must nevertheless bear in mind that the European direction is still the most important one for Russia. Its significance stems not least from the fact that Russia exports 50% of its oil and 63% of its gas to the EU,[8] and that energy represents 65% of all Russian exports to the EU. According to varying estimates, Russia covers 20–32% of the oil import and 40–50% of the gas import needs of the EU.[9] By 2020, the enlarged EU is expected to

---

[7] For more on this pessimistic approach to energy cooperation with Russia, see C.A. Paillard, *Gazprom, the Fastest Way to Energy Suicide*, Russie.Nei.Visions No. 17, Institut français des relations internationals, Paris, 2007. On Russia's problems with maintaining the level of gas production, see A. Riley, *The Coming of the Russian Gas Deficit: Consequences and Solutions*, CEPS Policy Brief No. 116, Centre for European Policy Studies, Brussels, 2006.

[8] See the website of the European Commission's Delegation to Russia (www.delrus.ec.europa.eu/en/p_217.htm).

[9] For the lower figures, see Y. Pozzo di Borgo (2007), op. cit. and J.H. Keppler, *International Relations and Security of Energy Supply: Risks to Continuity and Geopolitical Risks*, Directorate-General for External Policies of the Union, European Commission, Brussels, 2007 (retrieved from www.europarl.europa.eu/meetdocs/2004_2009/documents/dv/studykeppl/studykeppler.pdf); for the higher figures, see the *Washington Quarterly*, spring 2007, p. 93.

have increased its gas consumption by 50%. According to Russian estimates, by then Russia will cover 70% of the EU's gas imports.

3.   The EU and energy within the Northern Dimension context

The EU and Russia have institutionalised their energy relations by means of the 'energy dialogue', which is a key aspect of the EU–Russia 'common spaces', especially the common economic space. Since the new Northern Dimension functions as the regional expression of the common spaces, it is useful to assess the extent to which energy cooperation can be pursued within the Northern Dimension's agenda. Here it is also essential to draw some lessons from the failures of the policy's old format, with its mismatch between hopes and reality and its over-focus on EU-defined priorities (see chapter 1).

In 1998, the European Commission described the Northern Dimension area as having a huge "long-term potential for the exploitation of oil, gas and non-energy raw materials". Russia's hydrocarbon resources in particular were said to represent a potential strategic reserve for Europe's energy demands.[10] The European Council, for its part, defined cooperation on energy as a key area within the Northern Dimension framework.[11] In November 1999, the Commission identified several trends that would shape the future energy market in the region:

- the general movement towards globalisation and especially liberalisation, including competition among fuels;

- the continuing transition within Central and Eastern European countries, and also Russia, to restructure the market with the introduction of competition between energy markets and privatisation;

- the requirement for increased environmental protection; and

---

[10] See European Commission, Communication on a Northern Dimension for the Policies of the Union, European Commission, Brussels, 25 November 1998 (retrieved from http://ec.europa.eu/external_relations/north_dim/doc/com1998_0589en.pdf), p. 3.

[11] See European Council, Conclusions adopted by the Council on 31 May 1999, 9034/99, Brussels, 7 June 1999 (retrieved from http://ec.europa.eu/external_relations/north_dim/doc/pres_concl_06_99.htm).

- the emerging debate about fuel choices (more specifically, the role of gas, nuclear, coal and renewables).

The Commission additionally acknowledged the region's significance for realising the EU's energy strategy: "The Northern Dimension represents one essential frontier for security of supply due to the importance of Russian and Norwegian energy supplies."[12] Transit issues were described as a crucial element of regional energy policy to be addressed jointly, and energy cooperation with Russia was to be based on "the principles of the market economy and the European Energy Charter Treaty against a background of progressive integration of energy markets in Europe".

The first Northern Dimension action plan (2000–03) provided only a list of energy-related projects, with the focus on energy efficiency in north-west Russia and nuclear safety in Lithuania.[13] The second action plan (2003–06) was more ambitious. It promised attention on the development of infrastructure to provide more effective, safer and environmentally sound energy supplies. It called for closer collaboration on the further development and integration of energy markets, the strengthening of EU–Russia and Norway–Russia dialogues on energy, and cooperation with the Baltic Sea Regional Energy Cooperation. Finally, the action plan sought to promote energy efficiency and saving. A specific aim was to improve investment conditions in Russia's energy sector in order to upgrade the infrastructure, promote energy efficient and environmentally friendly technologies, and enhance energy conservation. Moreover, the implementation of what today is known as the Nord Stream pipeline was mentioned as part of the EU–Russia energy dialogue and the EU's trans-European energy network (TEN-E) priority transport axes (see also chapter 7).[14]

---

[12] See European Commission, Communication on Strengthening the Northern Dimension of European Energy Policy, European Commission, Brussels, 1999 (retrieved from http://ec.europa.eu/external_relations/north_dim/doc/energy.pdf), p. 11.

[13] See European Commission, "The Implementation of the Northern Dimension Action Plan", European Commission, Brussels (retrieved from http://ec.europa.eu/external_relations/north_dim/ndap/index.htm#impl).

[14] See European Commission, The Second Northern Dimension Action Plan, 2004–2006, European Commission, Brussels, 2003 (retrieved from http://ec.europa.eu/external_relations/north_dim/ndap/ap2.pdf), p. 22.

In 2006, the European Economic and Social Committee (EESC) encouraged closer coordination of regional cooperation and the EU–Russia energy dialogue to improve energy security and availability. The EESC also called for the establishment of a Northern Dimension partnership in energy, to promote the sustainable use of existing natural resources, energy efficiency and renewable energy resources, and the safety and environmental aspects of energy transport.[15] That same year, the "Political Declaration on the Northern Dimension Policy" invited development of energy-related projects by requesting "ND senior officials to examine the desirability of a Northern Dimension Partnership on Transport and Logistics, and to examine enhanced cooperation in the field of energy efficiency and renewable energy".[16] Yet, both the Political Declaration and the associated Northern Dimension Policy Framework Document failed to provide any details on the form or content of the envisaged regional energy collaboration.[17]

The official EU and Northern Dimension documents thus outline the scope and areas for regional energy cooperation and define the top priorities. These ambitious declarations notwithstanding, collaboration in the field of energy is still limping, owing to several factors, most notably the increasing politicisation of energy issues in both Russia and the EU. Furthermore, given that Russia and the EU are unable to reach agreement on how to proceed in their mutual relations at the grand level (i.e. the stalled negotiations on a new partnership and cooperation agreement) it is unrealistic to expect that cooperation in such a sensitive domain will work smoothly in the more narrowly defined Northern Dimension area.

---

[15] See European Economic and Social Committee (EESC), Opinion of the European Economic and Social Committee of 1 June 2006 on the Future of the Northern Dimension Policy, *Official Journal* C 309/91, 16.12.2006 (retrieved from http://eur-lex.europa.eu/LexUriServ/site/en/oj/2006/c_309/c_30920061216en00910095.pdf).

[16] See the "Political Declaration on the Northern Dimension Policy" (Helsinki, 24 November 2006) (retrieved from http://ec.europa.eu/external_relations/north_dim/doc/pol_dec_1106.pdf).

[17] See the Northern Dimension Policy Framework Document (Helsinki, 24 November 2006) (retrieved from http://ec.europa.eu/external_relations/north_dim/doc/frame_pol_1106.pdf).

4. Russia's energy strategy and the new Northern Dimension

The Northern Dimension area seems set to play an increasingly important role in Russia's energy strategy in the years to come. Over the past five years, several Russian energy actors have signalled their interest in the region. Mention has already been made of the aborted plan to transform Murmansk into a global oil hub. Another plan is to transform the Murmansk region – and the Barents Sea – into a new European and even globally important energy province through developing the huge Shtokman gas field as well as other offshore fields. The Murmansk region is also a principal strategic asset for the Russian military. The recent increase in Russian military activity in parts of the Northern Dimension area (regular sorties of strategic bombers, naval exercises, etc.) also testifies to Russia's strategic ambitions in the north. Making the north an area of 'soft' confrontation is, however, hardly conducive to creating conditions for mutually beneficial collaboration in the economic and energy sectors.

Depending on which approach the Kremlin chooses to take to the region and to its role in the overall Russian energy and political strategy, the Northern Dimension area may develop in various directions. At present, it is difficult to say which way the wind is blowing. President Medvedev himself, as well as Igor Shuvalov, first deputy prime minister responsible for economic policy, has repeatedly underlined the need for liberalisation and diversification: "Traditional state capitalism is a dead end for developing the economy."[18] In real terms, however, there is little evidence of concrete steps being taken.[19] This may mean that 'a liberal breakthrough' is unlikely. Moreover, the strategic terms through which Russian authorities view both oil and gas resources as well as military presence makes regional cooperation a matter to be dealt with by the presidential administration and the government rather than by regional-level decision-makers.

---

[18] See D. Medvedev, "We really do need to preserve this vast state – A state that has a great many problems, but also enormous potential", *Expert Magazine*, No. 13, 2005 (retrieved from www.kremlin.ru/eng/text/publications/2005/04/86313.shtml).

[19] To the contrary, Medvedev has for instance reassured Gazprom that he is not going to split up the company – see the article, "Gosudarstvo ne budet delit Gazprom, Medvedev", *RIA Novosti*, 17 January 2008 (retrieved from http://rian.ru/economy/20080117/97193267.html).

On the EU/European Economic Area side, in recent years energy collaboration has been lifted from a purely economic activity to the strategic and political domains, although the EU is still struggling to put together a comprehensive approach to energy cooperation with the outside world, including Russia. In the national discourses in some EU member states, especially those most dependent on energy supplies from Russia, the question of secure energy supplies is progressively being securitised. There is evidence of greater securitisation at the supranational level as well.

If energy cooperation is defined as a strategic matter by both Russia and the EU, then it will have to be dealt with not at the regional level and by low- and mid-level officials, but at the central decision-making level, in Brussels and Moscow.

5. Energy, the Northern Dimension and Russia: Some conclusions

The analysis above has shown that Russia and the EU approach energy cooperation from different angles: Russia is most interested in extending its market shares, securing its dominant position on the 'traditional markets', countering Europe's plans for diversification of supply, and increasing production capacity by attracting Western investments and know-how, without relinquishing control of its energy assets. By contrast, the EU is interested in ensuring continued energy supplies based on the principles of the Energy Charter Treaty, liberalisation of the energy market (including in Russia) and ensuring favourable conditions for European investments in the Russian energy sector.[20]

In addition, the growing political tensions between Russia and the West affect the prospects for energy cooperation and the possible development of an energy partnership within the Northern Dimension framework. After an initial pro-Western turn in the wake of the 9/11 terrorist attacks on the US, Putin's Russia gradually distanced itself from the West. Dmitri Trenin has described the new divide as Russia's decision to leave the Western orbit and instead embark on building its own 'solar

---

[20] See M. Menkiszak, *Russia vs. the European Union: A 'Strategic Partnership' Crisis*, CES Studies No. 22, OSW [Centre for Eastern Studies], Warsaw, 2006, p. 60; for a similar view, see D. Lynch, *Russia Faces Europe*, Chaillot Paper No. 60, European Union Institute for International Studies, Paris, 2006, p. 65.

system' based on the nation's own norms and values.[21] This shift has apparently also influenced Russia's strategic calculations with regard to energy collaboration with its Western partners.

In contrast to this securitised and oppositional image at the grand level, however, there is *some* room for framing energy sector cooperation at the regional level as a win–win game. One promising area is developing the energy efficiency of Russia's economy and focusing on renewable sources of energy. Both Russia and the EU have an interest in these issues, which could free up additional supplies to Russian and international customers. Energy efficiency and renewable resources could therefore form a suitable non-politicised platform for energy cooperation.

Concentrating on non-securitised aspects of energy collaboration may prove especially fruitful in the Northern Dimension context, where there is already considerable expertise as well as political and social interest in these issues. Importantly, both the local authorities and the Russian population have an interest in energy efficiency in the face of higher energy prices resulting from the gradual liberalisation of domestic energy markets.[22]

State actors interested in renewable sources of energy and in improving the energy efficiency of their economies always have both economic and environmental motivations. In the Russian case, such thinking stems from the understanding of the challenges that lie ahead. Russia's energy strategy until 2020 defines energy efficiency as one of four strategic directions. It proposes a systemic approach to energy efficiency, defines energy efficiency as being of strategic importance, and calls for a new legal and normative framework to implement it. The strategy also calls for cooperation between private and state actors.

There is a strong regional dimension to the Russian approach to energy efficiency. Most of Russia's federal subjects have signed regional laws on energy savings, and the regions together with the state are to

---

[21] See D. Trenin, "Russia Leaves the West", *Foreign Affairs*, July–August, 2006 (retrieved from www.foreignaffairs.org/20060701faessay85407/dmitri-trenin/russia-leaves-the-west.html).

[22] For more details on the issue of energy efficiency in Russia, see Energy Charter Secretariat, *Russian Federation: Regular Review of Energy Efficiency Policies 2007*, Energy Charter Secretariat, Brussels, 2007 (retrieved from www.encharter.org/fileadmin/user_upload/document/EE_rr_Russia_2007_ENG.pdf).

finance the federal strategic programme on "Improving Energy Efficiency". Between 2008 and 2015, a total of 71.1 billion roubles is to be spent on energy efficiency with 30.9 billion roubles coming from the federal budget, 18.5 billion from regional budgets and the remaining 21.7 billion roubles from non-budgetary actors.[23]

So far, official policies and economic realities have helped the Russian economy to become more energy efficient. Indeed, between 2000 and 2006, the energy efficiency of the economy improved by 23.5%, a figure much higher than what had been anticipated in the official energy strategy.[24] Nonetheless, Russia still lags behind other economies in the Northern Dimension area. Given that energy efficiency appears not to have been politicised, it seems possible that decision-making can be decentralised to the immediate stakeholders – the regional authorities. This would mean a huge potential for collaboration with Russia in promoting energy efficiency – and there is a chance that this type of cooperation may become a success story in the Northern Dimension context.

As regards renewable sources of energy, Russia includes these as one of its seven top energy priorities (the other six being gas, oil, coal, power generation, heat generation and nuclear energy). Even so, owing to its vast hydrocarbon resources and contrary to most other countries in the Northern Dimension area, Russia does not feel the same pressure to develop renewable sources of energy. This is also reflected in the energy mix, where hydropower stands for 6% of energy consumption and other renewables play a marginal part, whereas hydrocarbons – gas, oil and coal – cover almost 90% of the country's energy needs.[25]

According to the official energy strategy, renewable sources of energy are important as they may replace non-renewable sources of energy, limit

---

[23] For more information about the "Improving Energy Efficiency" programme, see website www.raexpert.ru/conference/2007/expert400/present/gordukalov.ppt.

[24] For more details, see A. Gordukalov, "O deiatelnosti Minsitersva promyshlennosti i energetiki Rossiiskoi Federatsii v sfere energoeffektivnosti", presentation, 2007 (retrieved from www.dena.de/fileadmin/user_upload/Download/Veranstaltungen/2007/12/Presentation_Michailov_Gordukalov_Minpromenergo.pdf).

[25] See the Energy Information Administration (EIA), "Russia", Country Analysis Briefs, EIA, Washington, D.C., 2008 (retrieved from www.eia.doe.gov/emeu/cabs/Russia/Full.html).

the negative ecological effects of the use of non-renewable sources, secure energy to customers living far away from the existing non-renewable sources of energy and limit the cost of transport of energy to remote areas. Peat and firewood have been identified as the primary sources of renewable energy to be exploited on a large scale. In the strategy, it is emphasised that Russia has both the resources and the expertise needed in this area, the only exception being expertise in windmills with production capacity higher than 30 kW. Still, bearing in mind the Swedish emphasis on biomass and the Finnish experience with peat,[26] along with the state-of-the-art expertise Denmark and Germany have in large-scale windmill farms, there seem to be good chances of making collaboration on renewable sources of energy a cornerstone of energy cooperation in the Northern Dimension area.

The rationale for paying more attention to renewable sources of energy seems to be the same all over the region, although the stress on specific issues may have a more local accent. Some actors, such as Sweden and Finland, have embarked on a strategy of strengthening their energy independence by putting an emphasis on renewable energy resources that are locally available. Such an approach towards helping to solve local energy dilemmas may also be applicable to Russia, and could be promoted without being seen as a strategic challenge by the central authorities in Moscow. In fact, Moscow's interest in taking measures to alleviate the country's energy security dilemma seems to be on the rise. The reason for such interest lies in the continuing boom of the Russian economy, which leads to increasing demand for energy at the same time as there are structural and infrastructural problems in the energy sector stemming from a long period of underinvestment. Local solutions to local problems may thus be welcomed.

Another factor concerns developments in oil and gas extraction. After a period of rapid growth during Putin's presidency, oil and gas production now seems to be stagnating. This will force Russia to look for other sources of energy (including renewables), which may boost the potential for cooperation with foreign partners facing similar energy dilemmas. Both Russia and other Northern Dimension countries have to survive in similar climatic and geographical conditions, amidst the growing shortage and rising costs of traditional fossil-fuel commodities. Cooperation on

---

[26] In Finland, peat currently makes up 6% of the energy mix.

developing renewable sources of energy and energy efficiency would also be in line with the EU's overall energy strategy, in which raising the share of renewable sources of energy substantially by 2020 is an important goal.

Cooperation among the Northern Dimension partners on these issues will depend not only on how they see their energy needs, but also on how they see each other and how they read the other Northern Dimension partners' intentions, including in a broader political context. For example, the sharpening of the tone between the EU and Russia in the wake of the conflict in Georgia in August 2008 may have a negative spillover in the Northern Dimension area. Nevertheless, mutual incentives for energy sector cooperation are strong. Indeed, this chapter has indicated that even though the EU may reconsider its energy collaboration with Russia, it is difficult to imagine a complete halt of relations in this sphere. If strategic interests are not threatened, the prospects for mutually beneficial energy cooperation in the Northern Dimension area are good. From this viewpoint, energy efficiency and renewables are the most promising fields for energy cooperation in the Northern Dimension area.

6.　References

Balzer, H. (2005), "The Putin Thesis and Russian Energy Policy", *Post-Soviet Affairs*, Vol. 21, No. 3, pp. 210–25.

———————— (2006), "Vladimir Putin's Academic Writings and Russian Natural Resource Policy", *Problems of Post-Communism*, Vol. 55, No. 1, pp. 48–54.

Bruggman, M. (2005), "Uspeshnyi god AO Kreml", *Inosmi.ru*, 17 August (retrieved from www.inosmi.ru/translation/221590.html).

Energy Charter Secretariat (2007), *Russian Federation: Regular Review of Energy Efficiency Policies 2007*, Energy Charter Secretariat, Brussels, 2007 (retrieved from www.encharter.org/fileadmin/user_upload/document/EE_rr_Russia_2007_ENG.pdf).

Energy Information Administration (EIA) (2008), "Russia", Country Analysis Briefs, EIA, Washington, D.C. (retrieved from www.eia.doe.gov/emeu/cabs/Russia/Full.html).

European Commission (1998), Communication on a Northern Dimension for the Policies of the Union, European Commission, Brussels, 25 November (retrieved from http://ec.europa.eu/external_relations/north_dim/doc/com1998_0589en.pdf), p. 3.

———————— (1999), Communication on Strengthening the Northern Dimension of European Energy Policy, European Commission, Brussels (retrieved from http://ec.europa.eu/external_relations/ north_dim/doc/energy.pdf), p. 11.

———————— (2003), The Second Northern Dimension Action Plan, 2004–2006, European Commission, Brussels (retrieved from http://ec.europa.eu /external_relations/north_dim/ndap/ap2.pdf), p. 22.

———————— (2008), "EU Energy in Figures 2007/2008", Directorate-General for Energy and Transport, European Commission, Brussels, June 2008 (retrieved from http://ec.europa.eu/dgs/energy_transport/figures/ pocketbook/doc/2007/2007_energy_en.pdf).

———————— "The Implementation of the Northern Dimension Action Plan" (website article), European Commission, Brussels (retrieved from http://ec.europa.eu/external_relations/north_dim/ndap/index.htm #impl).

European Council (1999), Conclusions adopted by the Council on 31 May 1999, 9034/99, Brussels, 7 June (retrieved from http://ec.europa.eu/ external_relations/north_dim/doc/pres_concl_06_99.htm).

European Economic and Social Committee (EESC) (2006), Opinion of the European Economic and Social Committee of 1 June 2006 on the Future of the Northern Dimension Policy, Official Journal C 309/91, 16.12.2006 (retrieved from http://eur-lex.europa.eu/LexUriServ/ site/en/oj/2006/c_309/c_30920061216en00910095.pdf).

Gevorkian, N. (2005), "Korporatsiia Rossiia", Gazeta.ru, 15 December (retrieved from www.gazeta.ru/column/gevorkyan/498063.shtml).

Gordukalov, A. (2007), "O deiatelnosti Minsitersva promyshlennosti i energetiki Rossiiskoi Federatsii v sfere energoeffektivnosti", presentation (retrieved from www.dena.de/fileadmin/user_upload/ Download/Veranstaltungen/2007/12/Presentation_Michailov_Gord ukalov_Minpromenergo.pdf).

Kennedy, P. (ed.) (1991), Grand Strategies in War and Peace, New Haven, CT: Yale University Press, p. ix.

Keppler, J.H. (2007), International Relations and Security of Energy Supply: Risks to Continuity and Geopolitical Risks, Directorate-General for External Policies of the Union, European Commission, Brussels (retrieved from www.europarl.europa.eu/meetdocs/2004_2009/ documents/dv/studykeppl/studykeppler.pdf).

Lynch, D. (2006), *Russia Faces Europe*, Chaillot Paper No. 60, European Union Institute for International Studies, Paris, p. 65.

Medvedev, D. (2005), "We really do need to preserve this vast state – A state that has a great many problems, but also enormous potential", *Expert Magazine*, No. 13 (retrieved from www.kremlin.ru/eng/text/publications/2005/04/86313.shtml).

Menkiszak, M. (2006), *Russia vs. the European Union: A 'Strategic Partnership' Crisis*, CES Studies No. 22, OSW [Centre for Eastern Studies], Warsaw, p. 60.

Orekhin, P. and E. Samedova (2005), "Korporatsiia Kreml uspeshno porabotala", *Nezavisimaia gazeta*, 26 July (retrieved from www.ng.ru/economics/2005-07-26/1_corporation.html).

Paillard, C.A. (2007), *Gazprom, the Fastest Way to Energy Suicide*, Russie.Nei.Visions No. 17. Institut français des relations internationals, Paris.

Pozzo di Borgo, Y. (2007), *Union européenne – Russie: quelles relations?*, Rapport d'information 307 (2006–2007), Sénat, Paris (retrieved from www.senat.fr/rap/r06-307/r06-30712.html).

Riley, A. (2006), *The Coming of the Russian Gas Deficit: Consequences and Solutions*, CEPS Policy Brief No. 116, Centre for European Policy Studies, Brussels.

Trenin, D. (2006), "Russia Leaves the West", *Foreign Affairs*, July–August (retrieved from www.foreignaffairs.org/20060701faessay85407/dmitri-trenin/russia-leaves-the-west.html).

10. FOREIGN INVOLVEMENT IN THE RUSSIAN ENERGY SECTOR: LESSONS LEARNED AND DRIVERS OF CHANGE FOR THE NORTHERN DIMENSION
MORTEN ANKER & BJØRN BRUNSTAD

1. Introduction

Business activity in Russia has been hailed as lucrative, in view of the country's strong economic growth and attractive assets. It has also been seen as risky, given the uncertain property rights, widespread corruption, cultural differences and generally high political risk. This two-sided picture applies to the energy sector as well. As energy is likely to be the most important business cluster in north-western Russia in the medium term,[1] the idea of facilitating cross-border cooperation in the energy sector has re-emerged in debates on the future course of the Northern Dimension (see chapter 9). In particular, this shift in the debate has been motivated by observations of the Northern Dimension's current relatively minor role in the major energy-sector projects that are set to shape the economic, environmental and transport development in the region (see chapter 8).

Perspectives on business opportunities in Russia have changed in exaggerated boom and bust cycles, at least partly owing to myopic assessments of the investment climate, which are far too coloured by vivid events at present and too little based on concrete evidence. In this chapter,

---

[1] See G. Dudarev, S. Boltramovich, P. Filippov and H. Hernesniemi, *Advantage Northwest Russia*, Sitra Reports Series No. 33, Sitra, Helsinki, 2004.

we seek a deeper understanding of more long-term patterns and trends underlying the development of Russia as an arena for energy sector investment and activity. We first examine the experiences of Norwegian companies operating in the Russian energy sector, drawing on interviews with representatives of these companies. Their experiences are used to elucidate the role of foreign companies in this sector. We then move on to discuss trends and drivers of change for the future development of Russia. These analyses form the basis for identifying areas where the Northern Dimension can play a constructive role in engaging businesses.

Our aim is not to tell the complete story of what business has done and can do in Russia, nor to present a recipe for instant success. Instead, we discuss some of the main uncertainties in Russia's future development and indicate how these uncertainties may affect long-term investment decisions and strategies, with implications for business-to-business cooperation and for how the public–private partnerships such as those planned within the Northern Dimension could be of help.

2.   The Norwegian case: Some success but modest activity

From a Norwegian perspective, the energy sector in the 'High North' is alluring. Norwegian oil companies have long chased the big prize in this game – participation in the huge Shtokman gas field in the Barents Sea – at last seemingly with success, as we return to below. But there are also other, less spectacular stories from which to learn. Norwegian supply companies thrive in Russia and a few smaller oil companies have successfully acquired stakes in the lesser oil fields. And although not yet setting a firm footprint in Russia, the experience of Norwegian power companies and consultancy firms in energy and energy efficiency may provide useful insights into other, less explored segments of the energy sector.

With some notable exceptions, Norwegian companies have been cautious about engaging in Russia in general, and in north-western Russia in particular. According to a report by Rambøll Storvik, in 2006 there were approximately 80 cases of Norwegian business involvement in north-western Russia.[2] Most of these were small-scale enterprises with fewer than 10 employees. Of the 80 companies, only 8 were involved in the oil and gas sector. A few were involved in energy efficiency projects and

---

[2] See F. Stålsett, *Prosjektrapport: Kartlegge norske bedriftsetableringer i Nordvest-Russland*, Rambøll Storvik, Kirkenes, 2006.

environmental projects related to the energy sector. Despite the small scale, we nevertheless consider the Norwegian experience in this field as relevant for the wider business community.

1) *Big oil: StatoilHydro's long way to something.* StatoilHydro's experience in Russia has been limited to two major projects. In the Kharyaga oil field located in the Nenets Autonomous Okrug, Hydro has had a 40% stake through a production sharing agreement (PSA) since 1996. And in the Shtokman gas and condensate field, StatoilHydro was approved for a 24% stake in the Shtokman phase 1 development company in October 2007.

Russian authorities are generally unhappy with PSAs of the Kharyaga type, regarding such deals as far too lucrative for the development companies and 'unworthy of a developed nation'. In consequence, the authorities have obstructed the Kharyaga PSA and criticised the operating company Total for low environmental standards and a sluggish development pace. Unlike the Sakhalin II PSA, however, in which Shell and the other consortium partners were forced to sell a controlling share to Gazprom, it seems that the Kharyaga license is not directly threatened, at least for now.

The Shtokman saga shows how unpredictable the Russian side may appear for international oil companies. After a long beauty contest, in which Gazprom postponed the partnership decision several times, there was a widespread feeling among international oil companies of being duped when in 2006 the Russians declared they would develop the field on their own. Then came a sudden turn of the tide, when Gazprom announced it had picked the French Total as its partner for the Shtokman development in July 2007. This move ignited suspicions of high-level political horse-trading. When President Vladimir Putin announced that StatoilHydro was to be given access to the project in an October 2007 telephone conference with Norwegian Prime Minister Jens Stoltenberg, this failed to dampen these suspicions. Although StatoilHydro certainly did receive high-level political backing, any questions of political horse-trading nonetheless remain pure speculation (see also chapters 8 and 9).

It is worth noting that the two non-Russian Shtokman partners are the same as the foreign stakeholders in the Kharyaga PSA. This could be mere coincidence, or it could reflect the Russian authorities' perception of the good track records of these companies in Russia. The actual content of the Shtokman partnership agreement is not to be revealed until 2009, so the price of the big prize is not yet publicly known.

2) Big oil: Aker Solutions and others gaining a foothold. Aker Solutions (formerly Aker Kvaerner) has been selling world-class engineering expertise to international and Russian consortia operating in the Russian offshore sector in the Far East and in the High North (Sakhalin II and Prirazlomnoye). The company aims high, and plans to establish itself as the leading contractor in the entire Russian oil and gas market.[3] After the acquisition of a majority share in the Astrakhan Korabl shipyard in 2005, Aker Solutions experienced negative pressure from the Russian authorities, including having their office raided by the police and having fines imposed. Aker Solutions finally decided to sell its share in Astrakhan Korabl in February 2008. The company has nevertheless amassed expertise and experience in operating in Russia and with Russian counterparts, and is clearly well positioned for further contracts.

Other Norwegian-based supply companies (among them Acergy, Reinertsen, Hydramarine, Øglænd and Havyard Leirvik) are also gaining a foothold in Russia.[4] In the construction work on the Prirazlomnoye offshore platform, Norwegian-based supply companies have provided some 25% of the total technology deliveries.[5] These companies tell differing stories about their experiences in doing business in Russia. Some report challenges regarding negotiation tactics, differences in business culture and bureaucratic foot-dragging, but regard those simply as additional hurdles, not major threats to business. Others have found it best to avoid relying on a Russian partner altogether.[6] Several of the companies have long-term strategies for working in Russia. Reinertsen is well established in

---

[3] See Aker Solutions, "Sakhalin – Concrete Advance in Russia", Aker Solutions, Oslo, 2003 (retrieved from www.akerkvaerner.com/Internet/MediaCentre/Featurestories/OilandGas/Sakhalin.htm).

[4] Here we refer to companies in the Norwegian oil and gas cluster, which includes Norwegian companies with headquarters in Norway as well as companies with substantial Norwegian ownership that operate on the Norwegian continental shelf but are based abroad (like Acergy).

[5] See the Nortrade.com article, "Norwegian Companies Attractive for Russian Partnerships", Nortrade.com, the Official Norwegian Trade Portal, Oslo, 2007 (retrieved from www.nortrade.com/index.php?cmd=show_article&id=255).

[6] Information obtained from interviews with the companies.

Murmansk, Acergy established a Moscow office in 2007 and Norwegian supply companies are now queuing up to take part in the development of the Shtokman field.

3) *Small oil: The adventures of Saga and Aladdin*. There are only a few smaller Norwegian oil companies that have invested in upstream assets in Russia. Saga Petrol and Aladdin have acquired licenses for small-scale onshore oil and gas fields through acquisitions of Russian license holders. Both companies were established quite recently and their experience with business in Russia is limited to two or three years. So far, the companies are very optimistic about their acquisition strategies. They have not met opposition from federal or local government, but on the contrary have been welcomed and received support from local authorities. Yet, it would be premature to draw substantial conclusions about a possible formula for success here.

4) *Big power: Scoping and waiting*. Unlike their Finnish and French counterparts (see chapter 11), Norwegian companies have not been very active in the power and heating sector in Russia. Statkraft has been scoping for opportunities, but has not made any decisive moves. One reason could be that the sector is currently in the midst of a massive transformation process with pressures for unbundling production, distribution and end sales of electricity, as well as the privatisation of the formerly dominant RAO UES. This situation makes it difficult to make long-term or even short-term risk assessments. Another challenge is the strategic element of the sector and the reluctance of Russian authorities to cede control. In that respect, this field resembles the oil and gas sector. Our interviewees confirm that there have been problems with the authorities changing the rules of the game and with informal players making decisions.

5) *Consulting, energy efficiency and new energy: Advising and aiding*. Advisory companies like Rosnor Energo and Scandpower have gained a certain foothold, providing services related to the market reforms underway in the Russian power sector. Several consultancies such as Norsk Energi and Rambøll Storvik have carried out small-scale energy efficiency projects largely paid for through Norwegian-sponsored environmental and development programmes. The common denominator for this category of actors is that they have made little risk investment – they are either just scoping, delivering consultancy services with relatively low risk or carrying out projects largely sponsored by Norway within an aid framework. Some of our interviewees claim that there is limited commercial potential for Norwegian consultancy business in Russia, not least because of the high

hourly costs in Norway. Moreover, on the industrial hardware side of the energy efficiency business, interviewees express doubts as to whether Norway has companies with the necessary technological know-how. Swedish, Danish and Finnish companies are said to have a competitive edge over Norwegian companies in this area.

What can we learn from the Norwegian experience?

Companies we have interviewed are generally positive about the business environment and opportunities in Russia. Yet, for several companies, high levels of corruption, extensive red tape and difficulties in finding reliable Russian partners remain significant barriers to business. Additionally, there seems to be a cultural barrier that must be overcome if one is to succeed in Russia.

It is hard to draw any substantial conclusions based on the experience of Norwegian firms in the Russian energy sector. There are too few Norwegian companies with such experience and those with relevant experience have normally been involved in Russia only for a short period.

Still, some tendencies can be discerned. For instance, the larger an oil or (particularly) a gas field, the more likely it seems that participation and possible partnerships will be decided at the top political level. The political winds in Moscow appear decisive for the success rate of existing projects and contracts, and to the quest for new projects. Conversely, there might be less politics – and more business opportunities – in small-scale oil field development. As yet, the increasing drive for state control in Russia has apparently not affected the few Norwegian companies involved in this area.

On the supply industry side as well, there seem to be good prospects in Russia. And this is not limited to internationally-managed field developments. Also, Russian-managed projects abound in business opportunities, with Prirazlomnoye as a prime example. In this business segment, the main competitive assets enjoyed by Norwegian companies would seem to be technological and managerial skills rather than political connections. From the experience of Aker Solutions, it would be tempting to suggest that it is currently easier and less risky to enter the Russian market solely as a provider of technology and services, than to aim for equity and control.

In the power and heat sector, trends are less clear. To be sure, there are business opportunities, but the risks concerning the future market are considered high. Norwegian experience in the power market is remarkably different from the Finnish one, with Fortum being one of the biggest foreign investors in the Russian power sector. Of course, Finland, as the largest importer of electric power from Russia, has closer ties to the Russian power market. Even so, the difference in both strategy and outcome between Norwegian and Finnish power giants is noteworthy (see chapter 11). In energy efficiency projects and renewable energy, the Norwegian experience is very limited. So far, most projects have been funded by the Norwegian government, and have in essence been a form of aid rather than profit-seeking business ventures.

3.   How the picture could change: Some driving forces

There are several important trends that will affect the business environment in Russia and the chances of success or failure for foreign companies. The Putin presidency led to massive changes. Some developments have become more predictable while others now seem more uncertain. In the following discussion, we look at a few key uncertainties that are likely to influence possibilities and risks for companies involved in the Russian energy sector, while we also aim at shedding light on some current trends that are important to understand when considering investment in Russia.

1) The Russian state is increasing its role in the economy, but will 'state corporations' work? One dominant trend in the Russian economy is the increasing role of the Russian state. This strengthening of the state is achieved partly through methods that in the West are regarded as illegitimate or at least questionable. How the role of the state in the economy will develop in the future is of critical importance to foreign companies operating at all levels in Russia. Yet, there are major uncertainties as to which sectors will be affected by the government's drive for control, what form state control might take and the consequences for the economy.

The Western business community has paid particular attention to re-nationalisation in the oil and gas industry, following the 2003–04 takeover of the main assets of Yukos by the state-controlled company Rosneft and the more recent pressure against Shell and TNK-BP to cede their shares in projects in Russia's Far East and Siberia. Growing state dominance is also evident in an increasing number of other sectors. The Russian government's work on defining strategic sectors in which Russian players are to have a majority stake is one example. Another is the creation and strengthening of the so-called 'state corporations' (see chapter 11).

A crucial question is whether such a strengthening of the Russian state's role in the economy can produce good economic results over time. On the one hand, it could help to create new, strong competitive sectors and national champions in Russia. On the other hand, the potential inefficiency of huge state corporations might vaporise the base of economic growth – in which case it would be an open question what Russia's response to a possible failure would be. It could be that the pendulum gradually swings back to better and more predictable conditions for international companies operating in Russia; but we might also see an increasingly introvert Russia with xenophobic tendencies, blaming the failure on external forces.

One test case of the consequences of a greater state role will be how the Russian side responds to the bids of international supply companies to participate in the Shtokman development project, at the possible expense of the development of a Russian gas supply industry.

2) The Russian economy shows strong growth in a period of high oil prices, but how robust is the economy? Thus far, in the 2000s, the Russian economy has grown consistently at 6–7% annually. Although growth is naturally associated with business opportunities, it is not at all clear what effect Russian economic development will have on the opportunities for foreign companies in the energy sector. High oil prices and strong growth could contribute to a better investment climate, but they could also support the surge of Russian nationalism and protectionism. Similarly, an economic downturn could mean a greater need for foreign investments, paving the way for good framework conditions for foreign investors; on the other hand, it might also increase economic risk.

Much depends on the nature of the growth. So far, growth has largely been driven by rising oil and gas export revenues, progressively supported by expanding domestic consumption. The Russian government has been building up the stabilisation fund since 2004, which was divided into the reserve fund and the national welfare fund from February 2008. At the same time, it seems that budget constraints are becoming softer. How robust will present growth trends remain if oil prices fall dramatically? The stabilisation fund will help to balance the budgets for some time, but a sustained oil price fall could threaten the growth prospects. And even with continued high export revenues, the government faces a huge challenge in handling the revenues in a sustainable way. Yielding to the temptation of increased budget spending could have severe consequences for the overall economic situation in the country.

Oil prices are also linked fairly directly to business opportunities in the energy sector, for upstream companies, supply companies, energy efficiency companies, power companies and consultants alike. Expensive foreign technology makes more sense when resource prices are high. But at the same time, high prices raise the resource rent. In Russia, as in many other resource-rich countries, this has spurred both nationalism and corruption, with the state and its leading actors striving to keep the rent for themselves.

3) Russia is approaching a gas supply squeeze, but will the response be adequate? Without substantial investments in upstream gas development or reform of domestic energy prices, Russia is likely to find itself in a gas supply squeeze some time before 2015, whereby it will struggle to cover its domestic consumption while also honouring its delivery obligations to the European market. Dealing with this challenge will affect a wide range of Russian policies and market conditions. Increasing import of Central Asian gas might be an answer, but this would appear to be a solely a short-term solution.

How will the Russian government approach the supply squeeze? Three options stand out: the government could try to boost production by opening up for massive, upstream field developments with foreign participation. It could also speed up implementation of the painful gas- and power price reform to cool down domestic demand, although with indeterminate effects on demand and possibly high political costs. Finally, it could launch substantial, state-sponsored energy efficiency programmes aimed at the domestic market with its immense potential for energy efficiency gains. And such programmes could create opportunities for companies with relevant expertise.

4) Climate policy is high on the global agenda, but how will it affect the energy market? Several international and global trends may influence business opportunities for foreign companies in Russia. One of the most prominent is the global climate-change agenda and possible alterations in global (and regional) climate policy. A strict global climate regime could affect the international demand for Russian hydrocarbons, but the impact is uncertain and the consequences for foreign companies in businesses related to the hydrocarbon sector even more so. On the other hand, a new global climate regime could open up opportunities in Russia for foreign companies involved in energy efficiency and renewable energy.

5) Gazprom is increasing its leverage in the European downstream gas market by swapping assets, but how would this impact the possibilities in Russia? Gazprom has set greater market access and market power in the European downstream gas market as one of its strategic goals. The company's major successes in this field have come through asset swaps, creating stronger vertical ties between Russian and German, Italian, French, Austrian, Dutch and other European energy companies. The Yuzhno-Russkoye deal may serve as an illustration of this strategy: Gazprom gained a 50% minus one share in BASF's gas distribution company Wingas by giving BASF a share in the Yuzhno-Russkoye gas field. The important question is how indicative this and similar examples are of what the future will bring. Ceding control of important downstream assets could be a prerequisite for participation in Russian upstream projects. For Norwegian actors, the relevant question will then be whether they have any tempting swaps to offer. Participation and partnership for Russian companies on the Norwegian continental shelf or in Norwegian gas pipelines could become a reality. But it is not clear whether the mature Norwegian shelf would be sufficiently interesting for Gazprom or other Russian companies.

Discussion

The state seems set to continue playing a central role in the Russian economy in the foreseeable future. The main uncertainties are how far this involvement will go, how it will be implemented and what effect it will have on property rights and foreign access to projects. Russia is headed towards a gas supply squeeze, but it remains to be seen what government strategies will unfold and when. There could be huge possibilities for foreign companies in upstream as well as in energy efficiency projects.

Trends towards swapping downstream assets for access to upstream development can prove disadvantageous for companies with small home markets and no access to downstream infrastructure. Norwegian companies and Nordic actors in general are at a disadvantage in this respect compared with, for example, German actors, with their access to key markets and networks.

Two questions are important in the discussion following the description of experience and future challenges for businesses in Russia. First, how can businesses adapt strategically to the challenges? Second, how and in what areas can the Northern Dimension help to promote well-functioning cooperation?

4.   Still grounds for a cautious approach

For firms engaged in business in Russia or considering involvement, past and present experiences provide an insufficient basis for future choices. When investing for the long term, it is necessary to identify the main drivers of change in Russia and assess how and the degree to which they can affect investment or contract possibilities. Some drivers have a fairly certain direction, while others are more uncertain.

Both past lessons and the analysis of driving forces indicate that it will remain important to be cautious when entering sectors of possible strategic significance for the Russian government. So far, the Russian centralisation and re-nationalisation of oil and gas assets seem to have affected the smaller players and the supply industry to a lesser degree than the major players, and oil assets less than gas. Nevertheless, the recent decision to let Total and StatoilHydro enter the Shtokman project shows that the door is not closed to big projects as long as international financing and technology is needed and – importantly – the Russian side can still exert sufficient control. The central question is how this new type of deal will play out over time – whether trust and win–win will prevail over distrust and discord, given the uncertainties that remain in Russia's business climate.

Often it may be safer and easier to become involved in small-scale projects that are below the radar of high politics or to avoid challenging the Russian need for control. The big equity prize might be within reach if the game is played right, but the costs and risks must be assessed carefully. When aiming for control there is always a risk of stepping on someone else's toes, and if that someone happens to be well connected, life can become miserable for the offender.

For companies involved in energy efficiency projects and also for those in the renewable energy business, the driving forces that may influence the power prices in Russia are of utmost importance. If, because of gas supply shortages, carbon fees, international emissions commitments or other reasons, Russia is forced to implement a painful gas and power price reform that substantially raises domestic power prices, there will be an enormous potential for energy efficiency projects. As Russia is the world's least energy-efficient country, there are huge possible challenges and gains in this area. But compared with the evident potential of German, Danish, Finnish and Swedish companies in this field, the question for Norwegian companies remains whether they would be able to take advantage of such a window of opportunity if it opened – or whether they would actually lack the necessary technology.

All in all, there are numerous good opportunities for companies doing or planning business in Russia. But there are also considerable risks. Some of the trends that can be observed in Russia today suggest that there is reason to be cautious about going into the Russian markets, while other development trends point to huge opportunities and an increasingly attractive market for investments. The key point for any foreign company seeking to do business in Russia is to have a strategy that is both robust and flexible.

Thus, it is crucial to study carefully a *range of development trends* in Russia, not only those that pertain to the market segment of interest in a narrow sense. Above we indicated some primary drivers to watch as a set of 'early warnings'. In this way, investors can determine at an early stage whether Russia is headed in the right or wrong direction in relation to their business plans. Based on that analysis they can trigger a predefined strategy for what to do with existing or planned investments: whether to exit, stay, enter or wait and see.

5.   How can the Northern Dimension make a difference?

We have focused on some principal driving forces and uncertainties within Russia, such as the state's role in the economy, the robustness of the economy, developments in the gas sector, global climate policy and Gazprom's strategy, and noted that they are likely to have an impact on the climate for foreign investment in the Russian energy sector. The main goal has been to point out the importance of analysing possible long-term tendencies and outlining strategies for the different trends. Part of the rationale for this is risk mitigation.

The Northern Dimension aims, among other things, at helping to build public–private partnerships in north-western Russia. The main effect of such initiatives for business is precisely risk mitigation. Project support through a range of Northern Dimension initiatives, including financial support and coordination, can help to reduce the risks and possible downsides of projects. Initiatives can also help in identifying possible partners and good projects, and in establishing cross-border contacts. Measures targeting issues such as easier border crossing, the fight against corruption and organised crime, and judicial cooperation, will also contribute to reducing the possibility of failure.

How does the Northern Dimension contribute to risk mitigation for foreign companies in the Russian energy sector? So far, the new Northern Dimension has been rather unexplored territory for energy firms. This means that experience is limited, providing little empirical basis for our analysis. Still, the current discussion of an energy partnership and substantial projects underway in the Northern Dimension area, such as Shtokman, can very possibly elevate energy issues onto the Northern Dimension agenda.

In general, large companies like StatoilHydro with a role in extensive projects as well as the major supply companies do not seek project support through policy initiatives like the Northern Dimension. Any financial support from partnership with governmental or intergovernmental bodies would be entirely marginal compared with the size of such projects. Furthermore, other more specialised organisations, like the Norwegian INTSOK,[7] are better placed to address the needs of big oil and oil supply companies abroad. Of course, companies can benefit from a general climate of cooperation and cross-border contact generated by Northern Dimension projects, but this is probably not a key ingredient in their success formula.

More important for these major oil companies than large, lofty multilateral cooperation programmes are bilateral contacts between governments and active state backing of their case. That Russian–Norwegian bilateral relations were fairly good and that StatoilHydro received full backing from the Norwegian government were probably paramount factors for a partnership deal in the Shtokman project. Should, on the other hand, government-level bilateral relations worsen significantly, that could cause problems for a company like StatoilHydro. But the dependency works both ways: if the principal oil players do well, that can strengthen the bilateral ties between their home country and Russia.

This perspective seems particularly relevant in the case of state-controlled and national oil companies. Success in Shtokman can have a positive impact on state relations between Norway and Russia, whereas failure could deal a blow to the bilateral ties between Norwegian and Russian political authorities. And a massive project like the Shtokman development will itself have an indirect effect on the Northern Dimension

---

[7] For a description, see "About INTSOK", INTSOK Norwegian Oil and Gas Partners, Oslo (retrieved from www.intsok.no/About-INTSOK).

agenda: when implemented, the project will have a huge impact on the general business climate in north-western Russia, thereby affecting the policy agenda of the Northern Dimension.

For the major power companies it is not clear how or whether initiatives under the Northern Dimension could be influential. It is stated that one of the possible areas for partnership support would be infrastructure programmes, but the extent to which that would facilitate investments in big power is uncertain. The strategic character of the power sector makes it more susceptible to shifts in governmental bilateral relations than to multilateral programmes. That notwithstanding, the Russian side has been seen to use the Northern Dimension as a platform for discussion and as a sounding board for its thinking on strategic sectors. The Northern Dimension could hence develop into a platform for intergovernmental dialogue and improved understanding of Russian views. Thus far, the Russian side has introduced the infrastructure and transport sectors to the agenda, and the power sector could be a future candidate for policy dialogue.

What our analysis therefore indicates is that the greatest impacts on energy issues within the Northern Dimension area stem from outside the Northern Dimension platform. For the present, it seems that the Northern Dimension on its own is most likely to make a difference and influence project opportunities in the areas of consulting, energy efficiency and new energy. These areas are far less politicised than the more strategic oil, gas and power sectors. The need for good projects is also great in these fields, and will be even greater as climate and energy supply concerns gain prominence. Promoting business cooperation in these areas could do much good for the region, while also creating market opportunities for European companies with pertinent expertise (see Figure 10.1).

Companies in the sectors of renewable energy and energy efficiency tend to be small, with clear limits to their capital base. Under the Northern Dimension Environmental Partnership, there are some opportunities for project support in these fields. Whether foreign companies will benefit from the Northern Dimension will depend on whether they have relevant competence and products to deliver. Small supply companies to the oil industry, typically sub-contractors, may also benefit from Northern Dimension projects.

For companies that stand to gain from support through the Northern Dimension there are various different possibilities. The general model for cooperation projects is said to be co-financing from Northern Dimension partners, as well as from international and private financial institutions where appropriate.[8] For Norwegian companies, however, there are already ways to seek state support for such projects. These schemes include INTSOK, Innovation Norway, the Norwegian Guarantee Institute for Export Credits and the Barents Secretariat. Particularly the investment fund of Innovation Norway seems a measure that resembles investment support through the Northern Dimension.

Figure 10.1 Directions of influence

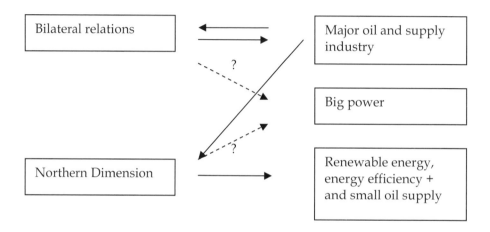

The Norwegian case indicates that it is vital for the Northern Dimension to be able to coordinate the various state-driven, international and non-governmental measures so as to avoid duplication and instead help to promote synergies from existing arrangements. In addition, we should note that the success of governmental investment funding has not been unambiguous. So far, investment funding from Innovation Norway has not been in high demand among Norwegian companies, nor been very successful in identifying the most profitable projects.[9] There is a double edge to any investment support sword. On the one hand, such support

[8] See European Commission, "Overview", Directorate-General for External Relations, European Commission, Brussels, October, 2007 (retrieved from http://ec.europa.eu/external_relations/north_dim/#Objectives).

[9] See Econ Pöyry, *Evaluering av fondene for Øst-Europa og Nordvest-Russland*, Econ-rapport 2007-103, Innovasjon Norge, Oslo, 2007 (retrieved from www.econ.no/modules/trykksak/publication_detail.asp?iProjectId=6731).

should not encourage unprofitable projects: unsuccessful business activity does not foster mutual trust, stability or broader cooperation. On the other hand, the very purpose of governmental investment support is to promote investment activity where it otherwise would not materialise. That means taking on more risky projects.

There are obviously also areas in which the Northern Dimension framework can be useful for companies working in Russia in more general terms. Infrastructure programmes, as well as programmes aimed at easier border crossings, combating corruption and organised crime, and judicial cooperation could all contribute to lowering the threshold for companies entering the Russian market. Furthermore, the Northern Dimension can have an important role to play as a provider of information, for example through informal channels such as the Northern Dimension business fora. These meetings may provide better information about business opportunities and enhanced understanding of emerging new policies, as well as contribute to an improved overall business framework.

6.   References

Aker Solutions (2003), "Sakhalin – Concrete Advance in Russia", Aker Solutions, Oslo (retrieved from www.akerkvaerner.com/Internet/ MediaCentre/Featurestories/OilandGas/Sakhalin.htm).

Dudarev, G., S. Boltramovich, P. Filippov and H. Hernesniemi (2004), *Advantage Northwest Russia*, Sitra Reports Series No. 33, Sitra, Helsinki.

Econ Pöyry (2007), *Evaluering av fondene for Øst-Europa og Nordvest-Russland*, Econ-rapport 2007-103, Innovasjon Norge, Oslo (retrieved from www.econ.no/modules/trykksak/publication_detail.asp?iProjectId= 6731).

European Commission (2007), "Overview", Directorate-General for External Relations, European Commission, Brussels, October (retrieved from http://ec.europa.eu/external_relations/north_dim/ #Objectives).

Nortrade.com (2007), "Norwegian Companies Attractive for Russian Partnerships", Nortrade.com, the Official Norwegian Trade Portal, Oslo (retrieved from www.nortrade.com/index.php?cmd=show_ article&id=255).

Stålsett, F. (2006), *Prosjektrapport: Kartlegge norske bedriftsetableringer i Nordvest-Russland*, Rambøll Storvik, Kirkenes.

11. STRATEGIC SECTORS OF THE RUSSIAN ECONOMY: IMPLICATIONS FOR DEVELOPING NEW NORTHERN DIMENSION PARTNERSHIPS
*KARI LIUHTO**

1. The emergence of strategic sectors in Russia

The new Northern Dimension agreed on in 2006 is structured around sectorally defined partnerships. Alongside the existing Northern Dimension Environmental Partnership (NDEP) and the Northern Dimension Partnership on Public Health and Social Well-being (NDPHS), a new partnership on transport and logistics is to be launched in autumn 2008, while the prospects for a partnership on energy are being considered.

Any steps in these new directions will mean an increasing need for cooperation between public and private bodies. Transport, logistics and energy are areas in which states as well as the EU as a supranational coordination institution issue legislation, regulations and strategic guidelines. Companies, for their part, are responsible for building ports, transport hubs and pipelines, along with extracting and processing energy resources, and distributing and selling energy to consumers. Also, pressure

* The author gratefully acknowledges the funding received from the Paulo Foundation (Paulon Säätiö), the Finnish Foundation for Economic Education (Liikesivistysrahasto), the Economic Research Foundation of Marcus Wallenberg (Marcus Wallenbergin Liiketaloudellinen Tutkimussäätiö) and the Foundation of Emil Aaltonen (Emil Aaltosen Säätiö).

to exploit the economic potential of the Northern Dimension area and to make the Northern Dimension a vehicle for practical cooperation accentuates the role of companies. Of particular interest will be their operating environment in north-western Russia, which is home to many energy resources, as well as a transit area for raw materials from more distant regions. Moreover, north-western Russia is a fast-growing market compared with the stalled growth in northern European EU member states.

For these reasons, this chapter concentrates on the operating environment for foreign companies in north-western Russia, while also examining trends with some reference to the experiences of Finnish, Norwegian and other non-Russian companies based in the Northern Dimension area. The Finnish case is particularly illustrative, as Finnish–Russian trade is intense and has generally been working well; therefore, any problems detected are likely to indicate similar or worse problems for other companies from the Northern Dimension area.

A key issue here concerns the effects of Russia's new policy of defining some parts of its economy as strategic sectors. President Vladimir Putin brought the idea into the global limelight in his annual address to the Federal Assembly in April 2005:

> Investors sometimes face all kinds of limitations, including some that are explained by national security reasons, though these limitations are not legally formalized. This uncertainty creates problems for the state and investors. It is time we clearly determined the economic sectors where the interests of bolstering Russia's independence and security call for predominant control by national, including state, capital. I mean some infrastructure facilities, enterprises that fulfil state defence orders, mineral deposits of strategic importance for the future of the country and future generations, as well as infrastructure monopolies…Some industrialized countries use this approach and we should also use it.[1]

Three years later, in May 2008, Putin signed a law on strategic sectors of the economy, restricting the participation of foreign-owned companies (see Box 11.1).

------

[1] See V. Putin, "Annual Address to the Federal Assembly of the Russian Federation", Kremlin, Moscow, 25 April 2005 (retrieved from www.kremlin.ru.eng/speeches/2005/04/25/2031_type70029type82912_87086.shtml).

Box 11.1 Summary and evaluation of the 2008 law on strategic sectors

Main sectors restricted:

- Nuclear installations and materials
- Ciphering-related activities
- Arms and military technology
- Aviation technology
- Communication services
- Metals and metal alloys important for the army
- Extraction of minerals on subsoil plots of federal importance
- Catching water biological resources (fisheries)
- Television, radio broadcasting, large-scale publishing and printing

Main ownership restrictions:

- Foreign companies are not allowed to have control over companies of strategic importance to Russia – foreign firms may own only up to 50% of such companies. If ownership reaches the 50% mark or more, foreign companies need permission from a commission led by the prime minister.
- Foreign state-owned companies need permission from the above-mentioned commission to own more than 25% of a strategic company.
- Stricter restrictions apply to the use of minerals on subsoil plots of federal importance. The ownership limit is set at 10% for private foreign firms and 5% for foreign government-owned firms.
- Foreign firms may own up to 50% of subsoil plots of federal importance if the plot is located on the continental shelf of Russia and the main partner is a Russian state-owned entity.

Some weaknesses in the law:

- It covers some sectors that are non-strategic for the country's defence and state security, like catching water biological resources, publishing, printing, television and radio broadcasting.
- It does not explicitly state what metals are deemed important for the army.
- The process of foreign companies' participation in strategic companies is highly vulnerable to administrative misuse and political choice.
- Ownership restrictions are not clear for foreign firms regarded as state-owned.

This new law forms only the tip of the iceberg, however – the explicit part of the strategic government policy. The implicit element of the policy is the creation of Russian-owned corporations in key industries of the economy ('national champions'). This latter aspect can be accomplished by using state finance such as funding capital received from the state or by means of favourable loans from Kremlin-friendly financial organisations. Moreover, the authorities in relation to the environment, construction and taxation, for example, as well as regional administrations, can slow down the operations of foreign competitors or other Russian corporations perceived as not loyal to the Kremlin.

By early 2008, Russia had formed several state corporations operating in fields such as strategic investments, nanotechnology, infrastructure, heavy industry and nuclear technology.[2] Further state corporations may be founded for modernising the road network, for developing fisheries and in the pharmaceutical sector.[3] In addition to such state-owned national corporations, the Russian government may treat private companies as national champions. This may be done to secure the loyalty of oligarchs or to establish the Kremlin's invisible but de facto control over private companies. Means of establishing control include issuing licenses for

---

[2] The term 'state corporation' refers to a hybrid of a joint stock company and a federal state-owned company. Upon their founding, these corporations become owners of state property in their own economic sector. Their financial reporting requirements are far less strict than are those of joint stock companies and they enjoy considerably more freedom in taking financial decisions. Their profits are not transferred to the budget; instead, they remain with the corporation, to be spent on the implementation of its statutory objectives. Finally, they are supervised directly by the president of the Russian Federation. See I. Wisniewska, "State-owned Corporations – A New Way of Managing the Russian Economy", *East Week Analytical Newsletter*, No. 37/102, 24 October 2007 (retrieved from www.osw.waw.pl/files/EastWeek_102.pdf); see also I. Wisniewska, "State Corporations – State Property in de facto Private Hands", *Baltic Rim Economies*, No. 1/2008 (retrieved from www.tse.fi/FI/yksikot/erillislaitokset/pei/Documents/bre2008/expert_article170_12008.pdf).

[3] See the *East Week Analytical Newsletter*, No. 37/102, 24 October 2007 (retrieved from www.osw.waw.pl/files/EastWeek_102.pdf).

natural resource exploitation, giving priority access to pipelines, inviting the company to 'friendly' auctions, offering low-cost state loans or guarantees and using the authorities to harass competing businesses.

2.   Impact on foreign direct investment inflows to Russia

The Russian stock of foreign direct investment (FDI) jumped from $5 billion in 1995 to nearly $200 billion by the end of 2006.[4] The annual FDI inflows in 2007 supported this growth trend by surging to $52 billion.[5] Still, without the re-nationalisation of Yukos and the introduction of strategic sector policies, Russia's FDI inflows would have been even larger. Indeed, Russia seems prepared to sacrifice at least some of its FDI inflows to ensure greater state control over certain sectors of the economy (Table 11.1).

Table 11.1 FDI and its significance in selected countries

	Inward FDI stock ($ billion)				FDI stock per capita ($)
	1990	1995	2000	2006	2006
Russia	–	5	32	198	1,398
Brazil	37	43	103	222	1,168
China, excl. Hong Kong	25	137	193	298	221
Poland	0.1	8	34	104	2,690
Ukraine	–	0.9	4	23	486
US	395	536	1257	1789	5,941

Source: UNCTAD, *World Investment Report*, UNCTAD, Geneva, 2002, 2006 and 2007.

It should be noted that some of Russia's FDI boom results from the repatriation of Russian capital. For example, during the current decade, the share of Cyprus, Switzerland and the British Virgin Islands has been 15–25% of annual FDI flows into Russia (Table 11.2).

---

[4] See United Nations Conference on Trade and Development (UNCTAD), *World Investment Report*, UNCTAD, Geneva, 2007.

[5] See Economist Intelligence Unit, *Russia: Country Report*, Economist Intelligence Unit, London, March 2008(a) (retrieved from www.eiu.com).

Table 11.2 FDI inflows to Russia by origin (%)

	1995	2000	2002	2003	2004	2005	2006	2007 Q3
UK	6	6	12	16	17	16	13	24
Netherlands	3	11	6	6	13	17	12	20
Cyprus	1	13	12	14	14	10	18	14
Luxembourg	0	2	6	8	21	26	11	9
France	4	7	6	13	6	3	6	5
Germany	10	13	20	15	4	6	9	4
Virgin Islands (UK)	1	1	7	5	2	2	4	2
Switzerland	15	7	7	4	4	4	4	9
US	28	15	6	4	5	3	3	2
Others	33	25	19	17	15	15	28	23

Source: L. Vinhas de Souza, "Foreign investment in Russia", *ECFIN Country Focus*, Vol. 5, No. 1, 2008 (retrieved from http://ec.europa.eu/economy_finance/publications/publication10969_en.pdf).

The repatriation of Russian capital may also explain why the emerging strategic sectors of the economy are not yet fully reflected in the statistics. For example, in 2007 17% of Russia's total foreign direct investment of $52 billion went into the mineral extraction industries.[6] That would mean non-Russian controlled firms investing some $10 billion in the sector – which seems unlikely without factoring in returning Russian funds (Table 11.3).

The same ambiguous pattern is evident at the regional level. To take the case of Finnish investment in Russia, an educated guess might set the cumulated Finnish FDI in Russia at some €3–5 billion, mostly invested in St. Petersburg and Moscow. Official statistics, however, indicate a stock of less than €2 billion (Table 11.4).

---

[6] See *BOFIT Weekly*, No. 15, 11 April 2008 (retrieved from www.bof.fi/NR/rdonlyres/C13F0945-DA93-47EF-8BDB-B595A18E7106/0/w200815.pdf).

Table 11.3 FDI inflows to Russia by sector (%)

	2003	2004	2005	2006	3Q2007
Agriculture, hunting and forestry	0.5	0.3	0.2	0.6	0.3
Mining and quarrying	19.3	24.5	11.2	16.6	17.3
Mining and quarrying of energy producing products	17.3	21.6	9.6	14.1	16.0
Mining and quarrying, except of energy producing products	2.0	2.9	1.6	2.5	1.3
Manufacturing	22	25.3	33.5	27.5	24.6
Manufacture of food products	3.4	2.3	2.2	2.5	2.5
Manufacture of chemicals and chemical products	1.2	1.9	2.7	2.8	1.2
Manufacture of metals and fabricated metal products	10.3	12.6	6.4	6.8	12.6
Manufacture of transport equipment	0.7	2.1	1.8	2.6	0.9
Manufacture of coke and mineral oil	0.6	0.2	15.1	7.2	3.8
Services	58.2	49.9	55.1	55.3	57.8
Construction	0.3	0.6	0.4	1.3	1.2
Wholesale, retail, repair activities	36.1	32.9	38.2	23.7	42.3
Transport and communication	3.8	5	7.2	9.6	6.5
of which communication only	2.3	3.4	6.1	8.5	2.9
Financial intermediation	2.6	2.5	3.4	8.5	2.4

Source: Vinhas de Souza (2008), op. cit.

Table 11.4 FDI flows between Finland and Russia (€ million)

	1998	1999	2000	2001	2002	2003	2004	2005	2006	2007
Finnish FDI stock in Russia	91	196	314	458	342	374	559	1,097	1,676	1,797
Russian FDI stock in Finland	272	241	241	306	449	338	366	378	431	446

Source: Bank of Finland, *Tilastoja suorista investoinneista Suomeen ja Suomesta, 2008*, Bank of Finland, Helsinki, 2008.

On top of this estimate comes the major investment by the Finnish power-generation company Fortum. In February 2008, Fortum won the auction for TGC-10, part of Russia's main electricity producer RAO UES. The deal in which Fortum acquired a 29% stake for €800 million was part of a wider electricity-sector privatisation launched in 2007. Fortum was also required to commit itself to buying a further stake of 34–47% through a share issue for €900–1,300 million. Should Fortum use its right to buy out the minority shareholders, such a move would raise the overall investment to around €2.7 billion. This energy sector deal is thus by a wide margin the largest investment made by a Finnish company in Russia. Most other companies have so far operated mainly in the consumer goods sector, as well as the metal, construction and forestry sectors (Table 11.5).[7]

Table 11.5 Largest Finnish employers in Russia

Company	Activities	Employees 2007
Fazer	5 bakeries, several AMICA catering firms	3,700
Stockmann	4 department stores (Seppälä, Hobby Hall)	2,640
YIT	Construction	2,154
Rautaruukki	Ventall, service centre	2,100
Stora Enso	2 sawmills, 3 packing factories	1,950
Sanoma	Magazines, kiosks, newspaper distribution	1,820
PKC Group	2 assembling factories	1,820
Atria	Meat product factory	1,500
Kesko	8 construction material supermarkets	1,440
UPM	Sawmill, plywood factory, logging company	1,210
Kemira	6 Tikkurila paint factories, logistics centre	1,200
Lemminkäinen	Several construction projects, Kaluga industrial park	1,000

Source: Ostint Oy, "Suomalaisyritykset työllistävät Venäjällä jo 35 000 ihmistä", *Kauppalehti*, 17 April 2008.

3. Main trends in Russia's sensitive sectors

The evolving Russian economy can be divided into the non-sensitive, economically sensitive, militarily sensitive and top sensitive sectors (Figure 11.1).

From the perspective of developing the new Northern Dimension partnership on transport and logistics and a possible partnership on energy, it is crucial to note that key activities within these spheres fall into the 'top sensitive' category. This means that in these sectors the Russian state will be an increasingly central actor that all partners must include as part of their strategies and plans. This proviso applies to the Finnish

---

[7] See the article, "Raising New Doubts about State Capitalism", *Moscow Times*, 10 October 2008.

Fortum's electricity sector investments and even more so to the Norwegian energy companies currently establishing a presence in north-western Russia (see chapter 10).

Figure 11.1 Strategic sectors of the Russian economy

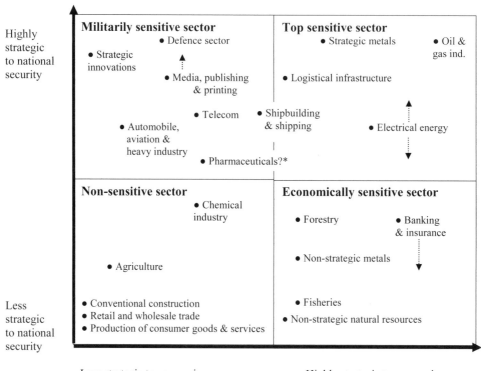

* The pharmaceutical sector has been given a question mark, as information on its positioning as regards the strategic sectors is not entirely clear.

Source: Adapted from K. Liuhto, "A Future Role of Foreign Firms in Russia's Strategic Industries", *Laboratoire européen d'Anticipation Politique/Europe 2020*, 2007 (retrieved from www.europe2020.org/spip.php?article393).

Straddling the top sensitive and the militarily sensitive categories we find pharmaceuticals, shipbuilding and shipping, all of which have assumed this status during 2007–08. The telecoms sector, in which Nordic companies are active in north-western Russia, belongs to the militarily sensitive category, as does strategic innovations (which has recently been elevated there). Non-strategic metals, fisheries and forestry, for their part, have recently jumped into the economically sensitive category. Of the latter two, fisheries are important for Norwegian interests and forestry for

Finnish and Swedish industries. At the bottom end, the consumer goods sector, where most Finnish companies operate, has remained relatively independent of state involvement (Figure 11.1).

These general trends are discussed in greater detail to highlight the possibilities of building new partnerships and promoting economic activity across borders in the Northern Dimension area.

The top sensitive sector

1) State takeovers in the oil business continue. The natural gas business is already strictly under state control. State-controlled Gazprom produces over 80% of the natural gas in Russia. It controls all gas pipelines and possesses an export monopoly, while the government decides on access to large gas fields. Even if the share of private companies in gas production should increase during the next few decades, and minority stakes be sold to foreigners, Russia's natural gas is bound to remain under tight state control.

In the oil business, the systematic takeover by the state has continued since the commencement of the Yukos affair in 2003. State ownership in publicly-traded oil firms increased from 32% in 2004 to 47% in 2007.[8] The role of foreign companies has become more limited as a result of the new law on strategic sectors, which restricts their access to projects in large fields. Global oil majors like Royal Dutch Shell have also experienced setbacks as they have been forced to sell some or all of the shares obtained in the lucrative production sharing agreements of the 1990s. The recent difficulties of BP with its Russian partners in TNK-BP may indicate a continuation of this trend. On the other hand, firms such as the Finnish Neste Oil, which is a petroleum product trader rather than a crude oil producer, have not been directly affected.

2) A Pyrrhic victory in the privatisation of the electricity sector. In July 2007, the Russian government approved a charter for the nuclear giant Atomenergoprom. The company will control all state-owned nuclear

---

[8] See Troika Dialog, "Who Owns Russia?", Troika Dialog, Moscow, 2008(a) (retrieved from www.troika.ru). Oil companies owned by regions or the state accounted for 15% of oil production in 2003. By the end of 2007, their share had already risen to 36%; see the article, "Sähkön hinta noussut Venäjän sähköpörssissä", *BOFIT Weekly*, No. 35, 30 August 2007 (retrieved from www.bof.fi/bofit).

assets, including uranium production, electricity generation and engineering assets. Furthermore, the state seeks to increase the share of nuclear energy from the current 16% to 25–30% of all electricity production by 2030. As the country's electricity consumption is growing, this means that Russia would have to build 42 new nuclear reactors. At present, it operates 31 reactors.[9]

Non-Russian firms face legal restrictions in the nuclear sector. They may yet find business opportunities, however. For instance, in November 2007, German Siemens signed a memorandum of understanding with Rosatom for collaboration in developing nuclear power facilities in Russia and abroad. The agreement envisages developing nuclear power reactors based on Russian design and using Siemens' technology. Similarly, Japanese Toshiba has signed a preliminary agreement to design and build power plants and to develop production capabilities for nuclear fuel.

Huge hopes were laid on the privatisation of RAO UES, which used to produce some 70% of Russia's electrical energy. It is definitely a positive sign that four foreign companies – Italian Enel, German E.ON, Finnish Fortum and German RWE – have managed to acquire strategic stakes in 4 out of 20 power generating units. At the same time, this is overshadowed by Gazprom's entry into the business. According to estimates, Gazprom and SUEK (Siberian Coal Energy Company) are set to gain control over more than 40% of the generation assets formerly controlled by RAO UES. Together they will also have a near monopoly on the fossil fuels used in power generation. SUEK is by far the country's largest producer of coal, while Gazprom is the natural gas export monopoly.[10] In other words, Gazprom and SUEK will be able to exert supply leverage on all other private power-generation companies.

---

[9] See the article, "President Putin's State-of-the-Nation Address to the Parliament Stresses Higher Spending on Economic and Social Development", *BOFIT Weekly*, No. 18, 5 May 2007 (retrieved from www.bof.fi/NR/rdonlyres/BB562C1B-0C0C-4B3D-863A-7AC117AEC680/0/we07.pdf); Troika Dialog, "Government Reiterates Aggressive Plans for Nuclear Development", Troika Dialog, Moscow, 19 March 2007(a) (retrieved from www.troika.ru); and the article, "Rosatom Set for Big Expansion", *Moscow Times*, 17 March 2008.

[10] See the article, "Gazprom and SUEK Reach Merger Deal", *Moscow Times*, 27 February 2008.

The Pyrrhic victory concerning the privatisation of Russia's energy sector also raises some doubts regarding the price reform pledged for 2011. There are some concerns that a full price liberalisation of industrial electricity prices may not take place. The liberalisation of electricity charges to private households is even less certain. The ministry for the economy has already proposed postponing the gas price liberalisation.[11]

3) Increasing state control over strategic metal producers and heavy industry. Some 70% of the metal and mining industry, which is important in energy production, is in private hands; the state's share is only 3%.[12] Yet, there are clear signs of the emergence of economic nationalism and consolidation here as well. Even without direct ownership, the Kremlin uses its indirect control through directors loyal to the state's strategic goals. A classic example of such a Kremlin loyalist is Oleg Deripaska, Russia's wealthiest person, with a fortune of $28 billion.[13] Russia's aluminium sector has de facto converged around Deripaska's companies Basic Element and Rusal. Now he aims at acquiring the country's leading metal producer Norilsk Nickel, which has large production sites in north-western Russia.

In November 2007, the Russian state founded Rostekhnologii to increase the competitiveness of the heavy industry.[14] Simultaneously, business in strategic metals, such as titanium, became concentrated in this state corporation. It would not be a major surprise if Rostekhnologii should proceed to acquire firms operating in the strategic metals sector, one by one.

---

[11] See Troika Dialog, "Economics Ministry Proposes Postponing Gas Price Liberalisation", Troika Dialog, Moscow, 2 April 2008(b) (retrieved from www.troika.ru).

[12] See Troika Dialog (2008a), op. cit.

[13] In July 2007, Deripaska even conceded that he would give up Rusal to the state if asked to do so; see the article, "Metal Moves", *Business Eastern Europe*, 11 February 2008.

[14] Rostekhnologii brings together the Russian weapons export monopoly Rosoboroneksport, the titanium producer VSMPO-AVISMA, the automotive manufacturer AvtoVAZ, the helicopter producer Oboronprom and several other companies; see Economist Intelligence Unit, *Russia: Country Report*, Economist Intelligence Unit, London, January 2008(c) (www.eiu.com). The company is headed by Sergey Chemezov, Vladimir Putin's former colleague from his time as an intelligence officer in Dresden; see I. Wisniewska (2007), op. cit.

A positive sign in this sector is that Renault acquired a blocking stake (25%) of Russia's leading car manufacturer AvtoVAZ through a $1.2 billion investment in March 2008. In the field of civilian aviation, Deutsche Bank has a 7% stake in the national carrier Aeroflot. Finally, in early 2008, the Italian Alenia was given the right to acquire a blocking stake in Sukhoi's civilian aircraft division.

4) The state is strengthening its role in logistics. In April 2007, Putin signed a degree on the acquisition of the petroleum-product pipeline operator Transnefteprodukt through Transneft, the crude-oil pipeline monopoly operator. In November 2007, Transneft's CEO Nikolai Tokarev, a former KGB general, stated that Transnefteprodukt would retain its independence within its new patron company.[15] Still, the acquisition and the appointment of Putin's former colleague to head the operation represent clear steps towards strengthening the state's grip over strategic logistics.

In November 2007, Sovkomflot started merger proceedings with the state-controlled shipping major Novoship. Once completed, this operation is expected to create the fifth greatest shipping giant in the world, with assets of nearly $5 billion. The merged company is expected to develop a strong focus on the Arctic region and the transport of energy supplies from Russia's Far East. It would operate a fleet of 113 vessels with another 36 on order, including ice breakers designed for Arctic shipping lines.[16] This implies the beginning of the consolidation of the shipping industry. The newly established, state-owned United Shipbuilding Corporation will support this trend.

Signals of growing state control over major seaports are becoming stronger. For instance, in March 2008, Transneft started construction of the Kozmino oil terminal on Russia's Pacific coast. In the Baltic Sea, Ust-Luga is considered one of the most strategically important ports and its further development ranks high on the Russian agenda.

It is not yet fully clear whether the pressure applied by both Russian authorities and the company Rosstroy in 2007 concerning the facilities of

---

[15] See Troika Dialog, "Putin Signs Decree of Accession of Transnefteproduct into Transneft", Troika Dialog, Moscow, 17 April 2008(c); Troika Dialog, "Transnefteproduct to Retain Independence; No Dividend Increase", Troika Dialog, Moscow, 2 November 2007(b) (retrieved from www.troika.ru).

[16] See the article, "Metal Moves", *Business Eastern Europe*, 11 February 2008.

the Finnish company Container Finance in Kronstadt was orchestrated by federal bodies or competing companies. After Container Finance decided to sell a major stake in two of its subsidiaries to Severstaltrans at the end of 2007, the situation calmed down. It is to be hoped that this partnership will prove sustainable and does not lead to a cuckoo strategy whereby the expanding newcomer throws the original owner out of the nest.

The militarily sensitive sector

1) Telecommunications: A mixture of stagnation and turbulence. Vladislav Surkov, a senior member of the presidential administration, has indicated that national capital has to be dominant in the ownership of strategic communications. The term 'national' capital seems to mean 'Russian' capital, but not necessarily state-controlled capital. Russian entrepreneurs playing on the team with the Russian state may thus qualify. At the same time, a distinction is made between trusted oligarchs and 'offshore Russians'.[17]

It is difficult to estimate the long-term role of foreign companies in Russian telecommunications. Major fixed-line telecoms companies seem to be classified as strategic. For example, any sale in the government's stake in the national fixed-line operator Svyazinvest would probably come under government scrutiny. The same most likely pertains to the long-distance services provider Rostelecom, which has a significant market share in several regions as well as in Moscow and St. Petersburg.[18]

The privatisation of Svyazinvest has been postponed several times. The Russian military has followed this privatisation very keenly and has probably slowed down the process. The army has also been concerned about the destiny of Rostelecom.

One of Russia's leading mobile telecommunication companies, Altimo, has created considerable turbulence in Megafon, which is partially owned by the Swedish–Finnish TeliaSonera, and in Vimpelcom, which is partially owned by the Norwegian Telenor. A business divorce between Altimo and Telenor may well be in sight. Altimo has several times offered

---

[17] See P. Hanson, "The Russian Economic Puzzle: Going Forwards, Backwards or Sideways?", *International Affairs*, Vol. 83, No. 5, 2008, pp. 869–89.

[18] See the article, "Strategic Sector Bill Clears 2nd Reading", *Moscow Times*, 24 March 2008.

asset swaps to TeliaSonera. A new page in this saga was Altimo's announcement to sell its stake in Megafon in exchange for Telia-Sonera's stake in Turkish Turkcell.

2) Main media assets taken over by the state and its loyalists. The most important electronic media are currently under direct or indirect state control. Also, some print media have come into the hands of Kremlin-loyal tycoons. The new law on strategic sectors aims at restricting the participation of foreign firms in the publishing and printing business. It covers large-circulation newspapers and publishing companies with the capacity to print 200 million pages per month, and periodicals with a circulation of at least a million copies. Broadcast media covering at least half the country are deemed strategic. Non-Russians are thus effectively excluded from holding majority stakes in nationwide television stations like state-controlled Channel One, Rossiia and NTV.[19]

Even if Internet service providers were not listed in Russia's 2008 law, no one can guarantee their non-restricted status in the future, especially if the political regime turns more conservative and nationalistic. The role of foreign firms in leisure-oriented print media, such as fashion, sports and the yellow media, seems to be accepted by Russia's ruling elite as long as political affairs and the main political figures are not touched.

3) Increasing risks for foreign firms in strategic innovation supporting Russia's defence industry. The Russian state wants to invest in the diversification of the civilian economy and to increase its competitiveness. The establishment of the state corporation in nanotechnology in 2007 was one means to that effect. The state's involvement might prove counterproductive, however, by restricting the formation of normal and sustainable competitiveness.

In the defence sector, the army needs technological innovations to make a serious comeback in the arena of the world's major military powers. According to the then first deputy prime minister Sergei Ivanov, "there is every reason to call the military-industrial complex the locomotive of diversification".[20] This assertion might have applied to the Soviet era, when most civilian high-tech goods were produced by the military-industrial

---

[19] Ibid.

[20] See the article, "Ivanov Sees Military Leading on High-Tech", *Moscow Times*, 21 May 2007.

complex. But if Russia should resort to this strategy today, the results would be far from certain. It is clear that a military-led reform will be much more expensive than a reform conducted by private entities. Moreover, foreign firms will most likely hesitate to participate in any innovation development run by the Russian army. In addition, many army-related activities are already classified as strategic and thus they have become off-limits to foreign firms.

The economically sensitive sector

1) Banking and insurance. Surkov has stressed the strategic importance of the financial system to the Russian state.[21] The law on the strategic sectors does not concern banking or insurance, but even if Russia joins the WTO, it is likely to restrict certain segments of this branch. In the context of the Northern Dimension, this sector is important in funding large-scale transport, logistics and energy projects, and there are signs that the Russian state wants greater involvement by Russian private financial institutions in the Northern Dimension.

At the end of 2007, there were more than 1,100 banks in Russia. Despite the large number of bank-like institutions, the sector is highly concentrated, with the five largest banks accounting for 42% of the assets in the sector. The three largest banks are all under state control. A positive trend here is the entry of foreign banks: in all, there are more than 200 foreign-owned banks in Russia, 62 of which are fully foreign-owned. In 2007, non-Russian ownership in banking grew from 16% to 25%, mainly owing to the initial public offerings of two major state-owned banks, Sberbank and VTB.[22] Indeed, in terms of foreign participation, banking and insurance have developed most favourably among the key industries. Several operations exemplify this trend:

- In February 2007, Sistema agreed to sell a 49% stake in the Rosno insurance company to German Allianz for $750 million, with Allianz expected to become the major owner of this company.

- In April 2007, the Belgian KBC Bank acquired the Russian bank Absolut for approximately $1 billion.

---

[21] See Hanson (2008), op. cit.

[22] See the article, "Pankkisektorin kasvu jatkuu nopeana", *BOFIT Weekly*, No. 8, 21 February 2008 (retrieved from http://www.bof.fi/bofit/seuranta/viikkokatsaus).

- In January 2008, French AXA signed an agreement to purchase a 37% stake in one of the largest insurers in Russia, Reso-Garantia, for €810 million – the largest foreign acquisition in the Russian insurance market.

- In February 2008, French Société Générale finalised its acquisition of control ownership in Rosbank with some $7 billion, representing what is probably the largest-ever foreign investment in the Russian banking sector.

Less encouraging are the activities of Kremlin-loyal oligarchs in the insurance world. Deripaska-led Basic Element has a dispute over ownership in Ingosstrakh. Although it is difficult to determine the real reasons behind the dispute, Oleg Ivanov, adviser to the State Duma Committee on Credit Organisations, has noted that "the Federal Security Service and other branches of the secret services do not buy insurance from firms with foreign investors. ...There is nothing in the law that prevents these kinds of deals. But the agencies have fears that foreigners on the board would access private information."[23] Whatever the real reasons, this dispute does not encourage other foreign insurers to enter Russia.

2) Forestry becoming increasingly sensitive. The total wooded area of Russia is some five times larger that of the EU-27. Nevertheless, paper and paperboard production figures in the EU-27 are some 15 times higher than are those of Russia.[24] Russia is the world's largest exporter of raw wood, accounting for one-third of all raw wood exports.[25] These figures may have motivated Putin to ask in his 2007 state of the nation address:

> Are we [Russians] really gaining maximum benefit from our natural resources? This question applies not only to oil, gas and mineral resources, but also to our forestry and water resources.[26]

---

[23] See the article, "Shareholder Spat Hinders Ingosstrakh Acquisitions', *Moscow Times*, 2007.

[24] See Eurostat, *The European Union and Russia: Statistical Comparison*, Luxembourg: Office for Official Publications of the European Communities, 2007.

[25] See the article, "Russia Raises Export Tariffs on Raw Wood", *BOFIT Weekly*, No. 7, 16 February 2007 (retrieved from www.bof.fi/NR/rdonlyres/BB562C1B-0C0C-4B3D-863A-7AC117AEC680/0/we07.pdf).

[26] See V. Putin, "Annual Address to the Federal Assembly of the Russian Federation", Kremlin, Moscow, 2007 (retrieved from www.kremlin.ru/eng/speeches/2007/04/26/1209_type70029type82912_125670.shtml).

The objective of raising the processing level of raw materials in Russia resulted in the export tariffs of raw wood rising from €10 per cubic metre to €15 in April 2008, with further increases planned to €50 from the beginning of 2009. These rises will force Finnish forestry companies to stop their raw material imports from Russia. Even though the Finns, as well as the EU, understand Russia's need to increase tariffs in order to improve the processing level of its paper and pulp industry, they also note that the tariff hikes may contradict the terms of the bilateral EU–Russian WTO accession deal agreed in 2004.[27]

Another problem is that the transition period is far too short. The construction of a modern paper mill is a strategic investment that costs around €1–1.5 billion and takes a long time. Furthermore, the foundations of the Russian paper industry are anything but firm. The state currently owns 96% of the forests. The remaining 4% is held by the regions.[28] Major foreign companies cannot simply rush into the Russian paper and pulp market, building new paper mills without guaranteed access to raw materials. An example here is the Finnish Ruukki Group, which withdrew from a planned project in Russia after failing to secure a priority position for obtaining wood from the Kostroma region.[29]

A welcome gesture from the Russian side would be to postpone the introduction of increased export tariffs planned for the beginning of 2009, and instead give foreign paper companies a five- to seven-year transition period to facilitate a proper analysis of the business and political risks of Russia in this capital-intensive sector.

Some Russian oligarchs have shown interest in the forestry sector. In particular, certain metal business oligarchs may well move into the paper and pulp industry as well. That would increase the political risks. The traditionally critical attitudes of Russian citizens towards private and

---

[27] See the article, "Higher Raw Wood Export Tariffs Now in Effect', *BOFIT Weekly*, 4 April 2008 (retrieved from www.bof.fi/NR/rdonlyres/85803501-CE19-4909-A3D3-2E22591CA89F/0/w200814.pdf); and the article, "Interregnum Delays WTO Accession", *Moscow Times*, 7 April 2008.

[28] See T. Karjalainen and T. Torniainen, "Venäjällä metsät säilyvät tulevaisuudessakin valtion omistuksessa", *Tieto & trendit*, No. 5/2006, March 2006.

[29] Yet, the two international companies International Paper and Mondi are already operating in the Russian paper and pulp sector.

foreign ownership of the forests also give the Kremlin political support for potentially restricting the access of foreign firms to the forestry sector.

3) Non-strategic metals elevated to economic significance. In the sector of ferrous metals, some oligarch-led businesses may assume the role of private national champions. Here also, Kremlin-loyal firms are always more favoured by the authorities.

4) Fisheries included in the economically sensitive category. Oddly enough, the fisheries sector has been included in the economically sensitive domain. One reason may be that the Russian navy wants to restrict the movements of foreign ships in Russia's territorial waters. Or it may be a result of the extensive corruption prevailing in the fisheries sector. In any case, ecological concerns are hardly the reason for including fisheries in the sensitive category.

The non-sensitive sector

Despite market-specific problems like tremendously increased corruption and 'normal' (i.e. not orchestrated by the federal level) bureaucratic abuse, the production and distribution of consumer goods and services have stayed below the Kremlin's radar. On the other hand, some Kremlin-loyal oligarchs like Deripaska are already engaged in the area of strategic construction.

Deripaska has expressed interest in investing heavily to develop Russian infrastructure and to create public–private partnerships. Through Rusal, Deripaska currently controls stakes in both Glavstroy and Transstroy. As Transstroy builds roads, ports and railways, it inevitably becomes more privileged than the majority of its competitors. Deripaska-run companies have also shown great interest in developing the cities of St. Petersburg and Sochi (Deripaska has pledged to invest $20 billion in St. Petersburg by 2015).[30] Even if Deripaska continues to focus on the development of major infrastructure projects in these two cities, his activities may distort competition in other construction-related sectors, especially when large projects are at stake. All this may also affect players like the Finnish construction company YIT.

---

[30] See the article, "Deripaska Holding's Tentacles Reach Farther", *Moscow Times*, 28 November 2007; and the article, "Deripaska Inks $20 Bln St. Pete Deal", *Moscow Times*, 30 November 2007.

Agriculture only narrowly stays within the non-sensitive sector. In March 2008, Prime Minister Viktor Zubkov intensified calls for the government to prop up Russia's agricultural industry and raise the domestic proportion of food products to 70% by 2012.[31] As food and agricultural products represented almost 17% of Russia's imports in 2006,[32] exporters of foodstuffs to Russia may experience challenging times in the near future.

4. Genesis of Russia's economic nationalism and the Northern Dimension

With regard to developing the new transport and logistics partnership or any other new partnerships where public–private cooperation is pivotal (as in the energy sector), the consequences of the new law on the strategic sectors are significant and must be taken into account. Although the new legislation does not prevent cooperation, it sets clear limitations for it. Moreover, we must bear in mind that the legal changes are only the tip of the iceberg: they represent the genesis of economic nationalism rather than its final form. The major aspects of economic nationalism in Russia are developed outside the realm of legislation. As such, it is the operations of state corporations and Kremlin-supported oligarchs that represent the main risks to any foreign investors.

On the one hand, it would not be surprising to see more state involvement in, for instance, the logistics and forestry sectors. This development might also assume an indirect format, through the use of Kremlin-loyal oligarchs. As long as state-owned companies are heavily involved in a sector, it is likely to remain sensitive; as a result, in sectors like electricity generation, the rules of international politics are more applicable than are those of international business.

On the other hand, FDI inflows to Russia can be expected to remain at a high level. Despite the strategic government policies, foreign companies are attracted by Russia's fast-growing private consumption. With regard to exploiting private capital to develop new Northern Dimension partnerships, this may generate considerable economic

---

[31] See the article, "Zubkov Calls for More Russian Food", *Moscow Times*, 26 March 2008.

[32] See the Economist Intelligence Unit, *Russia: Country Report*, Economist Intelligence Unit, London, April 2008(b) (retrieved from www.eiu.com).

dynamism in the Northern Dimension area as growth in the EU member states stalls. Most likely, the majority of future FDI deals will be conducted in the non-sensitive sectors of the Russian economy, especially in the private consumption-related branches. Major deals can also be expected in the sensitive sectors, but here foreign firms will have to be content with minority stakes.

What does this all mean in practice? To take the case of Finland, the overwhelming majority of Finnish firms are currently operating outside the strategic sectors, although the largest investments – both current and future ones – relate to the sensitive sectors. This tendency reflects the attractiveness of Russia's rapidly expanding, non-strategic, consumption-related sector and the coterminous need for large investments with Western involvement in the energy and other strategic sectors. At the same time, economic nationalism appears to be the driving ideology in Russia. Indeed, it would seem that Russia has abandoned economic policies in favour of the concept of a political economy. This means that political actors, regional administrations and private companies from the EU area and beyond must work together and in close contact with Russian authorities.

Putin's endorsement of the law on strategic sectors, signing it as one of his last acts as president, does not detract from the task the current tandem leadership faces of stopping the implicit spread of economic nationalism in Russia. At the grand level, the consequences of this implicit economic nationalism may dramatically worsen relations between Russia and the EU. Within the confines of the Northern Dimension, they may prove detrimental for developing the public–private partnership format. In this light, Medvedev's presidency will put his publicly voiced economic liberalism to a real litmus test. It is to be hoped that the test results will not prove too acidic for foreign firms operating in the Russian part of the Northern Dimension area.

5. References

Bank of Finland (2008), *Tilastoja suorista investoinneista Suomeen ja Suomesta, 2008,* Bank of Finland, Helsinki.

Economist Intelligence Unit (2008a), *Russia: Country Report*, Economist Intelligence Unit, London, March (retrieved from www.eiu.com).

———— (2008b), *Russia: Country Report*, Economist Intelligence Unit, London, April (retrieved from www.eiu.com).

————— (2008c), *Russia: Country Report*, Economist Intelligence Unit, London, January (retrieved from www.eiu.com).

Eurostat (2007), *The European Union and Russia: Statistical Comparison*, Luxembourg: Office for Official Publications of the European Communities.

Hanson, P. (2008), "The Russian Economic Puzzle: Going Forwards, Backwards or Sideways?", *International Affairs*, Vol. 83, No. 5, pp. 869–89.

Karjalainen, T. and T. Torniainen (2006), "Venäjällä metsät säilyvät tulevaisuudessakin valtion omistuksessa", *Tieto & trendit*, No. 5/2006, March.

Liuhto, K. (2007), "A Future Role of Foreign Firms in Russia's Strategic Industries", *Laboratoire européen d'Anticipation Politique/Europe 2020* (retrieved from www.europe2020.org/spip.php?article393).

Ostint Oy (2008), "Suomalaisyritykset työllistävät Venäjällä jo 35 000 ihmistä", *Kauppalehti*, 17 April.

Putin, V. (2005), "Annual Address to the Federal Assembly of the Russian Federation", Kremlin, Moscow, 25 April (retrieved from www.kremlin.ru.eng/speeches/2005/04/25/2031_type70029type829 12_87086.shtml).

————— (2007), "Annual Address to the Federal Assembly of the Russian Federation", Kremlin, Moscow, 26 April (retrieved from www.kremlin.ru/eng/speeches/2007/04/26/1209_type70029type82 912_125670.shtml).

Troika Dialog (2007a), "Government Reiterates Aggressive Plans for Nuclear Development", Troika Dialog, Moscow, 19 March (retrieved from www.troika.ru).

————— (2007b), "Transnefteproduct to Retain Independence; No Dividend Increase", Troika Dialog, Moscow, 2 November (retrieved from www.troika.ru).

————— (2008a), "Who Owns Russia?", Troika Dialog, Moscow (retrieved from www.troika.ru).

————— (2008b), "Economics Ministry Proposes Postponing Gas Price Liberalisation", Troika Dialog, Moscow, 2 April (retrieved from www.troika.ru).

————— (2008c), "Putin Signs Decree of Accession of Transnefteproduct into Transneft", 17 April.

United Nations Conference on Trade and Development (UNCTAD) (2002), *World Investment Report*, UNCTAD, Geneva.

———————— (2006), *World Investment Report*, UNCTAD, Geneva.

———————— (2007), *World Investment Report*, UNCTAD, Geneva.

Vinhas de Souza, L. (2008), "Foreign investment in Russia", *ECFIN Country Focus*, Vol. 5, No. 1, 2008 (retrieved from http://ec.europa.eu/ economy_finance/publications/publication10969_en.pdf).

Wisniewska, I. (2007), "State-owned Corporations – A New Way of Managing the Russian Economy", *East Week Analytical Newsletter*, No. 37/102, 24 October (retrieved from www.osw.waw.pl/files/ EastWeek_102.pdf).

———————— (2008), "State Corporations – State Property in de facto Private Hands", *Baltic Rim Economies,* No. 1/2008 (retrieved from www.tse.fi/FI/yksikot/erillislaitokset/pei/Documents/bre2008/exp ert_article170_12008.pdf).

PART III.
TOWARDS A NEW NORTHERN AGENDA

12. END COMMENT: EU–RUSSIAN RELATIONS AND THE LIMITS OF THE NORTHERN DIMENSION
IRINA BUSYGINA & MIKHAIL FILIPPOV

1. Introduction

This chapter looks at the significance and limits of the Northern Dimension within the broader perspective of EU–Russian relations. In theory, the Northern Dimension is part of the strategically connected multilevel interactions between the governments of the EU member states and Russia. Various scholars have already stressed the importance of the multilevel nature of EU–Russian relations, focusing on the interactions between the Union institutions and the Russian government, Russian bilateral relations with member states and cross-border cooperation at the sub-national level.[1] Building on this literature, we go on to investigate more specifically the implications of the strategic interconnectedness at all strata of EU–Russian relations.

Our theoretical premise is that representatives of Russia and the EU interact at multiple institutional levels, balancing several objectives at once. The key actors take into account consequences of interactions at all levels but assign differing significance (weights) to the outcome of various 'games'. In light of such a strategic linkage, choosing whether to collaborate

---

[1] See H. Smith (ed.), *The Two-level Game: Russia's Relations with Great Britain, Finland and the European Union,* Aleksanteri Series 2:2006, Aleksanteri Institute, Helsinki, 2006.

on one level could explain decisions made on others. Depending on the opportunities for cooperation at diverse levels, the existence of hierarchical or horizontal power relations on both sides and the perceived relative importance of attainable outcomes at each level, such a linkage across games could result in counter-intuitive strategies. In the following discussion, we focus on one of them: the dissonance between Russian foreign policy and its policy towards the Northern Dimension.

2. Does Russia welcome the Northern Dimension to compensate for political tensions with the EU?

By now, it will hardly be news that the Russian leadership is willing to sustain a certain degree of political conflict with Western counterparts as well as with many former Soviet republics. Regardless of the reasons for this willingness, a strategic linkage among various interactions with the outside world could lead Russia to a foreign policy strategy founded on a counter-intuitive trade-off – the better the economic relations, the more conflict can be introduced in political relations. For instance, the greater the mutual energy-trade dependence between the EU and Russia, the more political conflict with the EU the Russian government can afford without causing a rupture. Similarly, the growing political tensions with the EU at large could be 'compensated' for by cooperation on other institutional levels. Political tensions with the EU could stimulate the Kremlin to develop a more extensive framework of bilateral relations and to welcome regional programmes promoted by blocs of EU member states – such as the Northern Dimension.

To play this counter-balancing role, however, the content of bilateral relations and regional programmes must be strictly isolated from those issues of 'high politics' that serve as the context for tensions in EU–Russian relations. A programme of regional cooperation like the Northern Dimension thus has the greatest chances of success when it deals with specifically localised and non-political EU–Russian matters. It is less suited to deal with politically charged issues such as the development of democracy in Russia, freedom of the press, human rights, security or energy politics. Therefore, we posit that to be successful, Northern Dimension leaders must restrict the Northern Dimension by design to exclude certain issues – among these, Russian energy policies.

3.   Continued tensions in political relations between Russia and the EU

Relations between the EU and Russia are likely to remain tense for many reasons. Indeed, for politicians on either side there are few benefits to be gained from seeking compromises. In Russia, influential politicians can rely on the continuing tensions as a mechanism for generating rapport with a broad constituency. In the EU, relations with Russia represent a divisive issue. For some member states, the tensions with Russia have domestic political currency, whereas many key member states would welcome any moves that might help to reduce the tensions.

The situation is aggravated by the fact that the political systems of both the EU and Russia are currently undergoing a period of constitutional choice and political transition, although with very different starting points. Russia is essentially at the stage of setting its basic constitutional principles, choosing between a competitive democratic system and an authoritarian model. Currently, the high price of energy and natural resources on the international market make the authoritarian model attractive for the Kremlin.[2]

Energy trade relations with the EU are crucial to the Russian economy (see chapter 9). Economic objectives alone would require advancing cooperative relations with EU institutions as well as most of the EU member states. Unfortunately, domestic politics motivate the Russian government to continue picking numerous fights with the EU, the US and most of the post-Soviet states. These conflicts help the Kremlin to legitimise its authoritarian inclinations with the domestic audience, while continued cooperation allows it to profit from selling natural resources to the West at high prices.

In short, in the case of Russia, the high share of national revenue from resource exports creates the wrong incentives, not just for its own economic and political development (i.e. the 'resource curse') but also for its foreign policy. Domestic political calculations often encourage key players in the Russian government to wage uncompromising rhetorical or virtual battles with various foreign counterparts, while seeking to reach primarily the

---

[2] As Egor Gaidar has noted, energy prices tend to influence the shifts in Russia's domestic development; see E. Gaidar, *Collapse of an Empire: Lessons for Modern Russia*, Washington, D.C.: Brookings Institution Press, 2007.

domestic audience. The battles in these virtual conflicts are chiefly played out on government-controlled television channels, with politicians and pundits competing to present the most vivid and creative extremist stances: they convey an image of 'the Great Russia' as surrounded by unjust enemies and suffering from Western media biases.

4. The EU's strategic reaction

With the rise in energy prices after the turn of the millennium, EU–Russian relations began to manifest a growing detachment between their economic and political components: as Europe's reliance on trade with Russia increased, political relations deteriorated. Moreover, energy security came to define the most important lines of tension between Europe and Russia.

Russia's reputation in Europe as a reliable energy supplier had been built over decades of cooperation with the former Soviet Union and Russia prior to the leadership of Vladimir Putin. It was wiped out in a sequence of energy 'wars' between Russia and the former Soviet republics, although some observers have argued that Russia's energy policy tactics have been used "exclusively within the CIS [Commonwealth of Independent States] space",[3] and that energy deliveries to Europe outside the post-Communist region were never manipulated. The relationship is truly one of mutual dependence, as two-thirds of Russia's energy exports go to the EU. Russia does not have many market options for selling its natural gas and must rely on European demand. Furthermore, market prices for natural gas are much higher in Europe than in other potential markets such as Asia.[4]

Unfortunately for EU–Russian relations, Russian domestic political rhetoric and its hardline attitude towards the former Soviet republics makes Russia a prime candidate to fulfil the emerging political demand in Europe for a unifying external threat. Despite the impressive success of economic integration, the very principles, forms and limits of political integration in the EU are still subject to continuing debates among and within member states. The design and implementation of a successful common foreign policy could be a crucial step in EU constitutional

---

[3] See L. Póti, "Evolving Russian Foreign and Security Policy: Interpreting the Putin-doctrine", *Acta slavica iaponica*, Vol. 25, 2008, pp. 29–42.

[4] Towards the end of 2008, the price of Gazprom's natural gas for Europe peaked at an all-time high of over $500 per 1,000 cubic metres (information retrieved from http://en.rian.ru/russia/20081112/118261776.html).

development, as it could be used to justify further expansion of the political powers of European-level institutions. Yet, foreign policy is also a topic on which member states are very likely to disagree Anticipating such divergences over policies, member states are also likely to disagree about whether to commit to delegate foreign policy decisions to the EU level. Constitutional steps towards having a joint foreign policy require identifying an unwavering consensus among member states, or as Romano Prodi aptly stated, "Europe needs a sense of meaning and purpose."[5]

Could conflict with Russia emerge as an attractive candidate for becoming such a unifying issue – a basis on which to form the consensus needed for acquiring EU competence in foreign policy? Alternatively, it might be that the issue of fostering democracy in Russia could work to create a positive consensus in the EU. For a while, it seemed that the more positive consensus on the need for Russia to democratise could indeed unify the EU, but the stance taken by Russia itself unraveled that consensus. By 2000, the democratisation trend in Russia had been reversed and any grounds for such a positive consensus had vanished. The strategy of confronting Russia, however, is not feasible within the consensus-dependent EU institutions, where the biggest divisions vis-à-vis Russia are found between the Commission and the European Parliament.

5. 'High politics' conflicts and 'low politics' cooperation

It is reasonable to assume that while some actors in Europe focus more on relations between Russia and the EU at large, other key actors are more interested in good bilateral relations. Similarly, some players concentrate on specific issues – such as security, the environment, energy supplies or democratic development. In general we can expect the main actors to define their strategies by first taking into account what happens at all levels of interactions with Russia, and second, by assigning differing priorities to the interactions at various levels and to diverse issues. This means that the Council, the Commission, the European Parliament, individual member states, regional blocs and the sub-national governments of member states are all likely to pursue distinct and even contradictory strategies towards Russia. In addition, the same actor is likely to adopt alternative strategies for different institutional playing fields. For example, the French president

---

[5] See R. Prodi, "Shaping the New Europe", address to the European Parliament, Strasbourg, 15 February 2000.

can be expected to act differently in the European Council and bilaterally, and optimal strategies for Finland are likely to vary in the context of the European Council, the Northern Dimension framework, and in its bilateral dealings with Russia. Hence, lack of coherence in EU foreign policy is a natural reflection of its multilevel governance structure, and not so much a product of Russia trying to undermine unity through bilateral dealings.

The development of the Northern Dimension is a good illustration of how conflicts in the sphere of high politics do not necessarily diminish the opportunities for practical cooperation on issues of low politics. Even though political relations between Russia and the EU as a whole have become increasingly tense in recent years, the Northern Dimension initiative has managed to develop successfully. As many authors in this volume have shown, diverse forms of regional cooperation within the Northern Dimension have achieved much more than some early critics believed possible. Although the Northern Dimension has encountered various difficulties, it has not been significantly affected by the deterioration in EU–Russian relations, and perhaps most importantly, Russia remains committed to it.

A similar contrast exists between the current tensions in EU–Russian relations on the one hand and the friendliness of Finnish–Russian relations on the other. Although the 20th century was ridden with mutual territorial claims, interventions and repatriation of populations, with the winter war and the continuation war, and Finland fighting in the Second World War on the German side against the Soviet Union, a simple comparison of how the Russian media portray relations with Finland and with Estonia reveals a striking disparity. Russian television regularly reminds viewers about the crimes of Estonian Nazi collaborators, but it never portrays the Finns that way: Finland is always depicted in an amicable light. Apparently, as Timo Vihavainen points out, "history plays a very different role in Finnish–Russian relations than it does in Polish–Russian or Estonian–Russian relations".[6] When he visited Finland, the then President Boris Yeltsin apologised for the Soviet aggression; his successor Vladimir Putin went

---

[6] See T. Vihavainen, "Does History Play a Role in Finnish–Russian Relations?", in H. Smith (ed.), *The Two-level Game: Russia's Relations with Great Britain, Finland and the European Union*, Aleksanteri Series 2:2006, Aleksanteri Institute, Helsinki, 2006, p. 28.

even further and placed a wreath on the tomb of Marshal Mannerheim during his visit to Finland in 2001.

At the same time, the poor image of Russia in contemporary Finland is glossed over.[7] Considering that only Kosovo displays worse attitudes towards Russia, this situation demonstrates impressive restraint by Russian journalists. Similarly, although it provoked strong reactions in Finland, Finnish defence minister Jyri Häkämies' 'three R-words' statement in 2007 in Washington ("the three main security challenges for Finland today are Russia, Russia and Russia; and not only for Finland, but for all of us") went almost unnoticed in the Russian media. Neither was attention drawn to the news that Finland, normally a strong supporter of international initiatives, refused to sign the Ottawa Treaty ban on anti-personnel landmines, which it deploys on the Finnish–Russian border.

6.   The Northern Dimension – Insulated from high politics

The 1,340 km-long border shared by Russia and Finland itself guarantees that the Kremlin would not ignore major international initiatives by the Finnish government such as the Northern Dimension. Still, the success in implementation of the Northern Dimension relies on careful separation of regional cooperation in northern Europe from the issues of high politics that have been eroding EU–Russian relations.

As Pami Aalto points out, the Northern Dimension was specifically intended as an attempt to overcome the emerging division between the EU and Russia by dealing jointly with the practical functional problems of the north rather than struggling with issues of high politics.[8] It focused on the promotion of a few specific initiatives in Russia, avoiding controversies. Security issues were either excluded or dealt with on a very limited basis, as when addressing the 'civil protection' aspect of 'external security'.

Perhaps the most fortuitous decision was not to deal with matters of oil and natural gas supplies. Only nuclear safety and energy efficiency were included within the context of the Northern Dimension Environmental Partnership (NDEP). In chapter 8 of this volume, Indra Øverland notes that

---

[7] For instance, a 2004 Gallup poll showed that 62% of Finns had a negative opinion of Russia.

[8] See P. Aalto, *European Union and the Making of a Wider Northern Europe*, New York: Routledge, 2006.

nowadays the absence of "big issues related to hydrocarbons in the Northern Dimension is striking" in light of the significance of the north in energy production. Indeed, the importance of the north for the EU's energy strategy is well understood by the EU bureaucracy: "The Northern Dimension represents one essential frontier for security of supply due to the importance of Russian and Norwegian energy supplies."[9]

Yet, as Øverland explains, when the Northern Dimension was launched in the 1990s, energy was cheap and a less relevant topic. Since then it has become the hottest issue in EU–Russian relations, but fortunately, by design, the Northern Dimension has been shielded from the resulting disputes.

From the start, the Northern Dimension has been based on a partner-oriented and 'equal ground' approach that is open to equal participation by non-EU states. As Erwan Lannon and Peter van Elsuwege emphasise, "the fact that these partner countries have become involved in the process from the very beginning and participated in the Foreign Ministers' conferences on the Northern Dimension is rather unusual in the EU context. In other words, the partner countries were expected to be not only policy-takers but also policymakers."[10] Christopher Browning and Pertti Joenniemi agree that opening up for the participation of external partners as policy-makers is indeed the distinguishing feature of the Northern Dimension.[11] For both EU members and non-members, their involvement in the Northern Dimension creates venues for discussing issues of mutual interest on an equal footing. This partner-oriented and equal ground approach has guaranteed that the Northern Dimension would only deal with a limited set of issues that were acceptable to all participants. And as a rule, it has only dealt with issues of functional cooperation in areas of low politics.

---

[9] See European Commission, Communication on Strengthening the Northern Dimension of European Energy Policy, European Commission, Brussels, 1999, p. 11 (retrieved from http://ec.europa.eu/external_relations/north_dim/doc/energy.pdf).

[10] See E. Lannon and P. van Elsuwege, "The EU's Northern Dimension and the EMP-ENP: Institutional Frameworks and Decision-Making Processes Compared", in P.G. Xuereb (ed.), *The European Union and the Mediterranean: The Mediterranean's European challenge*, Vol. 5, EDRC, University of Malta, Msida, 2004, p. 25.

[11] See C. Browning and P. Joenniemi, "The European Union's Two Dimensions: The Eastern and the Northern", *Security Dialogue*, Vol. 34, No. 4, 2003, pp. 463–78.

7. A 'third way' initiative? Smart strategies of small steps by small countries

Over time, Finland skilfully transformed the image of the Northern Dimension from a foreign policy matter into a cooperative venture – "from a project of EU external relations to an initiative jointly owned by its four partners, namely the EU, Russia, Norway, Iceland".[12] It is noteworthy that the Nordic members of the EU are among the most cautious supporters of further European integration. Only Finland is in the monetary union, and even the Finns are sceptical on the subject of European defence. Thus, to an outsider, the Northern Dimension might seem like a framework for the countries of northern Europe to interact separately with the world and specifically with Russia (the 'third way'). It could even be viewed as the 'northern' alternative to the choice between the Western and the Eastern vectors of political and economic development. As Dmitri Trenin suggests, there is a possibility for the emergence of a new common global identity, a "[n]orthern" identity.[13]

It is often said that the Northern Dimension proves that the small states of the EU can get a lot done by pursuing 'smart small policies'. Contributors to this volume provide multiple illustrations to back the proposition that success in dealing with Russia has been tightly linked with the use of the 'umbrella of smallness'. While various specific details have accounted for the success of each separate case, a common denominator has been the relatively low salience multiplied by the magnitude of the issue at stake – all of them were below the radar of the central political leadership in Moscow. Thus, in chapter 6 on the partnership in public health and social well-being, Aadne Aasland notes that "much of the practical project collaboration with north-west Russia has taken place without involving policy-makers at the federal level". In chapter 5 on environmental

---

[12] See A.V.G. Vieira, "Dimensionalism in the EU External Relations and Its Implications for the ENP: The Case of the Northern Dimension", presentation at the Conference on "The EU in International Affairs", Brussels, 24–26 April 2008.

[13] See D. Trenin, "Introduction: The Grand Redesign", in A. Lieven and D. Trenin (eds), *Ambivalent Neighbors: The EU, NATO and the Price of Membership*, Carnegie Endowment for International Peace, Washington, D.C., 2003. The northern countries share many interests and their conditions are similar in many ways, including cold-climate economies depending heavily on the use of natural resources, short periods of agricultural growth and sparsely populated areas.

programmes, Nina Tynkkynen comments on how in some cases the lack of interest of the federal government and the decentralisation of environmental administration has opened up windows of opportunity. Sub-national governments, on the other hand, have been quite involved in Northern Dimension activities, as Western money went in to deal with pressing problems for which, in the grand scheme called Russian federalism, those sub-national governments were made accountable. Naturally, the success is very dependent on local actors' interests and commitment (see chapter 5).

It is important to bear in mind how precarious the balance of political influence between the centre and sub-national governments is in Russia, and how aggressively it has been maintained by the federal administration in recent years. Any advances in regional development that might tip the scales in favour of any single regional administration are certain to be keenly watched. As Ian Bache has argued, even in the EU the state remains a 'gatekeeper' in the policy-making process: it allows the sub-national units to participate, but not to significantly affect the policy outcomes (or, we add, policy balance).[14] In Russia today, successful cooperation at the sub-national level will continue only as long as the federal politicians allow it.[15] At minimum, sub-national cooperation must not contradict the political objectives of the national leadership; it is best when the national leadership simply does not care.

It is not by chance that cooperative venues tend to be at the sub-national level – this is required not only by politics but also by the technical arrangements involved in successful practical cooperation: avoiding political traps is an important component in any efficient arrangements of this kind. Attempting to negotiate joint ventures directly between nations involves huge and possibly insurmountable transaction costs, as those who

---

[14] See I. Bache, *The Politics of European Union Regional Policy: Multi-Level Governance or Flexible Gatekeeping?*, Sheffield: Sheffield Academic Press, 1998.

[15] For example, Igor Leshukov points out that the Northern Dimension could become attractive for St. Petersburg and some oblasts of northern Russia, provided that Moscow allowed the regional authorities to grasp the opportunities of cross-border cooperation with EU counterparts; see I. Leshukov, "Can the Northern Dimension Break the Vicious Circle of Russia–EU Relations?", in H. Ojanen (ed.), *The Northern Dimension: Fuel for the EU?*, Finnish Institute of International Affairs and Institut für Europäische Politik, Helsinki and Berlin, 2001.

speak for entire nations are preoccupied with divisive issues of high politics. Keeping contacts regional helps to keep the costs low. Alf Håkon Hoel describes in chapter 4 how Norwegian–Russian cooperation in fisheries management is insulated from high politics. Cooperation proceeds as a common practice, attracting scant political attention – attention that could prove dangerous, considering for example how Russia has over-fished its quota in recent years or the arrest of a Russian vessel at sea by the Norwegian Coast Guard. As Alf Håkon Hoel observes, it is mutually beneficial for the parties to keep a low profile and for their respective governments to look elsewhere:

> An important reason for this relative calm and isolation from high politics is probably that both parties have a strong interest in keeping the cooperation in fisheries management going. The cost of a breakdown could be severe, as both countries would then have to set unilateral quotas that would probably be far higher than are those dictated by management strategies aimed at ensuring the long-term sustainability of the fisheries.

Morten Anker and Bjørn Brunstad remind us in chapter 10 that this principle of 'going small' is even more important in connection with the Russian energy sector. From a Norwegian perspective, Russia's oil and gas industry is attractive mostly for small oil companies that can acquire stakes in *small* oil fields. They specifically caution that "often it may be safer and easier to become involved in small-scale projects that are below the radar of big politics or to avoid challenging the Russian need for control". Energy in Russia, of course, is always politicised; state gatekeeping is explicit – our thesis is validated by these authors. The issue is not the *economic* risks associated with running a large-scale oil extraction operation, but the *political* risks involved in an attempt to capture a noticeable share of the resource extraction market. The present-day success of the Northern Dimension integrationist strategy is largely owing to its superior ability to evade precisely such political risks. This is succinctly captured by Indra Øverland (chapter 8), who writes: "One could get the impression that cuddly multilateral cooperation is acceptable – as long as it does not deal with the really big issues, which are to be handled in bilateral or narrow, ad hoc multilateral settings."

8.   Geopolitical visions of the Northern Dimension

The role of the Northern Dimension has been changing with the changes of EU foreign policy towards Russia.[16] At the same time, the very success of the Northern Dimension has lain "in its ability to deal with localised issues regardless of the general climate".[17] Yet, those localised issues may not carry the weight required to attract attention at high levels, especially if contrasted with the enthusiasm over the Mediterranean process.

Russia has been mostly interested in Northern Dimension partnership programmes through which Western donors put up money to deal with pressing problems in Russia. The significance of those partnerships in economic terms has clearly declined with Russia's economic recovery. In 1999, after the three-fold devaluation of the rouble, the country's gross national product was about the size of Finland's. Only 10 years later, Russia can afford to spend billions of dollars on its various undertakings. Moreover, Western partners tend to keep track of their money in Russia, which makes their projects less attractive for corrupt bureaucrats and politicians than those that receive funding from the Russian government. But the Russian federal government allocates literally a penny for each dollar contributed by Western donors to Northern Dimension programmes. For example, the Russian government pledged €20 million towards the NDEP, which is expected to attract more than €2 billion from the West.[18]

Placing significant issues such as energy security under the Northern Dimension purview might seem like a logical step to raise the region's prominence. But it would put the future success of the Northern Dimension at the mercy of the evolution of EU–Russian relations. Energy politics has been controversial and this situation is unlikely to change in the near future. Thus, if successful regional cooperation and good-neighbourly relations with Russia are the greater priority, it is best to stay away from

---

[16] See P. Aalto (2006), op. cit.

[17] See C. Archer and T. Etzold, "The EU's Northern Dimension: Blurring Frontiers between Russia and the EU North?", *Nordeuropaforum*, Vol. 18, No. 1, 2008, p. 25.

[18] In 2006, the Russian government publicly pledged an additional €10 million towards the NDEP with expected Western participation of over €20 million. This brought Russia's total contribution during 2006–10 to €20 million (information retrieved from www.minfin.ru/ru/press/speech/index.php?afrom4=11.04.2006& ato4=11.04.2006&id4=4216).

energy issues or to restrict involvement to the least controversial aspects, such as renewable energy sources. Nevertheless, for politicians operating at the EU level and thinking in the high-politics terms of geo-political calculations, Northern Dimension expansion into energy policy is an attractive prospect.

9. The subsidiarity principle of EU foreign policy and the Northern Dimension

In a geopolitical sense, "the dimensionalisation is a form of exclusion. You become a partner in a given dimension if you are not entitled to become a member of the Union itself."[19] As Sami Moisio put it, "the Northern Dimension is at least as much eastern as it is northern".[20] In this 'eastern' perspective it receives "a precise geographical content: it is literally a border between Europe and its outside".[21] And in Brussels, the Northern Dimension is in fact 'located' in the EU foreign policy cabinets.[22] Conceptualised as a part of the EU's external relations, the Northern Dimension has been reduced to a regional application of the EU's Russia strategy.

An alternative future for the Northern Dimension could be based on a strategic decision to separate it from the controversies of high politics in Brussels and to maintain a certain degree of autonomy. The Northern Dimension already contains some important innovations compared with the EU's traditional foreign policy instruments, making such a separation easier to sustain. The Northern Dimension was created as a coordination framework for existing programmes, involving low extra costs for the participants. It operates with a combination of partner-oriented, equal ground and multilevel approaches that cut across the EU's pillar structure. Such a unique combination creates "a particular form of 'subsidiarity' in its foreign policymaking by accepting that the member states most concerned formulate and execute EU foreign policy in cooperation with those external

---

[19] See H. Haukkala, *A Hole in the Wall? Dimensionalism and the EU's "New Neighbourhood Policy"*, Finnish Institute of International Affairs, Helsinki, 2003, p. 7.

[20] See S. Moisio, "Back to Baltoscandia? European Union and Geo-Conceptual Remaking of the European North", *Geopolitics*, Vol. 8, No. 1, 2003, p. 95.

[21] Ibid., p. 96.

[22] Ibid., p. 97.

actors capable of generating the needed problem-solving capacity".[23] Subsidiarity of this kind enables the EU to establish multilevel foreign policy and to avoid "engaging in micro-management of every aspect of EU foreign policy" that could cause "ineffectiveness of its external policies".[24] On the other hand, the member states most concerned can avoid the controversies of high politics, focusing instead "on areas of cooperation where a regional and sub-regional emphasis brings added value".[25]

The subsidiarity principle of the Northern Dimension is distinctive from the vision of a multi-speed Europe or a Europe of regional blocs. It is best explained in a theoretical framework of multilevel governance that posits that the key actors can participate in European policy-making through a range of channels – from working within the European institutions to indirectly exerting pressure through regional, national and sub-national authorities. The resultant EU policy is the "outcome of overlapping competences, tensions and conflicts in a system of multilevel governance".[26]

Applying the subsidiarity logic to the future of the Northern Dimension, we could expect decision-making regarding specific, localised issues to be diffused across multiple levels of government – regional, national and sub-national – even though the European institutions would prefer to reserve a role in formulating common policy towards Russia. Different issues are likely to remain subject to the competence of different institutional players, based on the criteria of importance and commonality.

Such functional criteria for the involvement of diverse institutional players in decision-making on any given issue in the Northern Dimension means inviting to the table those players who 'own' it. As long as the Northern Dimension remains mostly a coordination framework for various

---

[23] See M. Filtenborg, M. Sicard, S. Gänzle and E. Johansson, "An Alternative Theoretical Approach to EU Foreign Policy: 'Network Governance' and the Case of the Northern Dimension Initiative", *Cooperation & Conflict*, Vol. 37, No. 4, 2002, p. 390.

[24] Ibid., p. 395.

[25] See the Northern Dimension Policy Framework Document (Helsinki, 24 November 2006).

[26] See G. Marks, F. Nielsen, L. Ray and J.E. Salk, "Competencies, Cracks, and Conflicts: Regional Mobilisation in the European Union", *Comparative Political Studies*, Vol. 29, No. 2, 1996, pp. 164–92.

programmes, assigning some aspects of issues associated with high politics to the Northern Dimension is likely to give the key role in Northern Dimension decisions on *those* aspects to EU-level institutions (the Commission and the Euro-bureaucracy). Such a move would reduce the role of the region, at least in that particular sphere of the Northern Dimension framework. Thus, it seems that our argument above, based on participants' rationality and nested games, falls neatly in line with the logic of subsidiarity, which also indicates that adding issues of high politics to the Northern Dimension is likely to be more appealing to the EU than to the countries of the region itself. For the latter, a more attractive option is to retain the Northern Dimension as a certain niche of localised relations with Russia and to avoid the controversies attached to high politics.

10. References

Aalto, P. (2006), *European Union and the Making of a Wider Northern Europe*, New York: Routledge.

Archer, C. and T. Etzold (2008), "The EU's Northern Dimension: Blurring Frontiers between Russia and the EU North?", *Nordeuropaforum*, Vol. 18, No. 1, pp. 7–28.

Bache, I. (1998), *The Politics of European Union Regional Policy: Multilevel Governance or Flexible Gatekeeping?*, Sheffield: Sheffield Academic Press.

Browning, C. and P. Joenniemi (2003), "The European Union's Two Dimensions: The Eastern and the Northern", *Security Dialogue*, Vol. 34, No. 4, pp. 463–78.

European Commission (1999), Communication on Strengthening the Northern Dimension of European Energy Policy, European Commission, Brussels, p. 11 (retrieved from http://ec.europa.eu/external_relations/north_dim/doc/energy.pdf).

Filtenborg, M., M. Sicard, S. Gänzle and E. Johansson (2002), "An Alternative Theoretical Approach to EU Foreign Policy: 'Network Governance' and the Case of the Northern Dimension Initiative", *Cooperation & Conflict*, Vol. 37, No. 4, pp. 387–407.

Gaidar, E. (2007), *Collapse of an Empire: Lessons for Modern Russia*, Washington, D.C.: Brookings Institution Press.

Haukkala, H. (2003), *A Hole in the Wall? Dimensionalism and the EU's "New Neighbourhood Policy"*, Finnish Institute of International Affairs, Helsinki, p. 7.

Lannon, E. and P. van Elsuwege (2004), "The EU's Northern Dimension and the EMP-ENP: Institutional Frameworks and Decision-Making Processes Compared", in P.G. Xuereb (ed.), *The European Union and the Mediterranean: The Mediterranean's European challenge*, Vol. 5, EDRC, University of Malta, Msida, p. 25.

Leshukov, I. (2001), "Can the Northern Dimension Break the Vicious Circle of Russia–EU Relations?", in H. Ojanen (ed.), *The Northern Dimension: Fuel for the EU?*, Finnish Institute of International Affairs and Institut für Europäische Politik, Helsinki and Berlin.

Marks, G., F. Nielsen, L. Ray and J.E. Salk (1996), "Competencies, Cracks, and Conflicts: Regional Mobilisation in the European Union", *Comparative Political Studies*, Vol. 29, No. 2, pp. 164–92.

Moisio, S. (2003), "Back to Baltoscandia? European Union and Geo-Conceptual Remaking of the European North", *Geopolitics*, Vol. 8, No. 1, pp. 72–100.

Póti, L. (2008), "Evolving Russian Foreign and Security Policy: Interpreting the Putin-doctrine", *Acta slavica iaponica*, Vol. 25, pp. 29–42.

Prodi, R. (2000), "Shaping the New Europe", address to the European Parliament, Strasbourg, 15 February.

Smith, H. (ed.) (2006), *The Two-level Game: Russia's Relations with Great Britain, Finland and the European Union*, Aleksanteri Series 2:2006, Aleksanteri Institute, Helsinki.

Trenin, D. (2003), "Introduction: The Grand Redesign", in A. Lieven and D. Trenin (eds), *Ambivalent Neighbors: The EU, NATO and the Price of Membership*, Carnegie Endowment for International Peace, Washington, D.C.

Vieira, A.V.G. (2008), "Dimensionalism in the EU External Relations and Its Implications for the ENP: The Case of the Northern Dimension", presentation at the Conference on "The EU in International Affairs", Brussels, 24–26 April.

Vihavainen, T. (2006), "Does History Play a Role in Finnish–Russian Relations?", in H. Smith (ed.), *The Two-level Game: Russia's Relations with Great Britain, Finland and the European Union*, Aleksanteri Series 2:2006, Aleksanteri Institute, Helsinki, p. 28.

13. POLICY RECOMMENDATIONS FOR NORTHERN COOPERATION
PAMI AALTO, HANNA SMITH &
HELGE BLAKKISRUD

1.   Introduction

In this volume, we have examined the lessons from various forms of practical regional cooperation in the Barents Sea and Baltic Sea areas, with a focus on engaging Russia constructively. We have also assessed prospects for cooperation in sectors where new institutional arrangements and structures are to be established or considered, such as transport and energy. Our overall policy research task has been to identify the potential role of the new Northern Dimension of the EU, Iceland, Norway and Russia in all this.

Let us now summarise our findings and policy recommendations with regard to northern regional cooperation thematically, in the same order as presented in the introduction to this volume: principles, policy environment, institutional structures and implementation. Throughout the discussion below, we also indicate how these findings can be relevant in the wider EU–Russia neighbourhood.[1]

---

[1] The recommendations are based on our earlier work within the project "The New Northern Dimension and the Possibility of an Energy Partnership – Cooperation between Finland and Norway", see P. Aalto, H. Blakkisrud and H. Smith (eds), *Energizing the New Northern Dimension*, Policy Paper, Jean Monnet European Centre of Excellence, University of Tampere, 2008 (retrieved from www.uta.fi/laitokset/

2.   Main findings and recommendations

1) Principles: How to put the equality principle into practice? The abstract principle of equality is best made concrete by ensuring that *objectives in all regional cooperation projects are jointly defined.* Activities under the aegis of the Northern Dimension are increasingly conducted in this manner. The experiences reported in this book show that jointly agreed objectives feed a sense of policy ownership. This is an important prerequisite for commitment, the development of trust and ultimately, success. Speaking of trust – defined as mutual expectations of the parties to honour their contractual or other obligations even if this cannot be legally guaranteed[2] – might appear odd in the present policy environment characterised by the Russian–Georgian war in August 2008. Even so, gradually developed trust is indeed a real factor in the regional cooperation experience of the north.[3]

Jointly defined *objectives must be based on the fundamental common interests of the parties.* In this way, they can be made durable in times of major political tension and economic uncertainty, as witnessed in autumn 2008. There is a wealth of fundamental common interests. Some may sound trivial, but it is worth mentioning each of them briefly to remind ourselves of the building blocks for a common future in northern Europe, especially in the midst of mutual tensions at the strategic partnership level.

International law can serve as an important starting point for thinking about fundamental common interests, but not much more than that. These laws are far too generic for most policy issues to be dealt with solely on that basis, so supporting principles and practices are needed (see chapter 4). And naturally, the EU–Russian controversy in interpreting the legal nature and consequences of Kosovo and the South Ossetian operations and arrangements further dilutes the role of international law as a shared fundamental interest that might help to structure mutual relations.

---

isss/monnetcentre/english/briefingpapers.php). The recommendations have been developed further in this book, however.

[2] See R. Bengtsson, "Towards a Stable Peace in the Baltic Sea Region?", *Cooperation and Conflict*, Vol. 35, No. 4, 2000, p. 363.

[3] For more, see also H. Rytövuori-Apunen, "Revisiting the Problem of Trust in Finnish–Russian Relations", in H. Rytövuori-Apunen (ed.), *Russia Forever? Towards Pragmatism in Finnish/Russian Relations*, Aleksanteri Series 1/2008, Aleksanteri Institute, Helsinki, 2008, pp. 121–63.

Sovereignty is a key concept in today's Russia and a widely shared principle in the wider European area, even though EU member states have delegated some of it to the EU. Drawing upon sovereignty, all states in wider Europe also underline the need for *secure and clearly demarcated borders*. At the same time, no one wants to seal those borders, not even in the circumstances of some remaining border disputes, which include the maritime border dispute between Norway and Russia in the Barents Sea, and the non-ratified land border treaty between Estonia and Russia.

Diplomacy in its bilateral and multilateral forms remains the primary means of solving conflicts among northern European countries. Where diplomacy has been lacking, as in Russian–Baltic and Russian–Polish relations, the best that the Northern Dimension can do is to provide a less controversial forum in which addressing practical issues is the rule. In this sense, the challenge for the Northern Dimension is to find regional cooperation projects in which the Baltic States and Poland can participate outside the shadow of sensitive foreign policy issues. Importantly, these must be projects in which these countries are willing and able to contribute financially.

The *market* is a widely shared principle in the wider European area. Russia's current trend of re-centralisation should not be confused with outright de-marketisation. What we are witnessing in broad terms is the creation of a state-led or state-supervised, socially-oriented, mixed economy in Russia. That model is not so fundamentally dissimilar from that of many EU economies, especially as the financial crisis of autumn 2008 has led states to reinforce their role in the banking sector and overall economy. Flows of foreign direct investment into Russia have continued to expand regardless of re-centralisation, the abolition and redefinition of production sharing agreements in the energy sector, heightened tariffs on exports of Russian timber and many sectors of the economy becoming viewed as 'strategic' and thus state-protected (see chapters 10 and 11).[4] Still, the full effects of Russia's operations in Georgia and the drop in energy prices in autumn 2008 may yet prove to affect the positive foreign investment trend.

---

[4] See also e.g. Bank of Finland Institute for Economies in Transition (BOFIT) (2008), "BOFIT Forecast for Russia 2008–2010", BOFIT Russia Desk, Helsinki, 11 September 2008.

The *environment* and its protection is increasingly a shared concern. This is clearly seen in the commitment to the Kyoto Protocol goals in the EU, Norway and Russia, with Iceland enjoying some exemptions. Many northern European companies have become integral participants in the EU CO_2 emissions trading mechanisms. Despite many doubts about Russian commitments to environmental protection compared with the eagerness of most of the Nordic states, environmental problems are receiving more and more attention in Russian planning.

In the *public health* sector, the bolstering of the Northern Dimension Partnership in Public Health and Social Well-being (NDPHS) is a shared goal and increasingly corresponds with national strategic priorities. Russian President Dmitry Medvedev has developed a high public profile in this arena in recent years. Public health is becoming perceived as a long-term security issue in Russia. Substantial extra federal funds have already been committed and are to be channelled to this sector in the short to medium term. One of the four 'national projects' coordinated by Medvedev prior to the 2008 presidential elections deals directly with health issues. There are strong signals coming from Russia that the authorities are considering spending significant amounts of money on this sector. This budget line increase may create a window of opportunity for augmenting the NDPHS.

Education and research is clearly an underexploited common interest. Russian universities are entering the Bologna process aimed at unifying degree structures across Europe. Efforts in this area are key to the EU's Lisbon goal of becoming the world's leading knowledge-based economic area. Education and research cooperation with Russian actors provides a cost-minimising long-term strategy not only in the natural sciences but also in the social sciences, where there is a large pool of human resources in Russia and simultaneously shrinking research opportunities in universities in the EU area. This area can provide a very interesting and cost-effective channel of cooperation in the long term, potentially leading to increased integration.

In the *cultural* domain, there has been a history of exchange and mutual learning, and a clear interest has emerged in building on that in the future. The worldwide significance of Russian artistic culture is obvious even for those with conflictual interstate relations. The European tradition of the welfare state and related policy approaches, on the other hand, has long been admired by the Russians.

Transportation and logistics is an area in which public–private funding partnerships are very much in the common interest. Such partnerships are also favoured by the Russian side, which faces a major investment challenge. Awareness of the extent of mutual coordination in this sector is only beginning to surface, however (see below).

Energy policy is a joint interest owing to EU–Russian energy trade in and across northern Europe. Both sides need each other. Russia's available energy transport routes mostly point towards the EU area. Only in the long term is there any prospect of Russia significantly re-orienting towards the Asian energy market. And this will not be a question of Russia's trading the bulk of its resources from the north-west eastwards, but rather of using eastern Siberian resources that are impractically distant from Europe.

Norway, the other main energy producer in the Northern Dimension area, is slowly becoming a significant regional supplier alongside its traditional global and Western European markets. The Scanled gas pipeline from southern Norway is projected to reach southern Sweden, possibly Denmark and in some scenarios even Poland. Norway supplies hydropower to the Nordic electricity market, which in the medium term is set to become part of the all-European grid and market, very possibly including Russia. As for large-scale projects, a good number of actors could stand to benefit from energy projects like the Shtokman field. It is not only about constructing rigs or supplying technology, but also about maintaining adequate environmental standards; controlling the levels of CO_2 that will be released during the extraction process (here Norwegian companies possess state-of-the-art technology); and building ports, terminals, roads, bridges and facilities for the army of workers.

A good example of continuing interdependence in the energy sector is the shared interest in *energy efficiency and energy saving technology and practices*, as well as *renewable energy*. This common interest exists regardless of whether the motive is to guarantee domestic supply in energy-importing countries or to ensure that enough fossil fuels are left for income-generating export. Furthermore, these issues are not as sensitive politically as for example questions of energy transport or field ownership.

Finally, all Northern Dimension partners have an interest in *maintaining the EU's presence in the north*, including the continued availability of its large funds. The transformative effect provided by the scale of European funding available should always be kept in mind whenever the institutional framework of Northern cooperation is discussed. Alongside the common interests in many sectors already enumerated, all northerners share the same structural problems of putting together the necessary funds, developing the hardware and software for mutual relations and all-European trade (in addition to other exchanges) in conditions of sparse population, wide geography and harsh nature, and in the midst of climate change (see Table 13.1).

Table 13.1 Common interests between the EU/European Economic Area and Russia

Common interest	Current/emerging activity
Respect for international law, sovereignty and inviolability of borders	Maintenance of secure borders with well-functioning and regulated cross-border traffic
Primary of diplomacy	Identification of non-controversial issues for drawing the Baltic States, Poland and Russia to the same table
Market principles	Support for state-supervised, socially-oriented mixed economies; regulation enabling foreign investment
Environmental protection	Kyoto commitments, linking of energy and the environment, bolstering of the Northern Dimension Environmental Partnership
Health	Public health investment, augmenting the NDPHS
Education and research	Bologna process, student exchange, research cooperation by pooling the shrinking university research opportunities in the Nordics and competitively priced and abundant Russian human resources
Culture	Cultural exchange, branding with 'northernness'
Logistics and transport	Public–private partnerships
Energy	Shtokman project and its support infrastructure; sharing of renewable energy technology, energy efficiency and savings technology
Maintaining an EU presence	Availability of funding and investment

Source: Authors' compilation.

2) Policy environment: How to compete/coordinate with other initiatives? It will be vital to *ensure that the EU's currently developed Baltic Sea strategy does not risk endangering the promising start made in the new Northern Dimension in engaging Russia in a mutually profitable way.* The passage of the Baltic Sea strategy through EU institutions so far seems to indicate that the Commission and the Council are aware of the possible conflicts between the two policies.

The European Parliament's resolution on the Baltic Sea strategy for the Northern Dimension, adopted on 16 November 2006, treated the initiative as a tool for refocusing the Northern Dimension into the relatively narrow confines of the Baltic Sea area.[5] The resolution also included several references to issues to which Russia is a crucial party, such as facilitating border traffic between the EU and Russia, and turning Kaliningrad into a "more open and less militarised pilot region" – without, however, consulting Russia in any manner at all, or even specifying any mechanisms for doing so.[6] Overlaps were evident with existing EU–Russia policies such as the roadmap for the 'common spaces', particularly the relatively promising work towards mutual visa-free access and the EU–Russia energy dialogue, not to mention priorities such as internal energy-market integration, where the EU's binding regulation is a far more effective tool than any strategy-drafting. In its Presidency Conclusions in December 2007, the European Council asked the Commission to prepare the strategy, but only noted that the strategy should focus on environmental issues, and that the Northern Dimension should remain the tool for cooperation with non-EU actors in the region.[7]

One way of avoiding duplication and undesirable overlaps would be to use the planned EU-centred Baltic Sea strategy to agree on proposals forwarded to the Russian side, or to agree on joint responses to Russian initiatives within the Northern Dimension. Even then, the added value seems ambiguous. The same can be done without any time-consuming strategy drafting process, given sufficient political will among the member states concerned. A more profitable use of the new Baltic Sea strategy would be to deploy it as a tool for engaging the Baltic States and Poland in regional cooperation, for example in the field of the environment. This

---

[5] See European Parliament, "A Baltic Sea Strategy for the Northern Dimension", European Parliament Resolution on the Baltic Sea Strategy for the Northern Dimension (2006/2171(INI)), P6_TA(2006)4094, 16 November 2006.

[6] Ibid.

[7] See European Council, Presidency Conclusions of the Brussels European Council of 14 December 2007, 16616/1/07 REV 1, Brussels, 14 February 2008.

would be a step towards engaging those countries constructively in case Northern Dimension cooperation involving Russia on an equal footing proves too sensitive for them at present. Deploying this tool could also speed up actions in this area, where quick results and inputs from all are needed to further the prospect of reviving the appalling state of the Baltic Sea eco-system.

3) Institutional structures: How to coordinate institutionally? It is important to invest time and adopt a mid- or long-term perspective to cooperation. A *learning-by-doing method* applies to all examples of established regional cooperation covered in this book. In the energy sector, such learning is only beginning, as this is at best an emerging field of northern European regional cooperation. The learning-by-doing method also means that there is no universal formula for success or failure (see chapter 5).

Thus, we conclude that *aiming at a very a rigid strategic document or setting up rigid institutional structures does not appear to be a useful way forward.* In fact, the lack of formal institutions, for which the 'old' Northern Dimension was often criticised, may be a blessing in disguise. After all, it is well known that by the early 2000s fatigue was setting in at the ministerial and senior policy-maker levels in the north, with the endless and too-frequent meetings under the various regional frameworks. In some cases, policy-makers turned up to face largely the same individuals, with largely the same matters on the table – only the name of the council was different. This is not to deny that the various regional councils in the north are important for making the case for extra attention and funding, and for selling project successes to interest groups at the national and sub-national levels. Yet, their simultaneous co-existence makes each project smaller and hence reduces the overall marketability of the results of cooperation, not least in larger countries where scale matters – such as Germany and Russia, or indeed EU institutions.

There is a clear case for *paying attention to competition among projects.* Bilateral and multilateral cooperation could also be better coordinated. When planning projects within the Northern Dimension framework, the possibility of competing projects under other existing or planned cooperation formats should be addressed and if possible eliminated. An illustrative example concerns railroad projects. The Finnish priority is the high-speed rail connection between Helsinki and St. Petersburg, which, after long talks and some delays, is set to become operational by 2010, while the Norwegian priority would be linking the Murmansk region to

Norway. Both these projects have been on the agenda for a long time but have been overshadowed by the priority the Russian authorities have given to the rail link between Kaliningrad and the rest of Russia via Lithuania. In general, only once one project has been finalised will Russia turn its attention to the next one. This tendency brings us back to the need to coordinate policy proposals on the EU side in which several member state governments are involved, compared with the one state bureaucracy on the Russian side (even if it is a complex one). Policy coordination should take place in the early stages of project planning, and if the EU's Baltic Sea strategy project can help, that would be useful. It is also important to note that projects involving national interests can be completed faster.

Avoiding unnecessary competition presupposes regular meetings and a policy direction, even if we do not recommend rigid institutional structures. In the new version of the Northern Dimension policy, the impetus seems to come from the experts of the steering group who have access to national and transnational interest groups. Continuing flexible coordination of the policy appears pivotal for the success of the Northern Dimension, but it will only work so long as activities are based on jointly defined objectives and grounded on the fundamental common interests of the parties. In the nuclear safety sector, flexible entry has also proven useful. EU member states and other states from outside the immediate Northern Dimension area have been drawn in – actors who might not perhaps have entered the policy at all if it were an all-inclusive, take-it-or-leave-it or one-size-fits-all package.

In more game-theoretical terms, to *continue to offer cooperation* is also an important institutional strategy even in conditions of soured overall relations between the EU and Russia. That the Northern Dimension policy was revamped in the aftermath of the Russian–Ukrainian gas transit conflict at the turn of 2005–06 shows that regional cooperation can proceed despite difficult conditions.

Cooperation can be offered in both *bilateral* and *multilateral* formats. Particularly successful examples of bilateral work include the Norwegian–Russian fisheries management regime (see chapter 4), as well as Finnish–Russian environmental projects. Multilateral successes have occurred even in cases in which the partners have been in conflict with each other politically. One such case is that of the Gulf of Finland Mandatory Ship Reporting System (GOFREP) involving Finland, Estonia and Russia (see chapter 5). Moreover, the examples of fisheries management and GOFREP show that within the Barents and Baltic Sea areas, *there remain specific sub-*

regional needs for policy-making, simply because regional differences are real. Learning across cases can be useful. For example, the experience in the Baltic Sea area will be of great value if and when a stronger need arises for monitoring maritime traffic in the Barents coastal areas as a result of increasing traffic from northern energy-extraction projects.

4) Implementation: How to develop existing partnerships and put into effect new and planned partnerships? The existing and planned Northern Dimension partnerships should be seen as important activities in their own right while also providing input into the broader common spaces of the EU–Russia strategic partnership. Using the partnerships as a testing ground presupposes good coordination between the strategic and regional levels. Once that is ensured, the Northern Dimension partnerships can provide platforms on which concrete and clear tasks are easier to define, funds and consortia can realistically be assembled, and impact can best be monitored within clear-cut issue areas and reported back to the funding bodies. Such a compact and transparent set-up enhances perceptions of real project returns and fits with the requirements of the public sector, supranational institutions and other funding bodies to show that their projects have tangible and measurable results.

In developing the Northern Dimension partnerships, depending on the particular case, there may be a need (on top of expert-level cooperation) to *include public information and other campaigns* directed at the broader population at the grass-roots level. Significant outcomes related to awareness-raising and policy returns in the areas of public health, the environment, and energy savings and efficiency can be achieved in this way, especially if accompanied by the provision of low-cost devices that help consumers to change their habits (see below). Towards these ends, a *project selection mechanism* needs to be further developed, to avoid situations whereby the Russian side comes to meetings with concrete proposals without getting any firm or satisfactory response, as happened in the unfortunate old Northern Dimension. Timescales should be flexible. Actors, their responsibilities, funding and evaluation mechanisms need to be clearly defined in all projects.

We propose the following policy recommendations for developing existing and potential Northern Dimension partnerships:

i) To develop the Northern Dimension Environmental Partnership (NDEP) further and generate trust, it is essential to move towards doing away with single-hull ships in the Baltic Sea. Such a regulation should not affect transport volumes or the operating companies significantly. Tankers are merely an exchangeable medium whereas the goods flow and core business would remain intact. But the measure would provide greater environmental security and help to strike one highly controversial question off the policy agenda. A similar need may arise in the Barents Sea; there the example of GOFREP could well be exploited. Overall, the list of priorities should be kept short to generate success stories supporting the whole programme. Besides flagship projects, smaller ones may prove successful.

For the Baltic States and Poland, the €10 million threshold for contributing to the flagship instrument, the NDEP projects, has proved too high. Solutions can be found, however, if there is sufficient political will. The Baltic States and Poland could well combine their efforts and contribute as a trio or quartet.

ii) As for the NDPHS, greater emphasis should be put on involving the Russian parties in the monitoring and evaluation of the public health programmes. The federal level should be widely engaged, although in some issues the federal district level will suffice, because of the decentralised decision-making in this sector in Russia.

Some projects require engaging the research community better, through funding research collaboration to create advocacy coalitions that are broad enough for achieving the stated project objectives. The partnership should work at drawing together a larger number of potential funders for projects, including funds for multilateral activities, and hence strengthening the independent role of the project 'pipeline'.

iii) As for the planned transport and logistics partnership, there is a great need for investment, which is best achieved through public–private partnerships. There is new legislation laying out the structure for such partnerships in Russia. Experience of how this has worked in infrastructural projects so far should be taken into account. It will also be useful to keep in mind that on the Russian side, the companies involved may be state-owned or state-controlled. Although the sector is increasingly seen as 'strategic', Russian authorities will most likely welcome the involvement of international financial institutions.

All non-infrastructural bottlenecks should be eliminated. This includes standardising transport-related technical and administrative structures, and developing spatial planning and transport corridor strategies together. For example, at present each party has its own transport strategy, even though we are talking about transport volumes where there is a shared interest in ensuring smooth flows. The roles of a Northern Dimension transport partnership, the EU's programmes for the trans-

European transport axes and the EU–Russia transport dialogue should be clearly defined.

The Russian side should be encouraged to abandon double invoicing at the borders in order to save time. It should also be encouraged to reduce the number of unnecessary border staff. Such a step would serve as an incentive for reducing multiple and unnecessarily time-consuming controls and release some of the workforce – a resource that is becoming scarcer in the country's north-west – for more productive purposes.

In energy transit, land-based pipelines should be encouraged and viewed as a trust-generating strategy to address the Russian–Baltic–Polish–Swedish controversy evoked by the Nord Stream pipeline. In return, transit fees should be lowered or not charged at all, against Gazprom's commitment for guaranteed long-term supplies priced competitively.

iv) Developing transport and logistics, as well as possible energy cooperation, must involve public–private partnerships. A thriving market environment is the key to greater involvement by private companies. To promote a mutually beneficial market environment, it may not be ideal to have each party supporting its own 'national champions'. If national champions are the rule regardless, partners should be informed of when and how these are to be privileged by the state.

A useful tool for developing a predictable business environment would be to create an independent expert team/forum of policy-makers, entrepreneurs and academics reporting biannually to the Northern Dimension steering group and to wider societal, political and business circles. The model of the EU–Russia Roundtable of Industrialists could help to develop this concept. National and cross-country comparative research measures might include systematically monitoring the success of various business strategies – acquisitions, 'go-it-alone', low-risk strategies, etc.

Supporting the underlying robustness and growth of the domestic consumption market in Russia will bolster Russia's economy and help to maintain a market for exporters from the EU and European Economic Area (EEA) outside the potentially volatile energy sector. Asset swaps in the fashion of German–Russian energy relations should be considered a model for overall economic relations; if no partner is available in the home country, allying with another EU area actor should be considered.

v) In the energy sector, a prerequisite for multilateral large-scale cooperation would be for the EU to first assume more competencies. This would be the best way of developing a more convergent approach to energy questions internally. Such a step could then pave the way for developing an external energy policy to match the record the EU has set in dealing with Russia in some other policy spheres. Today's prevailing bilateralism results in collective losses in EU–Russian relations that are characterised by a high degree of interdependence.[8]

Further alarmist security talk in energy policy should be consciously avoided, and the interests of energy buyers (security of supplies) and energy producers (security of demand) should be ensured. Energy chains should be considered jointly and responsibility for their development and maintenance shared. The strengthening of energy links between old and new EU member states should be continued, as this may help to reduce some of the former socialist countries' fears of being hostages to Russian energy (even though the energy supply may well be of Russian origin).

Every opportunity should be used to support the rise of domestic energy prices in Russia, as this will stimulate efficiency in energy use, spare non-renewable resources, reduce environmental impacts and help to maintain sufficient reserves for energy exports to the EU area. There should be a very proactive governmental policy at the EU and Northern Dimension levels on developing energy efficiency and savings, as well as renewable sources of energy, as these are in the interests of buyers, producers and transit states alike. Specific support in the field of sustainable energy should include the following measures:

- Technology transfers and the joint development of renewable energy technology should be promoted. German and Danish actors should be involved given their expertise in building large-scale windmill parks, as Russia has a strategic interest but lacks the necessary technology. Finnish and Swedish expertise can be useful in the exploitation of peat, which the Russian energy strategy identifies as the second, major 'new' energy resource. Icelandic firms could enter the picture, with their know-how in geothermal and wave energy.

- A Northern Dimension scholarship programme on renewable energy could be considered. In Russia there is considerable unexploited, latent technical expertise on these questions that could be brought into more integral contact with expertise in northern Europe and the rest of Europe.

---

[8] See also P. Aalto, "Conclusion: Prospects for a Pan-European Energy Policy", in P. Aalto (ed.), *The EU–Russia Energy Dialogue: Securing Europe's Future Energy Supplies?*, Aldershot: Ashgate, 2007, pp. 193–207.

- Commissioning a study on the 'ownership' of energy-efficiency issues in Russia should be considered, to shed light on the prospects for promoting and institutionalising the concept there.

- As a simple measure, the installation of heating regulators in households and blocks of flats should be supported financially and campaigned for at the bureaucratic and grass-roots level to popularise the good results attained in pilot projects.

- Environmentally viable wood-burning facilities should be promoted in Karelia, where coal is currently transported from thousands of kilometres away to feed the heating facilities.

- Finally, electricity should be a priority area in grid interconnection and market integration. In this sphere, there is relatively little alarmism and a fair amount of market development on both the EU/EEA and Russian sides. As a specific measure, the strengthening of grids on the Russian side should be supported, to erode opposition to cross-border electricity traffic at the level of local authorities and to deter threats of grid collapse as a result of increased load.

vi) A partnership on culture, possibly extending to research and education, might be considered to recognise the common interests towards each other's culture on both sides of the EU/EEA–Russian border. A partnership in this field would help the Northern Dimension to become a more useful testing ground and could serve as a regional example of the EU–Russia common spaces project in which culture, research and education make up one of the four key areas. On the other hand, education and research issues in the Northern Dimension might best be integrated as academic components into the other partnerships to provide additional support (as suggested above).

As for cooperation in higher education, useful lessons can be learned from evaluating the experiences of the Finnish–Russian Cross-Border University (funded by the Finnish Ministry of Education and the Ministry of Foreign Affairs), where the joint teaching of International Politics is arguably the field that is advancing most successfully. The work of the Norwegian University Centre in St. Petersburg could also be relevant. In research cooperation, the evaluation underway of the large-scale Russian programmes of the Academy of Finland's "Russia in flux" project (2004–07) can provide useful pointers as to future opportunities and directions.

vii) Finally, it is particularly recommended to set up and fund joint European–Russian research teams to study drivers of change in the

Northern Dimension area and to support the development of the partnerships. Further comparison of Finnish, Norwegian and other experiences of working with Russian actors would be useful. This could also include some non-northern countries, to widen the scope and bring in other experiences. Interesting 'new' actors could be Hungary, Greece, Turkey and Ukraine, which all have very different stories to tell of both expanding ties (Hungary, Greece and Turkey) and of problems along the way (Ukraine). Such a research fund could provide crucial input for the further successful development of cooperation within the Northern Dimension area.

3.   References

Aalto, P. (2007), "Conclusion: Prospects for a Pan-European Energy Policy", in P. Aalto (ed.), *The EU–Russia Energy Dialogue: Securing Europe's Future Energy Supplies?*, Aldershot: Ashgate, pp. 193–207.

Aalto, P., H. Blakkisrud and H. Smith (eds) (2008), *Energizing the New Northern Dimension*, Policy Paper, Jean Monnet European Centre of Excellence, University of Tampere (retrieved from www.uta.fi/laitokset/isss/monnetcentre/english/briefingpapers.php).

Bank of Finland Institute for Economies in Transition (BOFIT) (2008), "BOFIT Forecast for Russia 2008–2010", BOFIT Russia Desk, Helsinki, 11 September.

Bengtsson, R. (2000), "Towards a Stable Peace in the Baltic Sea Region?", *Cooperation and Conflict*, Vol. 35, No. 4, p. 363.

European Council (2008), Presidency Conclusions of the Brussels European Council of 14 December 2007, 16616/1/07 REV 1, Brussels, 14 February 2008.

European Parliament (2006), "A Baltic Sea Strategy for the Northern Dimension", European Parliament Resolution on the Baltic Sea Strategy for the Northern Dimension (2006/2171(INI)), P6 TA(2006)4094, 16 November.

Rytövuori-Apunen, H. (2008), "Revisiting the Problem of Trust in Finnish–Russian Relations", in H. Rytövuori-Apunen (ed.), *Russia Forever? Towards Pragmatism in Finnish/Russian Relations*, Aleksanteri Series 1/2008, Aleksanteri Institute, Helsinki, pp. 121–63.

GLOSSARY OF ABBREVIATIONS

AC	Arctic Council
BEAC	Barents Euro-Arctic Council
BRC	Barents Regional Council
CBSS	Council of the Baltic Sea States
CEE	Central and Eastern European
CIS	Commonwealth of Independent States
EBRD	European Bank for Reconstruction and Development
EC	European Community
EEA	European Economic Area
EESC	European Economic and Social Committee
EEZs	Exclusive economic zones
ENP	European Neighbourhood Policy
e-PINE	Enhanced Partnership in Northern Europe
EurAsEC	Eurasian Economic Community
FDI	Foreign direct investment
GOFREP	Gulf of Finland Mandatory Ship Reporting System
GUAM	Georgia, Ukraine, Azerbaijan and Moldova
ICES	International Council for the Exploration of the Sea
IDUs	Injecting drug users
ILO	International Labour Organisation
IMO	International Maritime Organisation
LNG	Liquefied natural gas
MNEPR	Multilateral Nuclear Environmental Programme
NGOs	Non-governmental organisations
NDEP	Northern Dimension Environmental Partnership
NDPHS	Northern Dimension Partnership in Public Health and Social Well-being
NEI	Northern European Initiative
NIB	Nordic Investment Bank

PAC	Partnership Annual Conference (of the NDPHS)
PCA	Partnership and Cooperation Agreement
PECs	Pan-European transport corridors
PSA	Production sharing agreement
SEA	Strategic Environmental Assessment
SES	Single Economic Space
SMP	Strategic Master Plan
TAC	Total allowable catch
TACIS	Technical Aid to the Commonwealth of Independent States
TEN	Trans-European transport network
TEN-T	Trans-European Network for Transport programme
UNAIDS	Joint UN Programme on HIV/AIDS
UNECE	United Nations Economic Commission for Europe
WHO	World Health Organisation

ABOUT THE AUTHORS

Pami Aalto is the Jean Monnet Professor at the Department of Political Science and International Relations and Director of the Jean Monnet European Centre of Excellence at the University of Tampere, Finland.

Aadne Aasland is a Senior Researcher at the Norwegian Institute for Urban and Regional Research, Norway.

Morten Anker is a Senior Consultant at ECON Pöyry, Norway.

Helge Blakkisrud is Head of the Department of Russian and Eurasian Studies at the Norwegian Institute of International Affairs (NUPI), Norway.

Bjørn Brunstad is a Foresight Specialist at ECON Pöyry, Norway.

Irina Busygina is a Professor at the Department of Comparative Politics and Director of the Centre for Regional Political Studies at the Moscow State Institute of International Relations (MGIMO) University, Russian Federation.

Mikhail Filippov is an Assistant Professor of Political Science at the Department of Political Science, Binghamton University, New York, US.

Jakub M. Godzimirski is a Senior Research Fellow at the Department of Russian and Eurasian Studies, Norwegian Institute of International Affairs (NUPI), Norway.

Alf Håkon Hoel is an Associate Professor and Chair of the Department of Political Science at the University of Tromsø, Norway.

Sigve R. Leland is a Researcher at the Department of Political Science, University of Tromsø, Norway.

Kari Liuhto is a Professor and Director of the Pan-European Institute at the Turku School of Economics, Finland.

Katri Pynnöniemi is a Researcher at the Finnish Institute of International Affairs, Finland.

Hanna Smith is a Researcher at the Aleksanteri Institute, University of Helsinki, Finland.

Nina Tynkkynen is a Lecturer at the Department of Regional Studies, University of Tampere, Finland.

Indra Øverland is the Head of the Energy Programme at the Norwegian Institute of International Affairs (NUPI), Norway.